Accursed Politics

Accursed Politics

Some French Women Writers
and Political Life, 1715–1850

❧ RENEE WINEGARTEN ❧

Ivan R. Dee

Chicago 2003

Illustrations of Germaine de Staël and George Sand copyright © Réunion des Musées Nationaux / Art Resource, New York. Illustrations of Alexandrine de Tencin and Manon Roland courtesy of the Library of Congress. Illustration of Claire de Duras courtesy of la Maison de Chateaubriand.

Library of Congress Cataloging-in-Publication Data:
Winegarten, Renee.
    Accursed politics : some French women writers and political life, 1715–1850 / Renee Winegarten.
        p. cm.
    Includes bibliographical references and index.
    ISBN 1-56663-499-7 (alk. paper)
    1. Women authors, French—Political activity. 2. Women and literature—France—History—18th century. 3. Women and literature—France—History—19th century. 4. Politics and literature—France—History—18th century. 5. Politics and literature—France—History—19th century. I. Title.

PQ149.W58 2003   2002041463

In memory of my husband Asher and my mother and father

And with affection for Hilda, Avril, Diane,

Elaine, Susie, Katie, and Olivia

Acknowledgments

MOST OF the following chapters—apart from "George Sand: The Struggle with Class" and the Prologue and Epilogue—first appeared in shorter form as essays in *The New Criterion*: "Madame de Genlis," September 1996; "Madame de Tencin," October 1997; "Madame de Staël," May 1998; "Madame Roland," October 1999; "Madame de Duras," November 2000. I am very pleased to have the opportunity to acknowledge here my profound debt of gratitude to the editor of *The New Criterion*, the distinguished critic and historian of art and culture, Hilton Kramer, without whom this book would not have been written.

Warm thanks are due my nephew David Godfrey for his unfailing patience and help with everything practical.

Contents

Accursed Politics

Prologue

In Search of a Political Voice

What else could one possibly write about today? When an unprecedented Revolution shatters the foundations of the world. How could one be concerned with anything else? The subject of politics is everything, it invades, absorbs and attracts everything: there is no thought, interest, passion but there. If a writer has some sense of his talent, if he aspires to reform or master his era, in brief, if he wants to grasp the scepter of thought, he can and should write on politics. . . . —ANTOINE DE RIVAROL, counterrevolutionary journalist, addressed these words to the poet Charles-Julien de Chênedollé in 1795 when they were both in exile in Hamburg

It is difficult to reconcile the views held in regard to women, because they are either contradictory or nonsensical. . . . —FÉLICITÉ DE GENLIS, *Mémoires*, 1825

Women whose influence in history has been either excessively emphasized or denied are often the radiant expression of a party.—LOUISE COLET, *Charlotte Corday et Madame Roland*, 1842

When Jean-Jacques Rousseau published in 1761 his once immensely influential novel *Julie, ou la Nouvelle Héloïse*, now little read, he chose surprisingly to have one of his women characters speak about politics. "Well, am I not being enmeshed yet again in accursed politics, *cette maudite politique?* I am lost, I am drowning in the stuff . . . ," writes Claire d'Orbe gaily, when staying in Geneva, to her friend Julie de Wolmar.[1] After mentioning that her father is deeply engaged in "politicking" with local magistrates, Claire remarks that she finds these discussions rather boring, and that she herself intends to say nothing about the government of Geneva to her friend. Despite this fine—and self-consciously ironical—declaration of intent, in fact she has already launched into a description of the equilibrium and harmony that prevail in this small republic and the virtues of its rule, as compared with what happens elsewhere in great monarchies. She means France, of course.

Several aspects of this convoluted passage in Claire's letter may strike the modern reader as odd. Claire professes to be overcome by "accursed politics" and bored by her father's involvement in political matters. She makes it perfectly clear in a lightly bantering tone that she intends to say nothing about these—but only after having described in the most rational, sensible, and straightforward manner what she considers to be good governance and the advantages of a small republic as compared with a great and overextended monarchy. These serious observations happen to coincide with those of the Geneva-born author himself, and he could easily have ascribed them to one of his masculine characters. Rousseau, who did not approve of women having anything to do with politics and exerting influence on political affairs, chooses to give his own views to a female personage in his novel and, moreover, one engaged in the act of writing. Claire's evasiveness in claiming that she will not talk about the subject of politics while actually talking about it proves immensely suggestive: it is a strategy that women, and notably women writers, will often employ with varying degrees of subtlety.

In a short space Rousseau uncovers a little of the archness and pussyfooting, the masquerading, the gap between what is professed and what is actually taking place, the sheer contradictoriness and the complexity characteristic of women's concern and involvement in politics in France in the eighteenth century and after. This is a theme bristling with inconsistencies, obfuscations, and even absurdities (as Félicité de Genlis, no friend to Rousseau, would later suggest). How to distinguish between, on the one hand, traditional pieties about woman's role and the lip service paid to these pieties down the ages by women as well as men, and, on the other, the way some remarkable women arrived at their political stance? What did they actually do? A great deal more than we are sometimes led to believe.

The present book grew out of a lifetime's love affair with French literature and civilization, and it seeks to counter received opinions about the relationship between women and politics and their supposed excessive or nugatory influence. It aims to portray some brilliantly gifted French women writers and to probe their responses to the tremendous political, social, and economic changes and upheavals through which they lived in the period before, during, and after the Revolution of 1789. What dreams, thoughts, and feelings, what sensibilities did they bring to a world that was collapsing about them or else in the throes of constant change? And why consider women writers in particular? It is in order to try to redress the balance, to see the world from their point of view. For they had political opinions, made judgments, and acted upon them. They also have much of value to communicate in their concern about the state of the society in which they lived, the government of the realm, their own political commitment and role. The aim is to present a different perspective through the experiences and the outlook of these individuals, these gifted women writers of distinct social origin and class, and the nature of their contribution to the political life of their country.

∽

IT IS NO SECRET that in the eighteenth and nineteenth centuries in France women were not only excluded from all offices of state but were also denied any ostensible involvement in public affairs. In theory they were not even supposed to show an interest in political matters, nor were they to "meddle" in them on pain of being labeled as women of low intrigue. As a result, some of the most active among them could make a signal show of coyness and caution whenever the subject of "accursed politics" was raised. This display should not be taken at face value.

Certainly it was not pleasant for a woman who valued her reputation to be categorized as an *intrigante*. Yet few people could be unaware that during the ancien régime, the Napoleonic era, and later the restoration of the monarchy, it was often through the intercession of women that men in search of favor or office had access to positions of power and influence. A higher grade in the military, an ecclesiastical place, election to the Académie Française, a sinecure, a title with highly desirable emoluments—for these an ambitious man made discreet use of the charms and intelligence of the women of his circle. Somehow the men in question do not seem to have considered this as political involvement on the part of women, or if they did, it could be disregarded. After all, this custom of sending one's wife or mistress, sister or woman friend, to solicit a minister was too useful for a man to be overly fastidious about it. Besides, these were the accepted manners of *le monde* or French polite society.

At the same time women were constantly being reminded that any connection with public life would bring them into disrepute, contempt, and ridicule. According to Saint-Preux, Rousseau's fictional alter ego, writing from Paris to his beloved Julie, French women might well discourse and decide on literature, history, philosophy, "even politics," but that did not mean they were esteemed for any power they exerted in this regard.[2] For French *galanterie*, with its endless flattery, was in truth merely superficial politeness and social custom. What it concealed, thought Saint-Preux, was nothing but scorn for women. Indeed, apart from snide remarks and contumely, women would have to endure openly crude anti-female diatribes that would turn violent in the corrosive and death-dealing words of partisan hacks during the revolutionary period. Later they had to suffer the jibes and insults of journalists on Napoleon's payroll.

The threat of losing their good name did not, however, prevent women from responding to political decisions that were taken in their day. How could it be otherwise for human beings endowed with intelligence and curiosity, with the capacity to feel, to think for themselves, and to write with ease, elegance, and acumen, as they were proving daily in their correspondence? Some women thought little of sending numerous long missives each day. Among these letters are to be found moving passages of psychological insight or compelling reported conversations that could easily fit into a novel with scarcely a word being changed. It was only a short step from writing vivid letters of description, comment, and discussion on topics of the day to one's family and one's absent friends, letters that were sometimes read and admired by a small circle, to composing novels in the form of memoirs or correspondence, a type of fiction in which women particularly excelled.

The Revolution of 1789 swept away an entire society that had offered intense pleasures to the privileged, while opening a path to new possibilities and often to troubled and melancholy reflection on human destiny. With the Revolution and the Terror came bloody spectacles of unspeakable cruelty, meted out equally to women as well as men. People from all walks of life, the eminent and the obscure, died by the guillotine. Many women who hitherto had led a relatively sheltered and protected existence, who had rarely ventured from their homes in town except to visit friends or to take the waters at Bourbonne, lost dearest members of their family and suffered the searing experience of prison and humiliation. Some had incredibly lucky escapes that read like fiction. Others were scattered around the globe in enforced exile and were now obliged to fend for themselves, frequently in reduced circumstances, in England, Switzerland, Germany, Spain, Russia, the French West Indies, or the United States. In order to live, noblewomen who had been presented at the court of Louis XVI and Marie-Antoinette now gave lessons, made gowns and trimmed hats, even took up farming.

How unlikely it would have been if thoughtful women had not reflected on their fate and on the political decisions taken without them that had had such a terrible effect upon their lives. Naturally they wanted to bear witness: they had something of importance to say to the world. Besides, in their long exile they had seen other manners, different ways of living and thinking. Sometimes their experiences imbued them with a newfound spirit of independence. They asked questions; they too wanted to know the reasons why their world had been shattered and what the future consequences were likely to be. At a reception and dinner in 1797, General Bonaparte, newly returned from his triumphs in Italy, stopped in front of a woman famed for her beauty, wit, and lively opinions, and for her salon frequented by the leading *idéologues*, as thinkers and intellectuals of the day were known. It was Sophie de Condorcet, widow of the liberal *philosophe* who had died in prison during the Terror. "Madame," said Bonaparte disagreeably, "I do not like women to busy themselves with politics." "General, you are right," replied Sophie de Condorcet. "But in a country where women have their head cut off, it is natural that they should wish to know why."[3] Bonaparte did not reply and moved on. Germaine de Staël was so taken with this telling repartee that she repeated it more than once in her writings. No mean wit in her own right, she probably wished that she had said it herself.

Nothing could ever be the same again. Despite those who would seek to turn back the clock after the restoration of the Bourbons, there was no real possibility of returning to the old ways that had led to disaster. Whether they wished or not, women had changed, as they demonstrated in their memoirs and their novels or in their writings on society, manners, and public affairs. Whatever might continue to be said ad nauseam about the proper role of women, limited to decent obscurity in the private sphere as dedicated wives and mothers, and their exclusion from the public realm if they wished to be respected, men of intelligence did as they had always done. In pursuit of their own advancement they consulted in private their wives, their lovers, their intelligent women friends, whose ideas they could borrow without acknowledgment. Manon Roland had commented on her husband's tendency to adopt her ideas as his own and believe he had invented them. Benjamin Constant did not make his mark as a liberal thinker before he set out to meet Germaine de Staël. According to the melancholy poet Chênedollé, known as "the Raven," who was present at dazzling conversational jousts at her home at Coppet in 1797, Benjamin Constant, brilliant as he was (and at his most scintillating with her), could not equal Germaine de Staël at her best. "She had lent him far more than she had taken from him," thought Chênedollé, referring to Madame de Staël's ideas.[4] To Benjamin Constant may be added the author of *René*, François-René de Chateaubriand, who was deeply indebted to his friend, the highly placed Claire de Kersaint, duchesse de Duras, for advice on the best ways of advancing his political career at court as well as for her intervention with the powers-that-be on his behalf.

After the Restoration, women continued to reign supreme in the Parisian salons that were often overtly political as well as literary in character. In the eighteenth century, in the decades before the Revolution, they had flourished outside the court at Versailles. As the noted literary historian Marc Fumaroli once observed, private discussions in the salons under an absolute monarchy served as a "counter-institution" vis-à-vis the power of the court. He even called this kind of private society of the salons "a kingdom within the kingdom."[5] With the restoration of the Bourbons after 1815, and the intense interest in revolutionary and postrevolutionary politics that flourished among the intelligent and the ambitious, some women were known for the particular political hue of their salons and the political celebrities and coteries they promoted. The liberal constitutional monarchist Claire de Duras welcomed people of various political shades as well as monarchists, provided they were not *ultras*, as the extreme right-wing royalists were called. *Ultras* were to be found in the salon of the marquise de La Rochejaquelein, romantic heroine of the first counterrevolutionary uprising in the Vendée and author of dramatic memoirs. Albertine de Broglie favored liberals—like her mother, Germaine de Staël. Others preferred to entertain Bonapartists. Since organized political parties in the modern sense did not yet exist, the salons provided an agreeable meeting place for the like-minded, where matters of the day could be freely discussed and women could exert an influence on public opinion.

There are at least two completely divergent views about the role of women in politics in France in the eighteenth and early nineteenth centuries. Both would appear to be right. They cancel each other out. That is why generalizations will count less in the present book than individuals with all their idiosyncrasies.

One theory proposes that the French condition is exceptional, and that women exerted an immense influence on politics in the eighteenth century without ever being permitted to hold any "office" except that of "*maîtresse en titre*," or "official mistress"—like Madame de Pompadour, whose place in Louis XV's life even enabled her to modify French foreign policy. This view of women's power behind the scenes, usually held by men, is wittily encapsulated in Montesquieu's satirical *Lettres persanes*, in the bemused comments of the Persian observer as he notes the strange behavior and customs of the French with regard to the latitude granted to the female sex. It is corroborated by the observations of numerous foreign visitors, among them Thomas Jefferson, then representative of the new American republic, who was amazed at the extent of women's political influence as he witnessed it in Paris. Many years later the realm of female political power (conceived as particularly deleterious) would be explored in the writings of those convinced misogynists, the bachelor brothers Edmond and Jules de Goncourt, who were among the first to probe eighteenth-century manners in their readable biographies of prominent women and their works of social history published in the 1860s.

The opposite theory—that of women's lack of empowerment—is elaborated, for instance, in the feminist pages of Choderlos de Laclos, notorious author of *Les Liaisons dangereuses*, pages that were not published in his lifetime. It can be found, too, in the feminist opinions of the marquis de Condorcet, eminent mathematician and ill-fated revolutionary. It was in eloquent terms that Louise de La Live, Madame d'Épinay, noted writer and benefactress of Jean-Jacques Rousseau, had complained bitterly about the position of women in public life—or rather the lack of it. In a letter to abbé Galiani in 1771 she declared: "Everything concerned with the knowledge of administration, politics, trade, is foreign and forbidden to women; they cannot and must not participate, and those are almost the only great matters through which men of education and learning can really be useful to their fellows, to the State, to their country. So all that is left to women are belles-lettres, philosophy, and the arts."[6] Preoccupied with the shortcomings of female education, like a great many women writers then and later, Louise d'Épinay reveals her pained sense of exclusion from what she regards as the truly important sphere of patriotic endeavor where a real contribution can be made to the well-being of the country. Almost a quarter of a century after her, Rivarol, famed for his savage wit and brilliant conversation, would proclaim to his friend

Chênedollé that after the Revolution the realm of politics is the only one worthy to occupy the serious attention of a man of talent. Where would that leave talented women?

～

MOST FORMIDABLE in shaping the sensibility of women, even the most independent-minded among them from Manon Roland and Germaine de Staël to George Sand, was the complex and tortured author of *Émile*, Jean-Jacques Rousseau. He casts a long shadow over them. That subtle nineteenth-century poet and critic, Charles-Augustin Sainte-Beuve, saw a clear divide between women who wrote before and after the advent of Rousseau. This division is not as clear-cut as he proposed, though it may serve as a rough guide. The political ambitions of Alexandrine de Tencin, who prospered before Rousseau and who died in 1749 (the very year he made his debut with his first discourse on sciences and arts), largely consist of attempts to advance her brother's career. It seems as if with her it is not really a question of ideas and ideals (as it is later with Manon Roland, Germaine de Staël, Félicité de Genlis, Claire de Duras, and George Sand). Yet the far-seeing Alexandrine de Tencin did loathe tyranny and the misuse of power by those who possessed it. She worried about the well-being of the country. After Rousseau, though, it is the noble causes of virtue, citizenship, the good of the people that loom large. Many women fell under Rousseau's spell even if they later managed to free themselves of it.

It was Rousseau's elevation of his own feelings, his cult of sensibility itself as a form of ennoblement, his constant probing of his own nature, his remarkable gift for self-justification, his concern with his own identity, authenticity, and selfhood that fascinated many and, in particular, women readers and writers. They tried to follow his example in seeking their own true voice. His influence on them was in some respects very strange, because although Rousseau depended on women and their generosity all his life, although he adored some of them with good reason, in his writings he always wished to keep them in their "proper sphere." They should remain ideally respectable and respected wives and, above all, perfect mothers. All this had little to do with his own eccentric conduct. As for marriage, he did not go through a form of it with his long-term partner Thérèse Levasseur until late in life. As for motherhood, he notoriously placed his infants in the foundling hospital because (so he claimed) he believed that Thérèse and her family would be a harmful influence on them. Visitors he entertained thought she was his servant, so in front of them he must have treated her like one.

Rousseau revealed in his *Confessions* how he liked to be dominated sexually: it is not surprising, then, that he feared female domination. Women, he thought, with their perpetual inclination to dominate, must therefore be kept well away from public life. In this regard Rousseau the rebel was firmly conservative. The devotee of Sparta and ancient Rome might find a few rare female heroines who had served the state in antiquity, but in his view there could be no such examples in France in his day, given the advanced and irreversible corruption of society—corruption brought about by what he saw as the disastrous feminization of French taste and culture.

Moreover, Rousseau thoroughly detested women writers as a species. What could be worse than a female wit, *une femme bel esprit*, obviously a pedant, a wife who took to writing for the public instead of quietly looking after her husband and children, as she should? "One of my great misfortunes was always having to associate with women authors," he remarked crossly in his *Confessions*. Born of modest parentage in the Republic of Geneva, he was rather a snob where the French aristocracy was concerned, and he said that he had hoped to avoid such tiresome encounters with scribbling women when he came to have dealings with members of the highest rank of the nobility. What a mistake! Here was the comtesse de Boufflers (mistress of the lofty, rebellious Prince de Conti) possessed of the mania for writing. She had composed for the Prince de Conti's private theatre at his magnificent summer residence at L'Isle-Adam a tragedy entitled *L'Esclave généreux* (*The Magnanimous Slave*). Rousseau "thought it his duty" to tell her that it was very like Aphra Behn's famous story *Oroonoko* (1688), regarded today as the first novel in English to promote emancipation of the slaves. It had been adapted for the stage and already translated into French.

The comtesse de Boufflers thanked Rousseau for his candor, but, she averred, she did not know Aphra Behn's work. She immediately ordered a copy, and she sent Rousseau a cutting from *The Spectator* about an occurrence in the West Indies on which she had based her own play—to no avail. Rousseau did not allow her the benefit of the doubt: he still accused her of plagiary in his autobiography, maintaining that he had offended his benefactress in a way that "neither women nor authors can ever forgive."[7] So he not only made known his unshakable belief that she had committed plagiary, most heinous of literary crimes, he also suggested that as a woman and an author she had never been able to forgive him. According to his distinguished biographer, the late Maurice Cranston, however, apparently nothing in her letters conveys any such impression.

What is at work here? It is some inner conviction on Rousseau's part that women who write are not to be trusted, whatever they may say in their own defense. This implies, moreover, that as writers women will betray all the underhand meanness of the literary genus, which in his growing paranoia Rousseau believed to be constantly directed at his innocent self by his rivals. (Sometimes, as in the case of Voltaire, he was not mistaken.) This deep-seated prejudice of Rousseau's against women who wrote and published did not just reinforce traditional stereotypes, it also formed part of a newly shaped and reasoned viewpoint of his own which, given his seductive prose, had an immense effect on generations of women writers. Rivarol called Rousseau "a master sophist, paradox incarnate, a great artist (as regards style)," adding perceptively if with misogynistic verve, "his epileptic eloquence must have been irresistible to women and the young. . . ."[8] Doubtless Rivarol had noticed—as would Félicité de Genlis—Rousseau's capacity for suddenly reversing his opinion and arguing against himself.

Rousseau's forceful distaste for women writers owed something to his enduring resentment at having served in the lowly position of paid secretary to wealthy women who felt the urge to write. There was the attractive Marie-Madeleine de Fontaine, Madame Dupin de Chenonceaux, famously chaste. Rousseau fell in love with her and was rebuffed. The daughter of Samuel Bernard, financier to kings, she was also the stepmother of Claude Dupin de Francueil, George Sand's paternal grandfather. It was the author of *Lélia*, determined to raise the consciousness of her sex, who would discover Marie-Madeleine's manuscripts with their advanced views on women when staying at Chenonceaux in the 1840s. In George Sand's view, "this remarkable and original woman never wanted to take the place in the republic of letters that she deserved. . . ." Perhaps it is regrettable, she added, that Madame Dupin de Chenonceaux did not develop and communicate her ideas. Marie-Madeleine did not append her own name to her husband's writing, "although I am convinced that she could have claimed the better part of it and its best ideas."[9] At the time when Rousseau was secretary at the beautiful château of Chenonceaux, his patroness was writing with her husband a work on the emancipation of women. It was said of her toward the end of the nineteenth century: "She wished above all that women should have a more serious education, and that they should not be excluded from public office and careers permitted only to men. . . ."[10] No surprise, then, that Rousseau had little sympathy for such concerns that ran directly counter to his own opinions. He was also annoyed at having to spend his valuable time at her behest in making extracts from the work on perpetual peace by abbé de Saint-Pierre. This farseeing dreamer, advocate of international courts of justice, was a writer whose views Rousseau did not share, since he thought them superficial, impractical, and absurd.

Yet another benefactress of Rousseau, Louise d'Épinay, showed him her novels, stories, plays, "and other rubbish," as he graciously expressed it.[11] Yet Madame d'Épinay was far from being a bumbling amateur, as Rousseau implies. She wrote among other works *Les Conversations d'Émilie* (1774), for which she won a prize some years later. Moreover she contributed comments on politics and literature to the prestigious *Correspondance littéraire*, edited by one of her lovers, Baron Grimm (with whom Rousseau had fallen out), and which circulated among the crowned heads of Europe. In her letters to abbé Galiani in Italy she reported on French political affairs in which she was passionately interested.

Remarkably, though, by the time Rousseau was complaining so vociferously about women writers as a whole, there had never been such an outpouring of works by women in France. Many of these writers were well known and highly esteemed as novelists by their contemporaries. Alexandrine de Tencin's *Mémoires du comte de Comminge* (1735), Françoise de Graffigny's *Lettres d'une Péruvienne* (1747), Marie-Jeanne Riccoboni's *Lettres de Mistriss Fanni Butlerd* (1757), with its oddly spelt heroine, were extremely popular. But the vast majority of eighteenth-century women writers—and the list is long—have remained in obscurity. In his invaluable edition of a number of important novels and stories by women in the eighteenth century and beyond, Raymond Trousson names at least forty who published fiction between 1735 and Rousseau's death in 1780. The woman writer either as novelist or journalist was thus a recognized and established phenomenon in Rousseau's own day when he was railing against it. Perhaps that was one reason why he objected so forcibly: there was no avoiding the creatures.

৵

IF ROUSSEAU STANDS at the beginning of our quest to ascertain the nature of the role of women writers in politics, it is not simply because of his great influence on them. It is also because he imbued them with a fresh sense of guilt at not fulfilling the domestic ideal, and because he fostered their inhibitions and reinforced their low self-esteem. Women for the most part lacked afflatus and genius, he wrote. They could succeed in minor works that require wit, taste, elegance, "sometimes even philosophy and reasoning."[12] They could acquire knowledge, learning, and anything else that might be attained by the effort of work. But as for celestial fire and sublimity, these would always be absent from their writings. This would prove to be a false prophecy.

It was Rousseau who, in *Émile*, his reflections on education, continued to propagate the notion that there was always some man behind every woman writer. (It has since been found that a woman often acts as muse and support to a male literary figure.) This mysterious and superior man was holding her pen, and in all likelihood he had written the entire work that for some obscure reason of *galanterie* had been published under her name. Since the intellect was commonly regarded as a masculine preserve, how indeed could a woman have ideas or give voice to them? For a woman to show signs of intellect was to be mannish and therefore unnatural. This view antedated Rousseau; he simply reinforced it, and it long outlasted him. Alexandrine de Tencin's fiction was said to be the work of her two nephews, one of whom she regarded as a "nincompoop" and the other as a wastrel. This particular prejudice was still current when George Sand produced the works of her maturity a century or so later, in the 1840s. Then—and afterwards—it was claimed that the pioneering socialist thinker Pierre Leroux had actually written the philosophical and political portions of her mighty novel *Consuelo* and its sequel *La Comtesse de Rudolstadt*. George Sand was certainly much moved by his ideas, but she had also studied books on political philosophy and had formulated social and political views of her own long before she met Leroux. Such prejudice about female incapacity has not entirely vanished today, and may surface when women writers of merit from the past are being discussed.

In the nineteenth century Sainte-Beuve would be among the first to take seriously the political and intellectual role of women authors, like Manon Roland, Félicité de Genlis, Germaine de Staël, Claire de Duras. Yet he vented his spleen elsewhere, in his private notebooks. There he dismissed the innovative educationist and popular novelist Félicité de Genlis—along with the English writer Fanny Burney, famous creator of *Evelina*—as two bluestockings, "fairly elegant examples of the pedantic vanity and egotistical chatter of the woman author." It was as if masculine authors (himself included) were never guilty of pedantry, vanity, or egoism. He also observed complacently that "the woman who chooses to become an author, however distinguished she may be, and even the more distinguished she is, loses her principal charm which lies in belonging to one and not to all"—a bizarre admission of male possessiveness. He went on to state: "Everything a woman gives to the public realm she takes away from reputation and true happiness."[13] This opinion was already old hat when Sainte-Beuve was voicing it. Even so eminent and distinguished a writer on public life as the politically active Germaine de Staël, who courted fame, had amazingly declared in her epoch-making study of German culture, *De l'Allemagne* (1810): "It is right that women should be excluded from public and civic affairs. Nothing runs more contrary to their natural calling than whatever would engage them in rivalry with men. For a woman fame itself could only prove to be a shattering bereavement of happiness, *un deuil éclatant du bonheur.*"[14] In short, if a woman wished to be happy in love (as she did herself), involvement in political activity, writing for the public, and being famous were not the ways to go about it. The struggle between the demands of the heart's affections and those of a literary and political career is far from new.

Who can tell what works were lost not only through prejudice against women writers but also through women's own inhibitions and timidity? As Voltaire's friend, the cultivated mathematician and scientist Émilie du Châtelet expressed it: "I am convinced that many women either remain unaware of their talents, through poor education, or suppress them out of prejudice and lack of mental courage."[15] Consider a passionate disciple of Rousseau like Manon

Phlipon, Madame Roland, who did not admire female wits. She did not believe, any more than her idol Rousseau, that women should write for the public. Yet she was an extremely gifted writer who could have produced works of real merit. What she did write is scattered in her letters-cum-essays to friends, her shorter pieces, and her considerable contribution to her husband's volumes. It was only in the long months of imprisonment during the Terror in 1793 that she was inspired to commit to paper her penetrating and moving memoirs in the hope they would be published after her death. She said, when it was too late, that she would have liked to write a history of France after the model of the well-known British republican historian Catharine Macaulay, whose volumes on English history she admired so much. With her keen insight and literary flair, Manon Roland was certainly capable of producing an important historical work on republican lines, if she had not been held back by her prejudices about women who displayed their talents and by her subservience to Rousseau. Paradoxically, Rousseau was at once an inspiration in her introspective probing and candor and a harmful influence on her attitude toward female authorship.

Even the celebrated Germaine de Staël took care not to be caught in the act of writing by her father who disliked the sight of a woman with a pen in her hand. "My father cannot tolerate a woman author," young Germaine Necker confided to her diary. In fact, Jacques Necker had literary ambitions himself, and he indulged them. He teased his precocious daughter, calling her *Monsieur de Saint-Ecritoire*, or Sir Writing Desk. Speaking of her mother's desire to write, Germaine observed: "Mamma loved writing; she offered it up to him as a sacrifice." Her father would explain his feelings to Germaine with fatuity all his own: "Just think how troubled I was," he said. "I did not dare enter her room without taking her away from a task that was more pleasing to her than my presence. Even when she was in my embrace I saw her following up an idea." His daughter commented demurely: "How right he was! Women are not really made to follow the same career as men"—while she took good care to ignore this limiting train of thought in her actions and writings throughout the rest of her life.[16]

One important consequence of the strong prejudice against women authors was an inclination to self-hatred, common enough in those who perceive themselves through the hostile eyes of others, and who end by absorbing the scornful opinion held by their critics and regurgitate it. "Do not think I am in favor of women authors, not in the least," wrote Sophie Cottin in 1800, not long after one of her most successful novels, *Claire d'Albe*, was published anonymously in 1799. Nature, she declared, in linking women's happiness to the sole duties of wife and mother, deprived them of genius only to keep them from "the vain desire to be more than they ought." If some women were allowed to write, she added, it could only be as an exception when they were no longer committed to their feminine duties. "And even then, I wish them to feel their shortcomings sufficiently to treat only subjects that require grace . . . and sentiment." Sophie Cottin's view that it was wrong for women to publish would strike even a moralistic stickler for etiquette like Félicité de Genlis as extraordinary and offensive on the part of a woman who had devoted much of her time to writing novels.[17] Yet even an extremely successful novelist like Sophie Cottin could find it necessary to repeat the refrain that Rousseau had uttered decades earlier.

To try to keep some perspective, though, it must be said that it was not only *women* authors who could be viewed with a degree of contempt. No less a writer of European repute than Voltaire had received little sympathy when the thugs of the chevalier de Rohan gave him a drubbing. That happened in 1726. In the years immediately before the Revolution that broke out sixty-three years later, however, some claim that the status of the writer had improved considerably. Others would believe that men of letters had become overly powerful. Debate has raged ever since over whether the *philosophes* were or were not responsible for the revolutionary cataclysm. Rulers would not be impressed by the idea of seeing men of letters in the corridors of power. Napoleon despised *idéologues* (whom he had once flattered for the sake of expediency) almost as much as he looked down on independent women writers, whom he favored with his customary intimidating parade-ground acerbity. He told his brother Joseph, whom he had made king of Naples, "You spend too much of your life with literary men and savants. They are coquettes with whom you should engage in relationships of *galanterie*, and you should never dream of appointing them your ministers."[18] Nor did Louis XVIII approve of "poets"—that is, men of letters in general—in positions of political power. "Take great care never to bring a poet into our counsels," said Louis XVIII in private to his closest advisers. "He will be a dead loss, those people are good for nothing."[19] Chateaubriand, whom he reluctantly had to accept as minister, spent a good deal of effort trying to prove to all and sundry that a man of letters could be a statesman, and doing so at least to his own satisfaction and that of poets like Lamartine and Victor Hugo who would later follow him into political life.

After the Restoration of the Bourbons, scorn for literary men lingered on among the more bigoted and benighted aristocrats. In 1822, in the salon of Armande de Richelieu (sister of the duc de Richelieu, celebrated as the governor of Odessa and now minister of Louis XVIII), the conversation turned to men of letters. Among those present was the liberal-minded Abel-François Villemain, distinguished professor at the Sorbonne, historian, and esteemed literary critic. One of those present asserted that until the Revolution men of letters were to be found in the best society. "No, no," retorted the aristocrat and royalist minister, abbé de Montesquiou, "Nothing is further from the truth." He maintained that writers were only "tolerated at table, they were not anybody's close friends." Plenty of examples were then quoted to prove the contrary, but abbé de Montesquiou would not be moved, despite his hostess's evident discomfiture. Times might have changed, but he went on to say a good deal more that wounded Villemain. Aiming to put an end to the discussion, another guest clumsily intervened, "Yes, men of letters were the dregs of society."[20] Villemain rose to make his exit. He said afterward that as he left he felt he had understood the Revolution. The anecdote is related in such a way as to show that sensible people now regarded such prejudice against writers as something stupid and absurd. It also reveals that it was not directed solely against women writers, even if they doubtless suffered from it more consistently, and although its consequences affected them in a more visceral and lasting manner. Women authors had more to lose and more profound psychological obstacles to overcome in the political as well as the literary realm.

If women were disfranchised, however, so was most of the population. Even when the vote was granted under the *Charte*, or Charter, of 1814, to much liberal rejoicing, it was limited to very few male citizens. In order to have the right qualifications to vote, men had to be in possession of considerable property, a condition that eliminated the greater part of the inhabitants of the country. In the early nineteenth century, political activity among the députés and the peers in Paris remained largely outside the purview of poor peasants and humble working people in the provinces, many of whom were illiterate. In this larger context, the political exclusion of women was far from unique. The limited male suffrage goes some way to explain the fact that for the most part women were not primarily interested in the vote until later in the nineteenth century. Along with the desire for a change in consciousness, they had more solid practical ends in view, like the ability to find a means to exert pressure in matters that did concern them.

∽

HOW, THEN, to try to discover what women themselves felt and thought? How to penetrate the mass of conflicting and contradictory evidence? Rather than addressing generalizations of dubious validity, I shall seek to concentrate on probing the experiences, the ideas, and the actions of six remarkable individual women writers. Their changing and developing attitudes and responses can be gauged from their letters, memoirs, novels, essays, and writings on society and politics, as well as from the observations of their contemporaries. These women writers cover a wide spectrum of divergent opinions, through various tones and shades of liberalism, conservatism, royalism, republicanism, revolutionary radicalism, and socialism. As regards religion, they include Catholics, lapsed Catholics, Protestants, deists, and seekers after some new religion of the future. Their economic and financial position varies. They do not all come from one class of society: there are women writers in the modest class of tradespeople, the bourgeoisie of high finance, the gentry or the higher ranks of the nobility, or molded by a mixture of several classes. All of them are involved openly or in subtle ways in the political life of their country, where in theory they were not supposed to be.

Doubtless the choice of these six writers might be ascribed in part to personal preference, to my appreciation of their varied literary talent, their adventurousness and fortitude, and the strength of their personality. If I have departed from the tradition that would constantly refer to them as "Madame de Duras" or "Madame de Staël"—at the risk of appearing to employ a tone of familiarity that does not accord with French style and manners—it is because this custom seems to render them in English more remote and less individualized. It was one of the advantages of a masculine pseudonym like "George Sand" that it stopped everyone from alluding to her as Madame Dudevant and thus permanently linking her to the husband she had left and later fought in the law courts.

The reader will find in the following pages no preoccupation with the vexed question of whether women exerted too much or too little influence, and no preconceived agenda of political feminism, political ideology, or literary theory. My distaste for ideology and theory, however, does not preclude my sympathy with the fate and cause of women, nor doubtless does it conceal traces of my inclinations to Orwellian-style humanism. I approached each of these six women with curiosity and was surprised by their intense concern with the changing society of their time, by their struggle to find an authentic political as well as literary voice, and by the degree of their involvement with the social and political affairs of their day. Apart from Germaine de Staël, they were not political thinkers as such but were mostly fascinated by political ideas or ideals. In their different ways, they seized the opportunity for action when it presented itself. As the following portraits should demonstrate, whatever obstacle may be placed in their path, there are always rare spirits who find some way to circumvent it.

ONE

Alexandrine de Tencin
Scandal, Intrigue, and Politics

THE COUNT: Oh! What you are defining is intrigue!
FIGARO: Politics, intrigue, what you will; but as I think of
them as related, rather like first cousins. . . . —BEAUMAR-
CHAIS, *Le Mariage de Figaro*, 1781, Act III, scene v

Do you think, Ibben, that it enters a woman's head to become the mistress of a minister in order to sleep with
him? What an idea! It is so as to present him with five or
six petitions every morning.—MONTESQUIEU, *Lettres persanes*, 1721

Infamous woman," "adventuress," "unfrocked nun," "*intrigante*"—
these were just a few of the epithets routinely leveled at Claudine-
Alexandrine Guérin de Tencin (1682–1749) during her lifetime. She
was commonly regarded as utterly unscrupulous, avid for money
and none too nice about how to acquire it, an ambitious political
manipulator who was fully capable of any dastardly act, not least
spying on behalf of a foreign power. Quite openly she was even accused of incest with her brother Pierre, a pillar of the church of
Rome—which made the salacious gossip all the more to be relished.
The public charge that she had intended to murder one of her nu-

merous lovers led to her incarceration in the grim fortress-prison of the Bastille.

Yet there were other voices among her contemporaries. Those who knew her well saw her not only as talented and farsighted but also as kindly, considerate, and actively helpful beyond their expectation or the call of duty. She was endowed with boundless energy (perhaps one reason why Stendhal would admire her) and unable to tolerate the lack of life and drive in others. Without being thought conventionally beautiful she was nonetheless strikingly attractive in a rather unusual way. Her steady sidelong gaze and half-smiling expression would indicate a person who prides herself on having seen into the depths of human folly and deceit, and who is not about to be readily duped. A woman of immense charm, wit, and intelligence, she could inspire, help, and encourage some of the outstanding and innovative men and women of her day who became her friends and allies. The venom of her opponents and her enemies suggests that she represented for them a challenging and subtly disturbing phenomenon: a woman who arrived, as it were, from nowhere, who made her own way and funded her own financial establishment, and who was disinclined to respect traditional norms and boundaries. She appears as one of the most extraordinary and intriguing figures in the rapidly changing society of early eighteenth-century France, the age of new and daring thinkers and writers with whom she associated so closely.

Alexandrine de Tencin was also the author of several important novels, published anonymously as was customary for women of the day. These included the celebrated *Mémoires du comte de Comminge* and the popular *Le Siège de Calais*, as well as *Les Malheurs de l'amour*, and her *Anecdotes de la cour et du règne d'Édouard II, roi d'Angleterre*, which she did not complete. With her the frontiers of the realms of fiction and reality were sometimes blurred when, for the sake of some cherished scheme or undertaking, she would try actively to transform recalcitrant facts into the shape required or envisioned by her roving and commanding imagination. One of her

Alexandrine de Tencin (Portrait by François-Hubert Drouais)

favorite ploys, for instance, was to compose—and send—elaborately fashioned anonymous letters or missives of invented provenance in order to influence the recipient to adopt a course closer to her own ideas and wishes. It was rather as if she were writing an epistolary novel, but in actuality instead of in literature. Besides being a political intriguer, as her critics and enemies claimed, she was also the inventor of quite complex fictional intrigues. Her most famous work, the often reprinted and highly esteemed *Mémoires du comte de Comminge*, a novel about enduring love and self sacrifice, was still reducing readers to floods of tears well into the nineteenth century. It was a tale that would be remembered by Félicité de Genlis and would arouse the admiration of Germaine de Staël, among other writers who were valued for their literary taste and discernment. Although this work does not seem at first to have much to do with the author as political manipulator, it proves to be a more subversive novel than may appear on the surface.

What really fascinated Alexandrine de Tencin was the "hidden face" of the cards, as she put it, though she was never very good at concealing her own hand.[1] A number of people guessed or knew or saw through her schemes. The fact is that there was scarcely an important political and economic crisis or social and cultural transformation in France in the first half of the eighteenth century with which she did not have some connection. These included the revival of the bitter conflict over Jansenism, a conflict to which Alexandrine was linked through her brother Pierre, who played a significant part in it. This quarrel turned on whether true allegiance was due primarily to the church of France or that of Rome, and it led to questions about whether the authority of the *parlements* or that of the king should prevail. In essence it was political as much as religious. Then there was the renewal of the intense debate between the "Ancients" who upheld the superiority of the writings of antiquity and the "Moderns" who numbered among Alexandrine's friends and who looked to the present and the future. This literary and aesthetic quarrel carried with it political undertones since it proposed a choice between tradition and change, authority and free inquiry. Alexandrine was also particularly closely involved in the risky fiscal reforms of the Scottish adventurer John Law, which ended in riches or bankruptcy for the speculators of the Regency. She would later figure, too, among the private critics of the monarchy, as a representative of the so-called "secularization" or growing lack of respect for the divinely instituted monarch in the person of Louis XV. While some people thought of her simply as a dangerous woman engaged in political intrigue, others among the most prominent figures of the era recognized and sought to use her considerable talents, just as she in her turn made use of their privileged position and advantages for her own ends.

What indeed did "intrigue" mean in eighteenth-century France? As Figaro would tell Count Almaviva, he could not see much difference between intrigue and politics. Their creator knew whereof he spoke, for Beaumarchais himself engaged in political intrigues. Under an absolute monarchy there were no political parties, only cabals, largely self-seeking individuals and factions, adherents of warring religious sects with their own political agenda. Men could regard themselves as servants of the public good, but if they cared about the standing or welfare of their country they often tended to associate these with their own and their family's interests. Titles, offices, and honors, with their accompanying privileges and emoluments, were in the gift of the monarch. Otherwise posts like that of tax farmer, an obvious source of enrichment, were available for purchase. An ambitious man who was neither presented at court nor in the royal service—and who was not well-to-do or supported by those who were—was likely to engage in some form of intrigue behind the scenes to obtain patronage and financial advantage and thereby advance his career. And since a woman who was fascinated by political power could not hold office, the only way open to her to have any influence on affairs was through some man and/or some cabal. But such conduct, when it became known, inevitably entailed the loss of her reputation and brought upon the offending female head the stigma of being regarded as an intriguer, and therefore as an unnatural or unwomanly woman capable of any crime in the book.

Alexandrine de Tencin appears as a frustrated political animal. Fascinated by the political game, she simply had to know the state of play and contrive somehow to be a party to it. She could judge—without any excess of charity—the leading political players of the moment. What she wanted was to influence the course of the game in a direction that suited herself rather than them. Astonishingly, it was a dream that came within an inch of fulfillment.

With tireless energy she worked for years to further the career of her brother, the equally disreputable Pierre Guérin, abbé de Tencin. There were those who suspected him of simony. Indeed, he would not be above creaming off a certain sum for himself from the pension he acquired for James Edward Stuart, "the Old Pretender" in exile, whom the French treated as "His Majesty King James III." Tencin's rise was rapid. Ingratiating, a social charmer (and aware of it), favored by the ladies, he was to make his name during the continuing struggle between, on the one hand, adherents of the authority of the church of Rome and the papal bull *Unigenitus* and, on the other, all those who followed the condemned principles of the Dutch Augustinian theologian, Cornelius Jansen, or Jansénius, whether out of religious faith or patriotic Gallic sentiment. Many in France disapproved of the way Tencin, loud supporter of the papal bull *Unigenitus*, hounded the aged and unworldly Jansenist bishop Jean Soanen from his diocese. But leading churchmen in Rome acclaimed Tencin as the hammer of Jansenist heresy. While her brother was busily at work in the provinces putting an end to Jansenists, Alexandrine was active in gathering support for him among members of the clergy in Paris. It was possibly the only time she favored tradition, authority, and the established order, and it served her as an excuse she could invoke and as a kind of insurance against her later less conventional activities. How far religious principle was what really concerned her (or her brother) remains questionable. The conflict certainly provided them with an important opportunity to further their ambitions, and they seized it.

From time to time, however, over the years, Tencin candidly expressed to his sister his serious doubts about his own abilities and merits as well as his longing for a quiet life in retirement. High positions, he felt, were beyond his strength and his capabilities: "Whatever you say you will not make me believe that I am worth anything."[2] He had acquired experience in ecclesiastical diplomacy, he admitted, but was he capable of dealing successfully with lofty matters of state? He did not think he could continue, he was not fitted for the role she had conceived for him. All this was not modesty but awareness of his own shortcomings, he insisted, as he returned to his refrain. Repeatedly Alexandrine (after Lady Macbeth) had to screw his failing courage to the sticking place. She scolded him and pushed him. It was she who helped him to rise from abbé to bishop, from archbishop to cardinal and ultimately minister of state in the king's council. She thoroughly enjoyed all this ceaseless activity on his behalf, this sense of being privately at the center of things, supremely in the know, suggesting possibilities, advising men who had the power to act in public affairs visibly as she could not. It was a perilous game, marked by obstacles and setbacks to be faced with courage and perseverance. Influence through her brother was the goal. If some "great engine" might bring him to power as minister of foreign affairs and ultimately as prime minister, she meant to be one of its principal levers.[3]

∽

HER EARLY LIFE reads like something out of her novels with their heavy fathers (and grasping stepmothers) who imprison disobedient sons or force their unwilling daughters into a convent. Alexandrine was the youngest of five children of an upwardly mobile family. In a few generations the Guérins, descended from a peddler or, according to some, an itinerant silversmith, had risen to be distinguished lawyers and magistrates, prominent figures in the administration and society of Grenoble. They had always married well and had acquired property through marriage, including the estate of Tencin that gave them the "de" of their noble-sounding name. In order to preserve the inheritance of his three elder children so that it should not be divided into five smaller parts, Alexandrine's father had opted for the church for his two younger offspring. It was then common practice, when the father's authority was absolute and mirrored that of the monarch. Unlike her brother, Alexandrine would not adapt well to her father's choice. At the age of eight she was sent to be educated with well-born girls at the convent of Montfleury, outside Grenoble. But it turned out that education was not the sole purpose. The time came when she was about sixteen that her father insisted she take the veil. She pleaded with him, making it perfectly plain to him and to any who would listen that she had no vocation for the religious life. He was not to be moved. If, afterward, Alexandrine was so keen to acquire money it was surely in part because the excuse of the want of it had forced her to become a nun against her will. And without funds, what chance was there for her to do as she wished?

Years later the ecclesiastical commission of inquiry that took place after her father's death learned of a grave act of tyranny. The young girl had received a letter from her father who threatened that, if she refused to make her vows, he would have her confined "between four walls."[4] According to a sympathetic witness, Alexandrine had always shown distaste for convent life, had scarcely obeyed its rules (which were fairly relaxed at Montfleury), and had made no secret of her desire for freedom. She was not released from her vows until 1712, when she was thirty, an age then—and for long afterward—usually regarded as the terminal point for a woman's sexual career. Many continued to speak of her with contempt as "an unfrocked nun," though her release had finally been granted in due ecclesiastical form.

The years of concentrating on one aim, the effort to obtain her freedom, doubtless gave her an insight into how to maneuver and manipulate those who could be useful to her. The experience also prompted a fairly jaundiced view of her fellow human beings. "The great mistake of intelligent people is their failure to credit that men are as stupid as they are," she once acidly remarked.[5] Fixed and determined she certainly was over the long haul to her freedom, but otherwise there seems nothing except her experience of enforced restraint to presage the passion for life, the boundless ambition, and the consciousness of her superior perspicacity that she was soon to reveal.

Free of the cloister at last, Alexandrine was launched into Parisian society by one of her elder sisters, the popular comtesse de Ferriol, who lived in a *ménage à trois* with her elderly husband and her lover, and who had attracted many leading English as well as French notables to her salon. Rapidly Alexandrine made up for lost time. According to contemporaries she was highly animated, with a mobile expression, seductive, and noted for her superior intelligence. Of this last quality there was never any question. Cardinal Gualterio bore witness to this superiority, asserting that it was impossible to hold out against the "ascendancy of the wit of this lady, who is supremely endowed with it."[6] She also had the great gift of putting people at their ease, whatever their station in life, and however timid or inadequate they might feel at their own shortcomings. She never married. Known as Madame de Tencin ("madame" being a courtesy title), she allowed herself on occasion to be thought a marquise (which she was not), and she acquired the title of baronne de Ré only by very dubious means at the end of her life. The list of Alexandrine's lovers is long (though how far the mere association of her name with theirs caused the gossips to put some of them in her bed may remain a matter for futile speculation). Many of them were persons of note and political influence, men who could be of service to her and her brother.

Among those who did not figure in this category was an artillery officer named Destouches. While he was absent on service she gave birth to their son. The baby was then deposited on the steps of the

Church of Saint-Jean Le Rond. He was to become the distinguished mathematician and *philosophe* Jean Le Rond d'Alembert, editor of the celebrated *Encyclopédie* along with Diderot. On his return Destouches found the infant and placed him with foster parents. Yet it appears that Alexandrine herself never took the slightest interest in her talented offspring, even when he became famous. She did not mention him in her will, leaving her property to her doctor, Astruc, one of her long-standing lovers. The eighteenth-century attitude to children could be famously cavalier: witness later that great humanitarian lover of Nature, Jean-Jacques Rousseau, who notoriously confessed to depositing all his children in the foundling hospital. But the stain on Alexandrine's reputation, as on Rousseau's, has remained indelible. The strange thing is that in her novels she alludes with tender feeling to illegitimate babies. It might be supposed either that her callous conduct preyed on her mind (an unlikely hypothesis?) or else that she thought fiction required a warmer, more generous, or more conventional attitude.

This was not the only scandal to be attached to her name. Along with many others, she seized the opportunity for enrichment provided by the rise of John Law, the wizard financier from Scotland whom the regent Philippe d'Orléans decided to employ in order to try to solve the problem of the huge national debt left by Louis XIV's expenditure on display and on disastrous wars. It was her brother Pierre who saw to the Protestant adventurer's conversion and received him into the Catholic church—for a large consideration, thought the ill disposed. John Law's solution to the nation's acute financial difficulties (a solution he had been hawking unsuccessfully around Europe) was the introduction of guaranteed paper money in place of gold. Alexandrine set up a finance company in the rue Quincampoix, in the banking district where John Law had established his bank. Her own enterprise was for speculators like herself, her brothers and sisters, and numerous friends and lovers. It appears that she made the largest deposit. When, after the frenzy of speculation, the crash came and Law fled the country, Alexandrine had managed to extricate herself in time with a considerable fortune. Some of her friends were not so lucky. One of her lovers, the now ruined banker Charles-Joseph de La Fresnaye, who owed her large sums of money, committed suicide in her apartment in the rue Saint-Honoré. La Fresnaye, his mind deranged, left a long libelous suicide note, accusing her of theft and of plotting to murder him.

A dispute over territory between two different branches of the law meant that Alexandrine was treated very badly. Although she was unwell, she was seized, forced to come face-to-face with the mutilated corpse, interrogated for seven hours, and imprisoned in Le Châtelet. From there she was taken to the dreaded Bastille where she spent nearly three months, at first in harsh conditions. Her health suffered. At around the same time, Voltaire was incarcerated in the Bastille for exercising his wit at the expense of the chevalier de Rohan, who saw to it that he received a thrashing. Voltaire's fame as a writer did not save him from prison, while the valets and their aristocratic master escaped punishment. Alexandrine had met Voltaire (though they did not warm to each other) at the country home of her sister, the comtesse de Ferriol, whose sons had been his close companions at the prestigious Jesuit College of Louis-le-Grand and remained his friends. He formed what he liked to call a "triumvirate" with them, the comte de Pont-de-Veyle and the comte d'Argental, of whom more will be heard. With a characteristic air of insouciance, Voltaire informed the comtesse de Ferriol that he and his fellow prisoner had been unable to exchange kisses through a hole in the wall like Pyramus and Thisbe. Alexandrine's innocence was finally proclaimed after slow legal procedure, and she was released, but inevitably some of the mud stuck.

Among her lovers there were far more powerful figures than Destouches and the unfortunate banker La Fresnaye. Alexandrine was briefly the mistress of the dissolute Philippe, duc d'Orléans, before he became regent in 1715 after the death of Louis XIV. Speaking of bedfellows who tried to engage him in political discussion, and possibly thinking of her, Philippe is supposed to have remarked that "he did not like whores who talked politics between the sheets."[7] She was present nonetheless at the free and easy *petits soupers*—or as some would have it, orgies—that he hosted at the Palais-Royal, among his friends and their various mistresses. Historically the dissipated regent does not enjoy a good reputation, but he began by trying to institute reforms (which inevitably led to upheavals) and only afterward reverted to absolutism. With the regent's court and his brief eight-year rule came a new cultural climate with a release from the authoritarian and somberly devout last years of Louis XIV and his influential morganatic spouse, Madame de Maintenon, years that had darkened Alexandrine's early life. She was not the only one who would breathe and act more freely with the advent of the Regency.

It was in the last three years of the old king's reign, however, that Alexandrine established herself in Paris. This was a period of intense European diplomacy, culminating in the Treaty of Utrecht in 1713 that ended the War of the Spanish Succession between France and Spain on the one hand, and England, Austria, and the Netherlands on the other. Opinion in France held that England had done rather well out of it in acquiring Gibraltar and other colonial possessions. The foreign diplomats who now entered Alexandrine's social circle were all eminent and highly gifted, and if they enjoyed her company she certainly must have had the qualities to hold their attention. Now that she had the opportunity to glean and impart views and information, she began to be regarded as a spy. She attracted Matthew Prior, poet and diplomat (and secret agent), who was in Paris during the peace negotiations, popularly known as "Matt's Peace." He was famed for his satires, his burlesque on the old ballad "The Nut-Brown Maid" where a wife's fidelity is tested, his light verse like that on the poet-lover who hides his real love for one lady behind pretended love addressed to another, as all three engage in a game of dissembling. The son of a Dorset joiner, Prior had risen through patronage and by deserting the

Whigs for the Tories. Lord Bolingbroke, the Tory statesman, teased Prior for leaving the "Nut-Brown Maid" to devote himself to Alexandrine.

Particularly notable and lastingly useful among Alexandrine's lovers was, briefly, the eminent statesman and writer Henry St. John, Lord Bolingbroke, like Prior a member of the comtesse de Ferriol's social circle. He, too, was in France during negotiations of the Treaty of Utrecht. The eloquent leader of the Tory party under Queen Anne, last of the Stuart monarchs, Lord Bolingbroke occupied high office during her reign, being in turn her secretary of state, secretary of war, and prime minister. He would flee to France after the death of Queen Anne in 1714, and live there in exile for a decade, devoting himself to political journalism in which he castigated corruption in public life. His views were to be published in *The Idea of a Patriot King* and other influential works. His writings would stir proponents of parliamentary reform in England as well as thinkers and activists of the American Revolution like Jefferson. The liberal Germaine de Staël would later treasure Bolingbroke's famous reflections on exile.

Bolingbroke was a great friend of the distinguished jurist and liberal political thinker Montesquieu, who was a frequent visitor to Alexandrine's salon when he came to Paris from La Brède, his château near Bordeaux. It has been said that Bolingbroke's ideas on the English constitution and the separation of powers influenced those of Montesquieu. This was the gifted English statesman and man of letters who was happy to associate with the intelligent Alexandrine de Tencin. Where she was concerned, one connection of Bolingbroke's would prove vital for the rise of the Tencins, and that was his enduring loyalty to the fallen Stuarts. On the accession of the Hanoverian George I, Bolingbroke immersed himself in serious plotting on their behalf and was charged with treason. He remained constantly in communication with James Edward Stuart. It was through Bolingbroke that Alexandrine and her brother Pierre would have lasting relations with the Old Pretender who lived in exile first in France and then in Rome. Indeed, it was through this Stuart connection that Tencin would ultimately obtain his cardinal's hat.

If Alexandrine had ever required a political reference, she could not have done better than apply to Lord Bolingbroke. In a letter to the Old Pretender, Bolingbroke declared: "I have been in commerce with a woman for some time, who has as much ambition and cunning as any woman I have ever known—perhaps as any man." A supreme if somewhat equivocal accolade in that age from a statesman of Bolingbroke's standing, thoughtfulness, and experience! And surely proof that in his eyes Alexandrine was not a mere frivolous meddler in political matters but a serious and useful player. He went on: "Since my return to Paris, she has, under pretence of personal concern for me, frequently endeavoured to sound how far I was engaged in your service, and whether any enterprise was on foot. Your Majesty hardly imagines that the answers I gave her were calculated to make her believe that neither I nor anyone else thought at present of any such design. A few days ago she returned to the charge, with all the dexterity possible, and made use of all the advantages which her sex gives her," he added tellingly.[8]

When Bolingbroke pretended to open his heart to her, suggesting that military action was impossible, "Upon this she launched into the present state of affairs, in a manner that I could see was premeditated." In her view, because of the aged Louis XIV's ill health, no military move could be made for the moment. But once the duc d'Orléans was confirmed as regent, doubtless some great enterprise would be undertaken. This could be construed as French engagement in war in favor of the Stuarts, who were about to embark on the ill-planned and disastrous expedition of December 1715. Bolingbroke reported to the Old Pretender, "she did not see why a marriage between you and one of his daughters might not be an additional motive to him, and a tie of union between you. I received this proposal merrily, as a sally of her imagination; and she let it pass." All the same, Bolingbroke was inclined to take her views seriously, for he continued: "But there must be more in it, because of her character, because of the intimacy she has had with the duc d'Orléans [the name is given in cipher], and because of the private but strict commerce which I know she keeps with one of his confidants, and the influence which she has over that man." All this was certainly a delicate affair, he admitted, but he could see a great advantage in winning over a man of such ambition and talents, so closely "allied to power." He awaited the Pretender's decision as to whether "any use may be made of this intrigue."[9] Bolingbroke did not make light of any of the feelers that Madame de Tencin put out because he was fully aware of her onetime intimacy with Philippe d'Orléans, and he knew of her liaison with the man "allied to power" to whom he refers, the future regent's chief adviser, abbé Dubois.

Alexandrine's influence with abbé Dubois is also confirmed in the memoirs of a writer of genius, the duc de Saint-Simon, who cordially loathed her and her brother. Grand partisan of the old aristocracy to which he proudly belonged, and whose privileges he urged the duc d'Orléans to restore, Saint-Simon would not be alone in accusing the upstart siblings of incest. In his writings they figure without the ennobling "de," so that Alexandrine appears as "Mme Tencin" and her brother as plain "abbé Tencin," as if Saint-Simon is not to be misled by any pretensions on the part of this shady lady or this dodgy cleric from Grenoble. "Tencin," he hastened to emphasize with no little contempt, was in truth simply a piece of land that served for the entire family. According to Saint-Simon, one of the regent's intimates, Alexandrine "became the mistress of abbé Dubois and before long his confidant, then the director of most of his plans and secrets. For a fairly long time this fact remained hidden, so long as the rise of abbé Dubois required a degree of discretion. But as soon as he was named archbishop, and even more so when he was cardinal, she became the 'public mistress,' openly in command of everything at his abode, and holding court at her own as being the real channel of favor and fortune."[10] It was through her, said the resentful Saint-Simon, that her beloved brother began to rise in the world since her lover Dubois found the amenable Tencin supremely useful and always ready to be of assistance.

Entrusted by Dubois with various diplomatic missions to Rome, Tencin made influential connections there among the princes of the church, including the humanist Cardinal Lambertini, who would become Pope Benedict XIV and be happy to correspond with Alexandrine and send her his portrait. Tencin also had a secret mission, which was to obtain the cardinal's hat for Dubois—an enterprise successfully accomplished and rewarded with various benefices. Alexandrine, too, acquired through her association with Dubois the wealth that enabled her to invest so largely in John Law's economic boom and profit from it. However much he was blinkered by caste prejudice, Saint-Simon was not altogether far from the truth in his account of Alexandrine's influential role with Dubois.

Witness, for instance, the dispatch of the Prussian ambassador to his sovereign on the important channel opened by a fellow diplomat, the distinguished Count Hoym, a handsome and wealthy bibliophile in the service of King Augustus II of Poland (the ruler who was the ancestor of Aurore Dupin, the future George Sand). As it happened, the highly cultivated Hoym was quite besotted with Alexandrine and was counted among her lovers. The Prussian ambassador noted that Dubois always received Hoym most favorably, along with Sir Luke Schaub, a Swiss-born English envoy (another of her intimates), thanks to the good offices of Madame de Tencin. Clearly, continued the Prussian ambassador, her friend Hoym viewed her liaison with Dubois as "a very suitable means" for penetrating the true intentions of the French court—the implication being that such an approach through the lady was a perfectly good model to follow.[11] How was it possible for diplomats to penetrate the "true intentions" of these exclusive courts if there were not some helpful agent to supply them with information they could then evaluate by reading between the lines? No wonder that Bolingbroke or Hoym seized on the means offered to them by Madame de Tencin, and that those in power in France were ready to use her as a conduit of their own. In any case, Louis XV himself would later favor an additional form of secret diplomacy alongside that of his official representatives.

As for Dubois, the story goes that Alexandrine had even helped him to become prime minister. The poet and novelist Jean-François Marmontel, who was often to be found in her salon, related this tale in his memoirs. *Se non è vero, è ben trovato*—even if it is not true, it is cleverly invented. Son of a modest provincial doctor, Dubois was one of the rare members of the lesser bourgeoisie to hold high political office. When, in 1715, Philippe d'Orléans became regent during the minority of Louis XV, his private secretary and confidant Dubois rose to be a power in the land. Never actually ordained, and notorious for his debauchery, abbé Dubois would move swiftly from abbé to archbishop and cardinal, much to the derision of the wits and *chansonniers*, or versifying satirists, the sardonic commentators and rumormongers who served as forerunners of today's yellow press.

According to Marmontel, who was himself of modest origin, Alexandrine had a dispatch sent in code by her lover, Count Hoym, to his government, where he spoke of how important it would be for the regent to choose a prime minister of low rank, someone like Dubois, who came from nothing, raised from the mud of the gutter, and who could be returned to his nullity whenever it suited his master to do so. The dispatch was duly intercepted and decoded, and the regent, amused by its impertinence, followed Hoym's advice. The tale is not entirely far-fetched because Alexandrine would always enjoy sending fake letters, taking care to use special paper if the missive was to purport to be written by a foreigner, making sure that the tone and the invented attendant details of the supposed letter writer sounded convincing. For her, novelist as well as political manipulator, it was all part of the gamble and the fun. Besides, it meant that she stayed secretly in command.

One thing is certain, however, and that is her own indifference to rank—except in so far as station and highborn persons might be useful to her. If she did inspire Hoym's dispatch, with its excessively derogatory language, it would have been tongue in cheek, simply as a person acting or overacting the part of a prejudiced nobleman. Could she have forgotten her own family's obscure origins? The theme of distaste for questions of noble birth recurs in her novels. In *Le Siège de Calais*, for instance, a bourgeois displays high-souled feelings "above his birth, and rare even in the loftiest ranks of the nobility." Elsewhere one of her heroines speaks of "this chimera of birth that men prize so highly." Yet another, in *Les Malheurs de l'amour*, declares, "I am not affected by birth or rank."[12]

That super-subtle dramatist Marivaux, creator of *Les Fausses confidences*, who came to Paris about the same time as Alexandrine in 1712, and who frequented her salon in the rue Saint-Honoré, observed that there was never any question of social status in her company. He depicted her with deep appreciation as Madame Dorsin in his novel *La Vie de Marianne*, at one point so carried away that he forgot his narrator was a woman and spoke in his own voice. "There was no question of rank or position in her home," wrote Marivaux, who was the son of a provincial official of the Mint. "Nobody remembered the degree of importance he had in society. . . . Here were men speaking to their fellows, among whom only the most cogent arguments prevailed over weaker reasoning, nothing else. It was minds of equal dignity, if not of equal strength, who were associating with each other. That is how a person evolved when with her, through the impression made by her manner of thinking that was both rational [*raisonnable*] and philosophical [*philosophe*] . . . and that is what caused everyone there to become like that," added Marivaux.[13]

Her way of thinking was thus rooted in reason in the manner of the *philosophes* who were beginning to make their mark. She was an intellectual before the word was invented, who encouraged others to shine as intellectuals, if Marivaux is translated into modern parlance. In his opinion, the only concern of the habitués of her salon, regarded without exception as persons and intellects of equal dignity, was to put forward "the most cogent arguments." This indifference to rank, this value placed on merit and the equality of intellect and reasoning may be seen as a vital element in Alexandrine's radical stance among the writers and thinkers of her day. It was one of the most influential aspects of her salon, to be followed by women who would inherit her mantle later in the eighteenth century.

∽

WHAT WENT ON in this leading salon besides the much-vaunted "conversation" to be viewed with such nostalgia by future generations? What was discussed, and is it possible to ascertain something of its nature in so fleeting an element as talk? By the 1730s and '40s Alexandrine's salon would become a sought-after place not merely for pleasurable society but also for independent thought and discussion. Its reputation extended beyond the shores of France, and with it her own, as Lord Chesterfield remarked to her in elegant French when introducing a certain cultivated Mrs. Cleland who was about to visit Paris and was dying to have an entrée. Lord Chesterfield, Tory statesman and man of letters, and a friend of Lord Bolingbroke's, had been introduced into Alexandrine's salon by Montesquieu. Known today chiefly for his worldly advice to his son, Chesterfield spoke warmly of her kindness and of "the qualities that distinguish your heart and mind from all others."[14] Allowing for the elegant flattery of the mask of *politesse* that was to be the butt of Rousseau, these words of praise for her mind as well as her heart are not so very different from those of Marivaux when he portrayed Alexandrine as Madame Dorsin in *La Vie de Marianne*. A more generous person emerges than the unscrupulous, single-minded *arriviste* depicted by her enemies.

In her salon there was an inner circle of intimates, known as the Seven Wise Men, some of them eminent, erudite, and already members of the Académie Française or the Académie des Sciences, friends who were always welcome and who came and went frequently, as they liked. Notable among these intimates were Fontenelle, Marivaux, and Duclos. A much larger circle embraced a number of gifted women. These included Voltaire's mistress, Émilie du Châtelet, with her absorption in mathematics and science: her jealous passion for Voltaire seemed bizarre to the more reasonable Alexandrine, who thought her "more deeply lovesick than all the novels put together."[15] Another friend was the protofeminist Madame Dupin de Chenonceaux, later benefactress of Rousseau. Then there was an actress who issued from the famous Dancourt theatrical dynasty—for Alexandrine was passionately fond of the theatre. Mademoiselle Thérèse Deshayes was the mistress of the immensely wealthy tax farmer La Popelinière, whom Alexandrine (a veteran matchmaker) blackmailed into marrying her protégée. Madame Geoffrin came in order to see how things were managed, so that she would be able to organize her own salon.

Distinguished figures in the realms of medicine, science, ideas, and erudition could be found in Alexandrine's salon as well as men celebrated for fiction, drama, and poetry, at a time when there was no distinction between branches of knowledge, between the so-called two cultures of modern times. The poet Piron, author of *La Métromanie*, appears to have been employed as a kind of house poet, writing amusing and flattering light verse in praise of Alexandrine herself, her doings, and her "heavenly abode"—to be introduced there far outweighed every other possession, he proclaimed.[16] Leading literary figures of the age frequented her salon: these included abbé Prévost, author of *Manon Lescaut*, along with the poet and dramatist Marmontel, who was a partisan of toleration and opponent of slavery. They joined the (then neglected) playwright Marivaux, with his undercurrents of social criticism, on whose behalf Alexandrine battled tirelessly for ten years to have him elected a member of the Académie Française.

Many of the habitués of her salon, whom she called her "menagerie" or her "pets" after some private joke, were challenging thinkers and reformers. Among them was the utopian *philosophe* abbé de Saint-Pierre, advocate of "perpetual peace," disarmament, and international arbitration (later to be so much admired by George Sand as the harbinger of many influential nineteenth-century humanitarian ideals). Abbé de Saint-Pierre had actually dared to publish a critical view of the authoritarian rule of Louis XIV. Outraged at such lèse-majesté, the maréchal de Villeroy, a trusted courtier, succeeded in getting its author excluded from the Académie Française along with others punished "for having told the truth," said Alexandrine.[17] She added amusingly that this was the first victory that the unlucky maréchal de Villeroy (defeated at Ramillies by Marlborough) had won over the enemies of the late king. Clearly, then, she herself was opposed to forms of tyranny, oppression, and the abuse of power, as might be expected after her bitter experience of them in her youth.

The leading habitué of her salon was the illustrious Fontenelle, always amiable and witty if coldhearted, curious about everything, the great popularizer of science in writings addressed especially to women, and leading proponent of the Moderns. Another keen advocate of the Moderns was the once well-known poet Houdar de La Motte, whom Alexandrine employed to write letters and sermons for her brother (much to Voltaire's wry amusement). Also to be found there at various times was the young abbé Mably, later famed as an egalitarian, and engaged by Alexandrine as her brother's secretary and adviser in practical matters. Then there was the tax farmer Helvétius, atheist and materialist, afterward author of *De l'Esprit*. Not least was Montesquieu, seven years her junior. She called him fondly "my little Roman," after his writings on the causes of the grandeur and decadence of the Romans. When he was having serious difficulty in France with the publication of his *De l'Esprit des lois*, originally published in Geneva, it was she who undertook to disseminate copies of the work at a time when she was already quite ill and nearing the end of her life. She was one of the first to recognize its importance. Only a few years before, she had been introducing forbidden books into the country, thumbing her nose at the authorities, according to a police report of 1745.

It seems highly unlikely that these eminent figures, some of them daring thinkers and reformers whom she entertained, men and women who were luminaries of the age in literature, science, philosophy, and political and social thought, were simply taking chocolate and playing card games like quadrille. Doubtless they did find relaxation in discussing questions of psychological motivation that have always intrigued the French, and such tricky subjects as whether it was better to have loved and lost or never to have loved at all. But it does not seem probable that their conversation was confined to society games. After all, the opportunity would have been too good to miss. There is the evidence of Marivaux in his portrait of Alexandrine as Madame Dorsin: he asserted that, under her rationalist stimulus, the habitués of her salon were seeking to put forward the most cogent arguments and behaving like rational *philosophes*. In his memoirs, Marmontel, too, suggests that serious discussion was taking place in her salon, although he treats it as a kind of ball game: "In Marivaux impatience to prove his finesse and wisdom was obvious. Calmly, Montesquieu waited for the ball to come to him, but he did wait. . . . Fontenelle alone let it reach him without seeking it, and he used with such restraint the attention he received that his subtle witticisms and his amusing anecdotes only took up a moment. Helvétius, attentive, discreet, harvested it all so as to be able to sow the seeds in the future."[18] Although it is not possible now to know exactly what kind of ball was being thrown from one to another of these distinguished writers and *philosophes*, at the least it may be deduced that in Alexandrine's salon significant matters that could lead to changes in public opinion were being discussed.

On the theme of whether the *philosophes* undermined the ancien régime—whether it was all the fault of Voltaire and Rousseau, whether men of letters played a large, a little, or no part in the origins of the French Revolution of 1789—much ink has been spilt without any conclusive result. Still, at least one contemporary witness alludes to their influence. "Yet the empire of men of intellect, without being visible, is the most widespread of all. The powerful command but the wits rule, because in the end they shape public opinion which sooner or later overturns all forms of fanaticism."[19] This famous observation was made public in 1751, shortly after Alexandrine's death. Its author was Charles Duclos, a novelist of humble origin, who had been a long-standing member of her inner circle. His writings remain an important source for the social mores of the day, and it is even possible that he based his remark partly on his experience of her salon.

In spite of their flagrant misogyny, the Goncourt brothers, writing more than a hundred years later, could not help being impressed by Madame de Tencin's political skills. Reluctantly they acknowledged that she was "the first of the political women to understand the power of pen pushers, to flatter and pamper this new party: the men of letters."[20] Given the influence attributed to writers and *philosophes* in the eighteenth century, Alexandrine may be seen as immensely important in bringing them together and, by her rational attitude and manner of thought, encouraging them to present to one another the "most cogent arguments." She appears as a catalyst in the creation of public opinion, the elusive but important new element that (in the view of Charles Duclos) was already leaving its mark.

∽

AT FIRST GLANCE Alexandrine de Tencin's novels might seem to have little to do with her political ambitions and maneuvers. Her cool comment that Émilie du Châtelet was "more lovesick than all the novels put together" suggests that in her fiction Alexandrine would not necessarily be intent on depicting mundane existence. Hers is a world that mingles elements of psychological insight and autobiography with high romance and adventure. On occasion she makes use of a setting in the past that is closer to fantasy than to historical fact—and yet this background can indirectly have close connections with her own experience. Three of Alexandrine's novels were published between 1735 and 1747 at times when she was busily involved in her political activities.

In Alexandrine's day—and for long afterward—the great model was Madame de La Fayette's *La Princesse de Clèves* (1678), originally entitled *Mémoires*. Reputable eighteenth-century critics of literature like La Harpe and Grimm actually placed Alexandrine's first novel, *Mémoires du comte de Comminge* (1735), on the same level. Much of the discussion of Madame de La Fayette's tale, praised for its limpid style, has concentrated largely on the love story and the psychological dilemma of the heroine and less on its historical and political setting, the court of Henri II in the sixteenth century. The king's mistress, Diane de Poitiers, rules the Valois court: the nobles can attain power only through submission to her, for her rule is "absolute" over the monarch and the state. "Ambition and *galanterie* were the very soul of this court" since both men and women were preoccupied with love affairs and political intrigues that were inextricably intermingled.[21] Madame de La Fayette evidently had in mind the politico-amorous cabals during the Fronde as well as life at the court of the young Louis XIV. This model of a political and historical background would be followed by Alexandrine in her popular novel *Le Siège de Calais* and in the first two books of her *Anecdotes de la cour et du règne d'Édouard II, roi d'Angleterre* (the third book being completed after her death by Madame Élie de Beaumont).

Unlike Madame de La Fayette's tale and some of Alexandrine's later work, *Mémoires du comte de Comminge* does not rely on a politico-historical setting, though it has political and social implications. The comte de Comminge relates the story of the tragic love between himself and his cousin Adélaïde de Lussan. Sensitive and noble souls, they are the unfortunate offspring of two feuding brothers. When Comminge's tyrannical father, whose hatred for his brother cannot be assuaged, learns of his son's love for the daughter of his enemy, he has the young man imprisoned. Seeking to free her beloved from his prison, Adélaïde decides to marry another, and in order to prevent (as she thinks) any jealousy on Comminge's part, she chooses the most hateful of her suitors, the comte de Bénavidès. Her bizarre decision—or most extreme example of self-sacrificing love—does not produce the hoped-for result in the suffering Comminge, who compromises her reputation. Bénavidès distrusts his wife, maltreats her, and keeps her sequestered. Comminge, believing her to be dead, takes refuge in a monastery and becomes a monk, though his love for Adélaïde is as passionate as ever. But she is not dead. On the demise of her tyrannical husband she can leave her prison at last. Disguised as a man "for convenience's sake," she rests for a while in the church of a monastery where she recognizes her lover's voice in the choir. The disguised widow is received as a monk, still full of love for Comminge. Only when she lies dying does she confess her errors to the assembled grieving community, and she dies in an odor of sanctity. Comminge in torment still feels his love for her more deeply than his religion, continues dreaming about her, and asks to be buried with her in a single tomb.

This is not the sort of story—a tale of unalloyed suffering and perfect love whose dénouement would prove a boon to future dramatists and opera composers—that one might have expected from the pen of the intriguer and confidante of Bolingbroke and Dubois. Yet there are elements in it that betray Alexandrine's hatred of the abuse of authority in the way Comminge's father imprisons his son for disobedience, or Bénavidès can persecute and seques-trate his wife with impunity. Religion, too, is treated oddly by the onetime nun and sister of a famous cleric. For a girl to marry a man she loathes for the sake of her beloved makes a mockery of the sacrament of marriage. To become a monk—the path chosen by the lovers—while dreaming constantly of the loved one, is to make a mockery of the religious life. And if Adélaïde dies a penitent, Comminge shows no signs of penitence at all, persisting in placing his love above everything else. The idea of their joint tomb seems a further curious challenge to received religion. These subversive elements are concealed within the all-powerful love story and may have worked subliminally on some of the numerous admiring readers of this potent tale.

Closer to the notion of historical background as found in Madame de La Fayette's work is Alexandrine's novel *Le Siège de Calais*, set in a fourteenth century of fantasy. The English are besieging the city. Various characters in the novel, including one of the heroines disguised as a man, vie in nobility and present themselves as burghers of Calais whose lives are forfeit. The book turns on three interlocking love intrigues. One concerns Monsieur de Canaple who returns late from the hunt to mistake Madame de Granson's bed for his own. Adventures, mistaken identities, secret marriages, betrayals, hidden pregnancies, and rejected and abandoned infants—these appear to have entranced Alexandrine's contemporaries. "Why satisfy one's vengeance at the expense of this unfortunate little child? Is he guilty of his birth?"[22] There is also the autobiographical note of unwilling incarceration in the convent. "How barbarous to force this wretched girl to be buried alive!"[23] This particular theme figures prominently in *Les Malheurs de l'amour*, in the story of Eugénie, sent to the convent at the age of six. The abbess is told that the girl is the daughter of a man with many children and little property, and that she is to be encouraged to take the veil. Loath to comply, Eugénie consults the abbess who tells her, "You are not made for the cloister. . . . These chains are very heavy when reason alone is obliged to bear them."[24] Eugénie has been constrained to become a religious in order to enhance her brother's fortune. When he dies, the family seeks her out. She learns that she has been sacrificed for him and that in reality she is a great heiress of high birth. Her decision to remain in the convent implies a rebuke, a criticism of contemporary hypocrisy and greed.

Alexandrine's most outwardly political novel is her *Anecdotes de la cour et du règne d'Édouard II, roi d'Angleterre*, the work she did not live to finish. Here there is much talk of "the place of affairs and intrigues." Queen Isabelle is imperious, proud, ambitious, and appears sweet-natured and kindly only "when her interest required it." King Édouard lacks courage and resolution—clearly essential for a monarch worth his salt. Madame de Surrey hates the government. If the duc de Lancastre shows magnanimity, it is only for the sake of his ambition. The ministers appoint men who serve their policy rather than those more suited to their office. There is a revolt because of a new tax. King Édouard has observed unbridled ambition in Mylord Lacey and has therefore kept him out of public affairs, and "through that had made of him a fanatical republican. Under the pretext of upholding liberty, Mylord Lacey seethed with jealousy against those who obtained the position he would have liked to occupy in government."[25] This insight into the mind of the disappointed seeker after power and place who turns "republican" and advocates liberty only in order to achieve his ends appears to foresee the rise of such figures among the future rebels and revolutionaries of the 1780s. The duc de Lancastre betrays similar tendencies to those of Mylord Lacey and seems likely to become the leader of a party. Lancastre makes a great show of virtue and is venerated by the people, while in secret he commits crimes and signal acts of injustice. His daughter is sacrificed to his ambition and forced into marriage against her will. From all this it is perfectly plain that what is said to be going on at the court of Edward II and his favorite Gaveston is not a million miles away from what is happening in France during the reign of Louis XV, as Alexandrine has observed and criticized it in her letters.

Since her novels were published anonymously there was much speculation about their authorship. Friends like Fontenelle, Montesquieu, and Piron had been sworn to silence. As usual there was a quest for a male author, and opinion settled on one or other of her nephews, Pont-de-Veyle and d'Argental. Pont-de-Veyle in particular was a popular choice, though he was known chiefly as a writer of witty light comedies and as a social butterfly. In fact it was he who asked his aunt to compose on behalf of a lady a letter to be addressed to the king. As for d'Argental, she thought him a ninny, incapable of anything serious. Montesquieu told comte Guasco in 1742 that he could not satisfy his curiosity about the authorship of the novels because "it is a secret I have promised not to reveal." But on the day Alexandrine died he felt free to let Guasco know that "Mme de Tencin is the author of *Mémoires du comte de Comminge* and *Le Siège de Calais*, works thought until now to be by M. Pont-de-Veyle, her nephew. I think only Fontenelle and myself are privy to this secret."[26] Abbé Raynal would later say that one had only to consult Fontenelle or Piron to know that she also wrote *Les Malheurs de l'amour*.

∽

ALEXANDRINE HAD EXPERIENCED a serious setback in 1723 with the demise of Dubois, followed shortly after by that of the regent. Efforts to win the favor of Cardinal Fleury were not producing the desired effect. Formerly tutor to Louis XV, and now in his seventies, Fleury was the new source of power after 1726. The king, having attained his majority, had begun to rule in his own name. Fleury wished to reach an accommodation between Jesuits and Jansenists, in whose bitter conflict Alexandrine's brother had become notoriously embroiled. Nor was Fleury so amenable to flattery, or to feminine charms and wiles, as his dissolute predecessor. On the contrary, as a traditionalist of advanced years he was profoundly suspicious of women who diverged from their conventional role. As Fleury saw it, "He [Tencin] has a sister, an unfrocked nun, who is no less disreputable than he, and who is the most active among female intriguers; she holds illegal assemblies in Paris, and charity prevents me from saying anything more." Decent people had urged him to banish her from Paris "because there is nothing she does not meddle with, and there would even be enough to put her on trial. She has been a spy for the late king George of England, but I have held out against all these requests to send her away although I am well informed of her intrigues," grumbled the cardinal in July 1729.[27]

Alexandrine de Tencin's cosmopolitan salon, frequented then by churchmen and foreigners, appeared to Fleury as a hotbed of intrigue and discontent. In the summer of 1729 the lieutenant of police kept her under surveillance and reported in petty detail to the powerful minister Maurepas. From police reports it was known who entered the house, at what hour they arrived and departed, whether they stayed for a meal (and what was served) or whether they played cards, but nothing really incriminating was uncovered. Nonetheless tongues wagged and eventually enough indiscreet talk was reported to Fleury to put him in a rage: "She has convinced fools that if her brother were made cardinal he would surely become prime minister, albeit after my death, for she does me the honour to consider this to be an impossibility while I am alive, even if she counts on this not being for long." In his view "so preposterous a fantasy could only be believed by some Iroquois newly landed from America," but he felt she was using this argument about Tencin's prospects to bind people to her brother. Furious at having his death discussed as imminent, the elderly Fleury saw to it that Madame de Tencin was commanded to withdraw "without fuss" some distance from Paris because, he maintained, he had proof of her involvement in "intrigues displeasing to His Majesty."[28] Internal exile was thus being employed as a punishment for recalcitrant females long before Napoleon used it so tellingly as a weapon against Germaine de Staël.

For Alexandrine it was a considerable blow to be banished from her Parisian home and her friends. She hastened to defend herself, claiming against all the evidence to have lived in retirement. Fleury knew that she had not been busy with her embroidery: "prudence requires that above all a person of your sex should only intervene in matters relating to her proper sphere." Alexandrine was not to be so easily silenced. "I must have explained myself badly in my letter," she told Fleury with no little imaginative flair. "In asserting that I did not intervene and have never intervened in current affairs, I may not have stressed adequately the distinction I make between knowing about things and intervening in them."[29] This was a nice distinction possibly invented on the spur of the moment. All the same, Alexandrine was claiming that at least knowledge of political affairs could rightly be regarded as part of a woman's proper sphere, and that she was not to be confined solely to trivial, domestic, or private interests. This was a highly important distinction in 1730 and one that sought to undermine the ideal notion of perfect reclusive womanhood that remained current then and later.

In her self-justification, Alexandrine spoke of her affection for her brother, owning that she knew about his activities and that she had distributed some of his writings on matters of religion—"but all that does not amount to having a hand in intrigues, or intervening in such affairs contrary to the propriety of my sex," she assured Fleury. It is difficult to resist a smile at the fencing of these astute characters, each of whom knew exactly what value to put upon the words of the other. Some notabilities who carried weight with Fleury interceded on her behalf. And when, on being permitted to return to Paris "for her health" after her unwilling stay nearby in the country, Alexandrine thanked Fleury profusely, requesting with an air of innocence his guidance on the line of conduct she should follow, it seems likely that she saw the humor of it. Fleury declined to act as her mentor: "Your sex encloses you naturally within certain limits which it is not necessary to recall to you, and you have far too much wit to fail to be aware of those you should suggest to yourself."[30] This interchange, with its requirement of feminine self-censorship, reveals with perfect clarity the traditional and official line on female engagement in politics—a line that could be strongly enforced by authority whenever it chose to pounce. At the same time the professed submission of the rebellious woman, fretting at the boundaries and limitations imposed on her, carries with it a flash of impertinence here and there in its affected disingenuousness. Both sides know perfectly well that at the first opportunity Madame de Tencin will, within reason, do exactly as before and as she pleases.

In concrete practical terms, though, Alexandrine's high political hopes were disappointed when, on the death of Fleury in 1743, Louis XV decided against appointing a prime minister. Although her brother was named minister of state, he never took charge of foreign affairs, nor did he attain the highest office. The current of feeling against him ran high—"anybody but Tencin as prime minister" was a view expressed by people in power. What a chance it would be for his sister the notorious intriguer to exert her influence on public affairs! "Who would have thought Tencin could be compared to Moses? Both of them saw the Promised Land, but neither of them entered it," gloated an acute *chansonnier* in pithy verse.[31]

༄

BUT ALEXANDRINE did not abandon her efforts. Like others, she was trying to find a way to influence the king's choice of chief minister through his choice of mistress. A new opening was glimpsed when Louis XV took as his mistress the ravishing and imperious young widow Madame de La Tournelle (whom he later made duchesse de Châteauroux, the name by which she is best known). She was one of five sisters, two of them having already preceded her in Louis XV'S bed. It appeared that she might be amenable to persuasion by Alexandrine's ambitious new friend, the duc de Richelieu. Great-nephew of the mighty and austere Cardinal Richelieu who had imposed absolute monarchy in the previous century, he was made of different mettle, being one of the most notorious and dangerous libertines of the age. A successful courtier, he was soon to be appointed *Premier Gentilhomme de la Chambre* (or first chamberlain), a position that carried with it the privilege of being able to approach the monarch every day. He was also a dashing soldier who would be promoted to maréchal de France. Some fourteen years younger than Alexandrine, the duc de Richelieu had become her great confidant and ally.

Alexandrine's fascinating letters to him, witty, racy, like easy and vigorous spontaneous everyday talk, are utterly different in tone from her novels written in the restrained classical language that was so much admired by her contemporaries. These letters of 1743–1744 allude to Hungary, Prussia, Austria, Sweden, and the prospect of peace, for the War of the Austrian Succession had been raging since 1741. They are also filled with advice and projects as well as suggested arguments, devices, and ruses, and they give voice to her contempt for the way in which the country is being governed—or rather not governed, in her opinion. "I tell you everything I am thinking and everything that comes to the tip of my pen," she wrote to the duc de Richelieu.[32] Overcome with impatience, she felt a pressing need to unburden herself. She knew about the surveillance of the post by Louis XV's *cabinet noir*, and she had serious doubts about whether this invasion of privacy could really be condoned. At least, if such a means were to be employed, it should be of use to the king and not to the three ministers who controlled it, including her enemy Maurepas. Alexandrine and Richelieu communicated with each other by means of a code. Mostly they employed private couriers like those of Pâris-Duverney, one of the Pâris brothers who ran an extremely powerful banking house. "They are wealthy beyond the dreams of avarice, they have many friends, every underground resource you can think of, and money to spread around," she told Richelieu.[33]

All Alexandrine's ambitions now revolved around the duchesse de Châteauroux (who, as it happens, was discreetly biding her time to influence the king and who was very suspicious of Madame de Tencin's indiscretion and her inclination to overplay her hand). Rather her than another, wrote Alexandrine to Richelieu, for "she cannot do worse than what we are seeing now."[34] In Alexandrine's view, "A skillful woman knows how to mingle pleasure with the general interest and, without boring her lover, contrives to have him do what she wants." This was surely her own credo.

Writing to Richelieu, Alexandrine comments that although all the king's ministers are incompetent "dwarfs," they throw their weight about even more than their predecessors under the Sun King himself—and what is worse, they "govern despotically."[35] Here is a charge that presupposes a desire on her part for less interference and greater freedom. Chief among her *bêtes noires* is Maurepas, who had played so significant a role in her own earlier misfortunes when she was kept under surveillance and banished from Paris by Cardinal Fleury. The overthrow of Maurepas would have been a cause for private rejoicing if only she could accomplish it. He had received vast sums for the navy and not one ship had put to sea, she asserted. Such corruption as his should be used as an argument to bring about his fall. "He is a deceitful rogue. . . . He would like his colleagues to be more inept than he is, so as to appear a person of merit. Maurepas will only be a great man in the company of dwarfs, and he thinks a *bon mot* or an absurd epigram worth more than a plan of war or peace. God grant that he does not stay much longer in his post, for our interests and those of France."[36] Here the good of the country is kept in mind, and it is not dissociated from personal ambition. Maurepas would be dismissed in the last year of her life and would spend a long period out of office.

Vanity is the chief failing of the French, she opines before Stendhal, a later *arriviste* from Grenoble who was to recommend Madame de Tencin to his sister Pauline as a model in the important art of pleasing members of all social classes. Observing the society of her day, Alexandrine notes a general cynicism or indifference regarding political matters: she finds that most intelligent people do not trouble themselves about public affairs; instead they spend their time either in litigation or at the opera. Their lack of involvement and their frivolous disregard are to be deplored. Consequently she foresees catastrophe: "The way affairs are being conducted, everything is inevitably going to the devil. . . . People carry on in a stupid way, but in the end they will do so many stupid things that there will be an upheaval in every aspect of public affairs. These are in a parlous state . . . all this will end in a thunderclap." According to her, "Unless God intervenes, it is physically impossible for the State not to come a cropper."[37] These prophetic words were written more than forty years before the French Revolution. While Alexandrine de

Tencin was not alone in foreseeing disaster and can be placed with the more farsighted among her contemporaries, it is noteworthy that here is a woman who sees herself as more preoccupied with "the general interest" and with "public affairs" than either the frivolous who should know better or the ministers in command of the country.

As for Louis XV, Alexandrine could not conceal her disgust and scorn for a ruler who appeared to take so little interest in the affairs of the realm and in the general good. "This monarch is a strange fellow. What is going on in his kingdom seems not to concern him, nothing bothers him," she wrote to Richelieu, absent at the wars. Her picture is presumably drawn from what she had been told by her brother, now serving in the king's innermost council. The king's ministers were more masters of the country than he was, she observed. "Once again in spite of myself I feel a certain degree of contempt for a person who lets everything ride according to the will of others. He needs to be ruled. The weight of the reins of State is too heavy for him, and since it is and always will be needful for him to entrust them to someone else, I should have preferred it to be my brother."[38] With similar candor she reminded Richelieu that "we have no connections"—for the Tencins had no powerful aristocratic family to back them, as was commonly the case with those in pursuit of political power. He could therefore count on their gratitude if he supported them in their ambitions.

When the duchesse de Châteauroux finally persuaded Louis XV to put himself at the head of his armies, Alexandrine remarked that this had required no small effort: "Between ourselves he could not command a company of grenadiers, but his presence will do much; the people love the king out of habit. In the eyes of the soldiers and the people, a king of any sort is what the Ark of the Lord was for the Hebrews."[39] Alexandrine de Tencin's portrayal of Louis XV as a man bored by his role remains one of the most damning on record. The Goncourt brothers thought she painted a portrait of Louis XV's weaknesses unequaled by any historian they knew.[40] Indeed,

Alexandrine had the impression that she herself was more bothered than the king about the country's welfare.

It was a stroke of ill luck for the Tencins that the duchesse de Châteauroux, who had decided to follow their advice at last, was suddenly taken ill and died tragically at the age of twenty-seven. Her successor as *maîtresse en titre*, or official mistress, Madame de Pompadour (sustained by the powerful bankers, the Pâris brothers), although acquainted with Alexandrine de Tencin, had no need of her political acumen, having a sufficiency of her own. It was indeed the end of Alexandrine's aspirations. She and her brother were now in their sixties. Alexandrine had certainly acted as the prime mover, because after her death in 1749 Tencin retired to live comfortably in his archbishopric in Lyons, and he made no further effort to advance his political career.

ℐ

IN HIS deliciously satirical *Lettres persanes*, Montesquieu has his Persian visitor to France express astonishment at the influential political role of Frenchwomen. With some rhetorical exaggeration he was pointing to a real phenomenon. And perhaps Alexandrine's "little Roman" might have had his hostess in mind. According to Montesquieu's Persian mouthpiece, "These women constitute a sort of republic . . . it is like a new State within the State." Here in France were women who did not hesitate to speak to the minister on behalf of some courageous young colonel or some worthy abbé who had been overlooked. Such women were not necessarily royal favorites, for "there is no one who holds a position at court, in Paris or the provinces, without some woman through whose hands pass all the favors he grants and sometimes the injustices he can cause."[41] Alexandrine herself gave some useful career advice to her young protégé Marmontel: she urged him to choose his friends among women rather than men, "because by means of women you do all you want with men."[42] Men, she declared, were too busy with their own affairs to bother with yours, whereas women, if only out of idleness, would turn over in their minds how best to serve your interests.

Yet how frustrating this subordinate place as the adviser and agent of men must have appeared to a seriously enterprising and imaginative woman like Alexandrine de Tencin, supremely conscious of her superior abilities, can readily be guessed. Still, even crumbs from the table of power must have seemed better than nothing to the actively ambitious woman, and for some the element of secrecy may well have added a certain spice.

Alexandrine de Tencin had the pent-up energy of the years she had been forced to spend in the convent, energy that exploded into her many love affairs and her urge to influence matters of state. Devotion to her brother's career was a way of focusing that energy. She could be daring to the point of rashness in her obvious desire for a political role, indiscreet, apparently indifferent to scandal, and in revolt against heavy-handed authority in all its forms. This forceful woman was "If need be, a statesman [*homme d'État*]," proposed Piron in one of his versified allusions to her.[43]

Such political principles as Alexandrine de Tencin possessed have to be deduced from her own words and attitudes. That she wanted a strong monarch who really cared about the welfare of the realm seems evident, since she thought weak rule could lead only to the disaster she feared would come unless matters were taken in hand. Whatever her own political and financial intrigues, she disapproved of corruption, want of seriousness, failure of duty among ministers of the day. She thought women as well as men should occupy themselves with the fate of the country and be appreciated for doing so. Above all, she hated both private and public despotism. Her contempt for the powers-that-be, extending to the monarch himself, suggests that she felt she could do better if only she had been given the opportunity. She could scarcely have done much worse than those who were then in command of the destiny of France.

TWO

Manon Roland
The Making of a Revolutionary

> The habit of concentration, the study of history, the taste
> for philosophy . . . these would lead to my love of the
> organization of politics; not that petty intrigue which
> passes for politics in royal courts; not the futile knowl-
> edge of the newsmonger on which gossips pride them-
> selves and which only fools find amusing; but politics
> regarded as the art of governing men and developing
> their happiness in society.—MADAME ROLAND, *Mémoires*,
> 1793

If anyone helps to overturn conventional notions about the role
of women in politics in eighteenth-century France it is Marie-
Jeanne (Manon) Phlipon, later Madame Roland (1754–1793). It was
not just the upheavals of the French Revolution of 1789 that inspired her concern with history, society, and the art of government,
as it were out of the blue. On the contrary, she had been interested
in such subjects since she was a girl, claiming that she took her
treasured copy of Plutarch's lives of the great men of antiquity to
church to read instead of her missal when she was about nine. For
her, Plutarch remained one of the principal sources of her dream of

austere republican patriotism and heroism. To him would be added over time many authors in the fields of philosophy, theology, and history as well as literature. Deeply studious, she loved reading, even works by the most difficult thinkers, and she read widely for self-instruction and in order to acquire self-knowledge. In this way she was indeed well equipped to hold her own in any political discussion.

Young Mademoiselle Phlipon was a Parisian to her fingertips. As a girl she went shopping in the market with her mother. Accompanied by her devoted maid, she would visit her grandmother who lived on the charming Île Saint-Louis. Manon Phlipon comes to resemble those bourgeoises, or "women of the Third Estate" as they were called, depicted by Chardin with such refinement. For most of her early life she lived in a house on the Quai de l'Horloge, close by the Pont-Neuf, a vital artery of the old capital. The Pont-Neuf area was then one of the main centers of information in Paris where, in that age of official state and ecclesiastical censorship, purveyors of news and rumor—often indistinguishable—could contrive to offer their wares. If you were trying to find a friend of yours, it was said that sooner or later you would run into him there. When Manon looked out from her window over the Seine she could follow the animated scene; when she stepped out of the house she could scarcely fail to hear gossip about the latest financial crisis or scandal in high places.

It was on the busy Quai de l'Horloge that her father, Pierre-Gatien Phlipon, respectably established master engraver, kept his studio and also taught a number of young pupils or apprentices who boarded with him and his wife. Manon liked to recall that the milieu she knew in her youth was that of artists, albeit "not those of the front rank."[1] Her father's circle embraced figures who have left little trace. He associated with the painter Pierre-Étienne Falconet (son of the eminent sculptor); Nicolas-René Jollain, member of the Académie Royale de Peinture et de Sculpture, and sometime keeper of the king's pictures, who would later fall afoul of the great radical

Manon Roland (Portrait by Adelaide Labille-Guillard)

artist David during the Revolution; Nicolas Guibal, disciple of the successful decorative painter Natoire. There was also the sculptor L'Épine, "right-hand man" of the more celebrated Pigalle. Phlipon's colleagues do not appear to have belonged with the unlucky struggling artists and writers on art who were unable to find patronage and who, because they quite naturally resented being excluded, swelled the growing number of critics of varying caliber, *libellistes*, or scurrilous pamphleteers, *chansonniers*, or satirical poetasters, and protesters against the regime that denied them access to a decent livelihood. Yet one of her father's friends, whom Manon thought sufficiently talented to warrant a place in the Académie Royale de Peinture, was excluded because he was a Protestant.

Manon who, as she owned, was always "all eyes and ears" when anything interesting was being said or done, felt pleased that she had frequented artists in her youth and had listened to their intelligent discussions on serious aspects of art—and in all likelihood on matters of the day as well, since these were virtually inseparable. Even if these particular artists were not personally deprived, it is unlikely they would have failed to speak of the political and social controversies that were raging in the sphere of art. Talk about conditions in the art world entailed the appeal to "public opinion," a theme that began to figure increasingly in discussions on cultural affairs and social reform, and one that would prove of immense concern to her. The conversation and debates of artists seemed to Manon so much more enlightening and satisfying than the talk of tradespeople who were blinkered by their sole concern with commerce, or the chatter of members of the minor gentry she encountered who valued nothing but pedigree and rank while enjoying privileges that were not based on merit.

Her father taught her drawing and engraving, for which she showed considerable talent. He also took her to the leading Paris exhibitions of paintings and *objets d'art*, delighted to reveal his expertise as he pointed out significant details to her. Her interest in art would never wane. Having visited with a friend the studio of

Greuze, moralizing painter of bourgeois life, she returned there two years later, this time accompanied by Mignonne, her maid. By then Greuze was exhibiting his work outside the official Salon. Manon saw *The Father's Curse*, that icon of the bourgeois family, admiring the variety of passions depicted with "force and truth," though she now found it "too grey."[2] She spent some time in conversation with Greuze: she had the painter almost to herself, for there were few visitors present. At that period Greuze was isolated and humiliated, a focus of controversy. Manon's curiosity was aroused: she had to see for herself what was going on. Throughout her life she would be up to the minute, whether the manifestation in question was some fresh attack on a powerful minister or the current fashionable absorption in mesmerism.

Her mother, esteemed and adored, was pious without being fanatically devout, a more sober figure than her ebullient husband, much less bohemian, and more sensitive and perspicacious than he was. She encouraged Manon's passion for history and literature, and her inclination to devour any book that came her way, no matter how controversial, including the anti-clerical writings of Voltaire which devout ladies of Madame Phlipon's circle regarded as deeply dangerous and pernicious. Manon had tutors for history, geography, and arithmetic as well as for the subjects considered essential for girls—like music, singing, and dancing. She could play the guitar to a very high and even professional standard, according to her teacher who had instructed no less a personage than Marie-Antoinette. Whatever her daughter's talents in the arts, however—and they would be widely admired by connoisseurs—Madame Phlipon wanted them to be kept within the domestic sphere that was judged proper to Manon's station and her sex. On no account should they be produced in public or practiced professionally—a view with which Manon concurred for most of her life.

At the same time her mother inculcated all those solid bourgeois values of simplicity, probity, decency, modesty, thrift, and hard work, together with a deep distaste for laziness. Manon was also led to disdain an ostentatious style of life such as that current in court circles, especially around the much criticized, frivolous, and spendthrift Marie-Antoinette, or among certain prominent members of the aristocracy. Their excesses were known through word of mouth and the scandal sheets of the pamphleteers. Still, what Manon later called "the manners of the Parisian bourgeoisie" of her day allowed for considerable expense in dressing up for two hours of parading in the Tuileries gardens on Sundays, or for family visits, baptisms, and weddings.[3] Her parents had suffered the misfortune of losing six children in infancy, Manon being the sole survivor. They naturally concentrated all their affection upon her. It is scarcely surprising that their cherished and gifted daughter grew up with a sense of her own value, rightness, importance, and, above all, an ability to think for herself.

It was on the subject of religion that Manon began to differ quietly from her mother. Doubts arose. In particular she found that she could not accept the doctrine of papal infallibility. As for the concept of eternal punishment and damnation for those who—like Socrates—lived before the rise of Christianity, it seemed to her cruel, unjust, and absurd. All this was in the air, conveyed through the work of Voltaire and other *philosophes* of the Enlightenment like abbé Raynal and Diderot, whom she admired. Once Manon had rejected the teachings of the church on one point, the spirit of inquiry was bound to take her further—as Diderot, writing in 1771 at the height of the conflict between the king and the *parlements*, held that it necessarily would do. Once the majesty of heaven was under attack, declared Diderot, it was impossible to stop there, and the assault against kings who ruled by divine right must follow. Manon would become an unbeliever, though ready to attend church "for the good order of society and the edification of my neighbor," or perhaps more properly a deist after the manner of Voltaire.[4]

Long before she had reached that stage of doubt and denial, however, she had been stirred by "romantic ideas about the cloister" drawn from poems and novels (though not from those of Madame de Tencin, where the relegation of unwilling girls to the convent is shown as a form of the abuse of authority and power, a theme that would remain a question of serious critical debate). It was at her own wish that in May 1765, when she was eleven, Manon entered the convent occupied by the nuns of the Congrégation de Notre-Dame, in the rue Neuve-Saint-Étienne, as a boarder. She loved the peace and silence of the convent and was soon the nuns' star pupil. During the year she spent there she grew close to two sisters, Sophie and Henriette Cannet, who issued from the higher bourgeoisie of Amiens and who were to have a lasting effect on the course of her life. The younger sister, Sophie, became her intimate friend.

In the most remarkable series of letters that Manon wrote to the Cannet sisters over the ensuing years, letters that fill large volumes, she discovered her vocation as a writer. Manon would later admit this to herself, even going so far as to call her letters to Sophie "the origin of my taste for writing, and one of the causes which, through habitual use, increased my facility in it."[5] She found writing letters a pleasure because she felt they offered an opportunity to broach many diverse subjects and adopt different tones of voice. They could be a way of dramatizing her existence, too. She would write letters for her father, imitating his manner; for a certain lady of the minor gentry who, despite her rank and her pretensions, was too ignorant to write her own; and eventually for her husband in his professional and public life. And it was she who would correspond with her husband's radical friends, future luminaries of the Revolution, because he was too busy and preferred to leave the task to her since she enjoyed it so much.

What made Manon decide so resolutely against becoming a professional writer when there were many talented women who were practicing the serious moral essay as well as certain forms of journalism, and most notably the art of the novel, with singular success? When a cultivated masculine friend prophesied that Mademoiselle Phlipon would indeed write a book one day, she declared vehemently that she would rather eat her fingers—a pretty drastic solution. The force of conventional opinion, powerful as it was, would scarcely have been sufficient to quell an independent spirit like hers. Was her reluctance largely due to some personal experience?

Introduced by male admirers of her talents into various intellectual milieux of the capital, young Mademoiselle Phlipon found many of the women celebrities of the day absurdly pretentious. At the amateur concerts given in the salon of Madame L'Épine, the Italian singer who was married to the sculptor friend of her father's, or when attending the reading circles where women writers were to be seen displaying (as she thought) too much flesh along with their accomplishments, she was far from impressed. The well-known author Madame de Puysieux, for instance, onetime mistress of Diderot, or the prolific novelist Madame Benoît, whose work (Manon claimed) was already on the wane, offended her by their vanity and their posturing. Originally she had believed that a woman author who wrote on moral subjects must be someone deemed worthy of respect, but this proved to be far from the case.

Keen observer as she was, she noted with dismay the attitude of the men who were present. She saw that they ridiculed women authors alone for the very faults men themselves shared. Manon came to believe quite early that the publicly acknowledged woman author lost more than she gained from her celebrity. Such a person, she maintained, was despised by men and criticized without mercy by members of her own sex. Besides, if her writings were poor, she was an object of mockery; if they were good they were stolen from her. When forced to recognize her merit, men tore her character—as well as her manners, her behavior, and her gifts—to shreds, to such a degree that any reputation she might have acquired for her intelligence was counterbalanced by the public examination of all her faults. Clearly the perils of celebrity appeared particularly daunting for a talented woman, and the one thing Manon was not prepared to risk was ridicule.

In some respects Manon may be considered a professional writer manqué. She wrote a great deal in her youth. She once sketched a metaphysical dissertation, planned a philosophical novel, and had been persuaded to submit an essay on women's education to a provincial academy—anonymously, of course. She had even written a lively account of a journey into the country disguised as her cousin's maid, and had fantasized about the advantages of traveling in men's clothes. But that was as far as it went. Nothing was to be for the eyes of the public under her own name. From her memoirs it would appear that she later had regrets on this score as on others. She came to feel that she could have made her mark in France as a serious historian to equal the eminent Mrs. Catharine Macaulay, whose history of England in numerous volumes, written from a radical republican perspective, Manon deeply admired. Such an ambition was surely not beyond her talents.

On one rare occasion she was to compose, in her own (married) name, a reply to a certain Varenne de Fénille who had criticized her husband's contribution to a debate on a universal language, sponsored by one of the many provincial academies that served as the cultural associations of the day. This debate was prompted by Antoine de Rivarol's celebrated *Discourse on the Universality of the French Language* (1784). After a few conventionally coy remarks about a woman's place, Manon went on to support her husband's advocacy of English. She observed that relations with the young American republic, its constitution and commerce, would eventually lead to the choice of English as the universal language.

Then, with a light touch, she launched into a spirited appraisal of English poets and novelists, culminating in a dazzling defense of Shakespeare. In an age that still largely endorsed Voltaire, who criticized Shakespeare for bad taste, ignorance of the famous three unities, and failure to aspire to the elevated tone that characterized French tragedy, Manon recognized with enthusiasm Shakespeare's unique genius. She saw that if he chose to show common people alongside those of high birth it was precisely because "that is how they exist in nature."[6] Her keen admiration antedates by more than forty years that of Stendhal in *Racine et Shakespeare* (1823) and the heady intoxication of Romantics like Berlioz with Shakespearian poetry. Moreover, Manon wanted to know why Varenne de Fénille was not "curious" enough to try to find out why the English admired a dramatist whose style was so different from that of the French. This letter, virtually a short essay, shows what an acute literary critic was lost to posterity.

Manon was driven to consider writing for the public at the end of her life, when she saw that the favorable verdict of public opinion was essential for her aims to be appreciated and her position understood. For it was in dire circumstances, in prison, in the last months of her life in 1793, that she felt impelled to write her memoirs. By then she knew that she had little chance of survival and that the work, if it appeared in print at all, would necessarily be published posthumously. She intended to tell the whole truth: "I shall tell everything, absolutely everything, it is the only way to be of use."[7] This was a highly creditable if impossible aim. Principally she wished to leave behind her "moral and political testament" and at the same time to preserve her husband's reputation and her own in the eyes of the world and of future generations. These aims are not entirely compatible.

"Can I write?" was her first question on entering the prison gates. The memoirs are immensely compelling, powerful, and impressive, but they are disjointed—a broken monument. Perhaps it is their very disjointedness that makes them all the more moving today. Trusted friends who were allowed to visit her concealed the completed sections of the manuscript and smuggled them out of the prison at great risk to themselves. One, when in fear of immediate discovery, burned the pages in his possession. They could not be replaced. Manon was devastated. So essential to her sense of her own being was the composition of her memoirs that she said she wished she herself had been consigned to the flames.

Whereas many of the numerous memoirs of the Revolution were composed by survivors long after the event, often with total recall and the benefit of hindsight, a few were penned during the upheaval, and hers in particular come as it were hot off the press, written with passionate urgency. While protecting her image, they nonetheless offer a unique insight into the life and reflections of a Frenchwoman who was very conscious of her class—and, as far as I know, there is nothing to compare with them from the hand of "a woman of the Third Estate" cut off in her prime.

ᗧ

ONE OF THE MOST telling moments of Manon's early life had occurred in 1776 when at the age of twenty-two she tried to call on the celebrated recluse, Jean-Jacques Rousseau. She failed to get past Thérèse Levasseur, Rousseau's long-suffering mistress, who by then was his wife. As for Manon's letter, Rousseau in his reply thought, or affected to think, that it was written by a man. What this adventure demanded in the way of enterprise, daring, and energy for a young woman of the day, brought up to be careful of public opinion (as indeed Rousseau himself advised in *Émile*) may readily be supposed.

Disappointed but not disillusioned, Manon wrote to her dear friend Sophie Cannet in Amiens: "His genius has warmed my soul. I have felt it set me aflame, uplift and ennoble me."[8] It was not just his novel *Julie, ou la Nouvelle Héloïse*, qualified by her as "a masterpiece of feeling," that seized her imagination, but also his *Discourse on the Origin of Inequality*, his *Social Contract*, and other works that contained "countless interesting truths in connection with government."[9] Political matters ceaselessly occupied her thoughts. Despite Rousseau's faults of character (for which she found excuses), in her eyes the self-styled "lover of truth" remained not just a genius but a friend of humanity, its benefactor, a man of virtue, and "a citizen"—high praise indeed.

This admiration would never fade, and it was perhaps all the more intense because she had discovered Rousseau fairly late, when she was emotionally vulnerable on account of her mother's sudden decline and untimely death in 1775. He joined her favorite authors:

Plutarch, of course, and Montaigne (lauded for his probing self-inquiry and candor). She told Sophie Cannet that she loved Rousseau "beyond all expression. I carry Rousseau in my heart." He is "my breviary," she declared.[10]

As if all this were not enough, she once confessed, in a strange cry addressed to "divine Rousseau," her idol: "You are like me. I find myself in you. You transform me *into you, or you are none other* than myself" (her emphasis).[11] She owned that she was inclined to merge into literary personages or characters, whether real or fictional, who seized her imagination. Given her passionate enthusiasm for Rousseau, it is no surprise to learn that some years later she made a pilgrimage to Ermenonville, where the author of *Les Confessions* then lay buried on an island in the park. The inscription on the cenotaph, recorded in a delicate sketch by Hubert Robert, ran: "Here lies the Man of Nature and of Truth." With her husband Manon would also visit sites associated with Rousseau when they were in Geneva, the great man's birthplace. She waxed indignant at the way he had been persecuted.

Clearly this *exaltée*, who would become the supreme political heroine of the French Revolution for Stendhal and Carlyle, was already an exceptional young woman when she discovered Rousseau. "I admit that I do not feel I am made for ordinary things," she had told Sophie.[12] Yet her background was ordinary enough. She came from what she herself called—in 1777—"*la moyenne classe*," the respectable lower middle class of artisans-cum-artists, craftsmen, tradespeople, as distinct from those she defined as the "common" or "the most numerous" class. It was a vital distinction.

At that time the lower orders of the trading bourgeoisie, to say nothing of the plebs, were not even regarded as forming part of what was acknowledged by the aristocratically minded intellectual elite as society as a whole. As for *le monde*, or Parisian "society," it constituted an influential world of its own. Writing some fifty or so years earlier, the Scottish financier John Law had already observed that the common people in France "are not, so to speak, of any class." In a rigidly fixed hierarchy such creatures fell outside the social categories that were regarded as being of any significance. Alexandrine de Tencin's protégé Marivaux, in *La Vie de Marianne* (1734), spoke sarcastically about the persistent French concern with the upper crust and indifference to all other sections of society: "Leave the rest of men there; let them live, but see that they are never portrayed." Nature could perfectly well have avoided letting them be born, added Marivaux with biting irony. The noted critic Baron Grimm, writing in 1753, could still condemn a novel because "its characters are all people who have no existence whatever in society" since they belonged to the lower orders. "Those who go on foot are not part of society . . . ," wrote Rousseau's alter ego Saint-Preux angrily when describing his reactions to life in Paris. "The most numerous class almost counted for nothing," declared Manon Roland in 1789.[13]

In perceiving herself to be a member of "*la moyenne classe*," Manon was making an important statement. She was already staking a claim to a place in a society where people would be judged on their merits and not on their social status. Her origins were unlike those of the liberal Germaine de Staël, which lay in the better situated and ever-rising bourgeoisie of high finance that often bought its way into the nobility, or those of the radical-turned-conservative Félicité de Genlis, who was descended from the old aristocracy of the *noblesse d'épée* with its military and naval traditions.

When the nineteenth-century poet and critic Sainte-Beuve came to consider the destiny of Madame Roland, he suggested that the question of social status or class could scarcely be eluded. He observed: "She marks a date, that of the introduction of solid merit and grace into the middle class where it was to play thenceforward an ever increasing role. From her onwards, what before had scarcely been boldly usurped began to be owned as a right."[14] It is striking that he chose Manon Roland to head the women who came after Rousseau and were indebted to that great eccentric, rather than Germaine de Staël whom he admired in equal measure. Perhaps it was because he sensed Manon's proximity to the naturalness, candor, spontaneity, and plain speaking of Rousseau, son of a Swiss watchmaker, the absence of flummery and pretension where rank was concerned.

Following Rousseau's *Confessions*, where her idol spoke openly about his sexual experiences, Manon would write frankly in her memoirs about such matters as menstruation and female sexuality (to Sainte-Beuve's protestations of distaste). In graphic detail she related the unwanted sexual attentions of one of her father's young apprentices when she was a girl. She did not even hesitate to convey the shock and disappointment of her wedding night. It must have seemed to Sainte-Beuve (who was no hermit) that these were not the kind of remarks to be made to the general public by any woman who prided herself on her feminine modesty and *pudeur*, and that there might even be a social and political agenda underlying the nature of these revelations. She appeared to some degree a woman in advance of her day. In her memoirs she would allude to her imaginative sensibility, her "wandering and romantic imagination," her "romantic mind."[15] She could have found the word "romantic" in one of her favorite writers, the Scottish poet James Thomson, melancholy lover of nature, virtue, and liberty.

In some respects Manon's revealing letters to Sophie and Henriette Cannet foreshadow her memoirs, at times resembling a personal diary. Here can be found, conveyed at length, not only the day-to-day details of her domestic life but also her moods, feelings, thoughts, and opinions. She recounts her almost unbearable distress at her mother's death. Then she has to endure her father's changed ways, his rapid decline into dissipation and near ruin. This unfortunate development she turns into a vivid family drama with herself as the central suffering victim. Here, too, are portraits and judgments of the people she encountered—what she liked to call her study of men. This is accompanied by her unrelenting self-analysis (the acknowledgment of "a strong dose of amour-propre," for instance). She felt the need to write, and in these letters she could test her writing skills and refine her style. Indeed she was already a frustrated author, enraged when she thought that letters of hers were lost or had been intercepted by the censors.

Some of these letters report on her reading and presuppose similar interests in her friends or stimulate discussion between them. On occasion they are like didactic literary or political essays. Among the most singular is the one dated January 5, 1777, that gives her account of Jean-Louis Delolme's study of the English constitution. It occupies many pages and offers an insight into her political views at the time, some twelve years before the Revolution. Delolme, a Swiss republican, was "a truly political mind" in her judgment, and he presumably confirmed her republican inclinations.[16] For Mademoiselle Phlipon became a republican in spirit long before Robespierre. (According to her, in the summer of 1791 the Incorruptible was still asking with a nervous laugh what exactly a republic was.)

Moreover, it appeared to her, as a convinced Anglophile, that the English were enjoying genuine liberty at a time when the French had to labor under the irrational constraints of absolute monarchy. Obliquely, in his *Lettres philosophiques*, Voltaire had already implied as much. She felt nothing but contempt for "the insulting Asiatic luxury" of the French kings, which would have been known to her as to many others from the *libelles* and *chansons*, the partly accurate and partly fictional written and spoken scandalous revelations of pamphleteers and satirists. In her view of English history, the arrest and execution of Charles I in 1649 clearly set an example to the world at large (as indeed it did). As for the "Glorious Revolution" of 1688, with the Bill of Rights it had established the true principles of societies. And this was not all she conveyed to her friends as she reflected on Delolme's work.

By expelling James II, a king who had violated his solemn oaths, the "Glorious Revolution" had affirmed—or rather reaffirmed—the right of oppressed peoples to resist tyranny. The violation of the royal oath would be one of Manon's chief accusations against Louis XVI after his attempt to flee abroad and his arrest at Varennes in

June 1791. For he had sworn, however unwillingly, to uphold the constitution. With the removal of a despotic royal house, the English Revolution of 1688 demonstrated to everyone that nations do not belong to kings, she declared; on the contrary, legislative powers are rightly assigned to parliaments alone. There must be elections and freedom of the press. These, then, were the advanced ideas circulating among intelligent convent-bred young ladies in Paris and the provinces in the 1770s.

They were to be among the convictions that Manon would carry with burning intensity into the French Revolution. She kept at least one copy of her résumé of Delolme's views which, in August 1784, she was able to offer to Louis-Augustin-Guillaume Bosc, one of her radical-minded friends who was then an official in the postal service. In this way she appears as a conduit of republican tendencies in the years before the Revolution. Two years earlier, in August 1782, she had been railing against the citizens of Geneva who, it seemed to her, were totally unworthy of liberty because they had failed to fight for their freedom with sufficient energy. They should have defended to the last so dear a treasure as liberty, and, rather than submit, they should have "died in the ruins." At the mere thought of their spinelessness, "I am seized with impatience . . . and my blood boils," she told Bosc.[17] At the beginning of the Revolution the words she would employ would not be very different.

It was not only from books that Manon derived her political views, though some of these works were very challenging. Apart from histories of ancient Greece and Rome, she delved into a study of the revolutions in England and another on Spanish conspiracies against the Venetian republic. She had even read the *remontrances*, documents published by the lawyers of the Parisian and provincial *parlements* in their long and increasingly bitter conflict with the king. The more radical such defiant challenges to royal power were, the more they appealed to her. She also read the *papiers publics*, the journals of the day. Much of her information was drawn from travelers she encountered. If she met a Frenchman who had served in the colonies, in Pondichery or Louisiana, a Genevan who had lived in Russia, a Prussian, a Corsican sea captain who had visited Senegal (which she knew as the important entrepôt for the slave trade), she seized the opportunity to question them. A "poor black" she met at Vincennes aroused her sympathy. From all these encounters she formed an historical and political map of Europe in her head, as she put it.

When she came upon some "Americans" (who turned out to be wealthy slave-owning inhabitants of the French colony of Saint-Domingue) she did not hesitate to ask them about the progress of the War of Independence and "the condition of the insurgents." As she wrote to Sophie in October 1777, "I am very pleased to think as you do about the importance of this revolution. I regard it with keen interest, and I wish for the liberty of America, as just vengeance for the violation of natural law in that unhappy continent, so little shaped for unhappiness."[18] Together with sentiment in the style of Rousseau, the note of intransigence, morbid violence, and revenge can already be heard—that tone of ruthless ancient Roman severity, or what passed for it in eighteenth-century France. There was, at the same time, a kind of self-assurance or self-congratulation at the advances that had been made in political thinking, presumably by Rousseau in particular. "We know more about the true principles of good policy in the last twenty years than all the governments of antiquity," wrote Manon to Sophie.[19]

The consequence of this sense of progress in political thinking meant that one could now be certain as to what true political principles were, who was in possession of them, and who was not. This attitude would lead to the notion of "true patriots" (oneself and one's friends) and "false patriots" (one's opponents) as well as to some serious misjudgments. A number of those who were thought to be true would unluckily turn out to be false. While Manon's high principles were directed to the service of humanity, she had an extremely poor view of the generality of men, an opinion repeated many times in her letters and memoirs. She does not appear to have noticed, acute as she was, the contradiction between her passionate devotion to the regeneration of humanity and her convinced misanthropy, doubtless fostered to some degree by personal experience. Manon's charm and intelligence, and more particularly the prospect of her dowry, had attracted a number of suitors. Unfortunately her father—now a merry widower—lost most of her portion in gambling and dissipation. Various suitors faded quietly away along with her financial prospects. She did become really attached to an impecunious young writer of superior social position named Mammès-Claude-Pahin de La Blancherie, who failed her in this respect. He had even invited her to write for his journal. The difficulty was that she had cultivated her sensibility, as the eighteenth century would have it, and she had educated herself above her station. "Had I lived with Plutarch and the philosophers just to marry a merchant without feelings similar to my own?" she was to ask rhetorically in her memoirs.[20] There were a few intelligent and well-traveled men, somewhat advanced in years, who shared her interests, gave her access to their libraries, escorted her to literary or musical gatherings, or to public sessions of the Académie Française. She might have been on the brink of committing herself to an arrangement with one of these gentlemen when her affairs took a sudden and more hopeful turn.

✍

IT WAS THROUGH Sophie Cannet in Amiens that Jean-Marie Roland de La Platière came to call with a letter of introduction when he visited Paris in 1776. He was known as a liberal-minded advocate of free trade. At that time he was serving as the extremely conscientious and hardworking official inspector of manufactures in Picardy, whose headquarters were in Amiens. A bachelor past forty, he had traveled widely in Europe and he was acquainted with eminent savants. Tall, thin, with sallow complexion and receding hair, he visited Manon for the first time on January 11, 1776. As she reported to Sophie, they touched lightly on a number of interesting persons and subjects, including "Rousseau, Voltaire, travels, Switzerland, the government, etcetera."[21] Here was someone with whom she could discuss literature, philosophy, and politics—a friend, mentor, and guide. Roland might be domineering, but he also appeared "austere," high principled, a man of learning, experience, and integrity. "I believed I saw that as regards politics and conduct he held true principles," wrote Manon to Sophie, revealing her own priorities as a young woman of twenty-two.[22]

There followed an odd on-off courtship that lasted some four years. What soon became obvious was that Roland was in no hurry to commit himself. He was a very proud, dour, irritable man, set in his ways. His superiors in Amiens disliked his overbearing, highhanded manner. One called him "uncontrollable . . . a man who seeks to run everything . . . good for giving orders but not for obeying them."[23] He was also touchy, suspicious, and secretive. He did not want Manon to continue her intimate confessional friendship with Sophie Cannet. Manon did sacrifice it, but with no little regret, because she thought a woman needed to have women friends. Neither Sophie nor Manon's father were to be told about the warmth of the developing association and understanding between Roland and Mademoiselle Phlipon.

Manon lost no time in their burgeoning correspondence in enlightening Roland at length about her moral values, her love of "virtue," her views on the good society. The letters she wrote to him provided her with yet another opportunity to recount her situation in life and dramatize her feelings and responses. There were times when he became seriously irritated by all this, asking her to be less of a phrasemaker, to moderate her long dissertations, calling her endlessly argumentative or *"la sempiternelle raisonneuse."*[24] For her part, she was not at all pleased by his inflexibility and his lack of sympathy and understanding. All the same, she knew how to soothe and flatter his masculine vanity. Happiness in marriage certainly depended on the collaboration of both parties, she informed him, while urging him: "Be my master, my support, my crown; let your spirit inspire me, elevate and improve me. Your will shall be my law. We shall study a little together because the pleasures of the mind do not fade away . . . you will enlighten me, I shall think with your ideas. I shall become more worthy."[25] Constantly she assured him directly and obliquely that he was her superior and that this was just what she wanted. Yet in her turn she was irritated by his obduracy, for he could not brook contradiction, and some of his unsympathetic or insensitive comments she found hard to take. It was the clash of "two superiorities."

The question of social position was not long in coming to the fore. Roland issued from landowning gentry in the Lyons area, though his family was not particularly well-to-do. His place in the social hierarchy was therefore superior to hers. Manon was quite conscious of this social distinction when the prospect of marriage was seriously discussed: "The place I occupy is not unworthy of me, since I can exercise virtues in it. Nor do I consider myself unworthy of another situation where they could be practiced in a different way. If the hand of a husband . . . were to raise me to a rank far above my own, I should ascend to it gratefully and without surprise."[26] In her various accounts of her life she had revealed to Roland—frankly if unwisely, given his suspicious temperament—her father's gambling and the fact that Phlipon now had a mistress. Roland took this badly, putting the worst construction on it. His parents, when they finally heard of his project to marry a person of lesser social standing whom they had never met, and moreover a woman without a dowry, whose father was apparently on the brink of dishonor, naturally saw the marriage as a misalliance.

Nonetheless Roland eventually wrote to Phlipon in cold tones of the strictest formality, asking for Manon's hand in marriage and fully expecting her father to be flattered by the offer. Phlipon, annoyed at being kept in the dark, felt offended by Roland's conduct and tone, and he refused his consent. The two prideful men clashed, seemingly indifferent to her feelings. "My family, ordinary and obscure for the most part, is not damaged by any stain that reflects on me," she told Roland proudly. "My dowry should not matter to one who desired to do without it and who could do so."[27] Whatever her father's shortcomings, she added, he was not dishonored, nor was he scorned but was generally regarded as "a respectable artist." She offered Roland his freedom, and he took it.

Manon let Roland know that she was moved to despair and thoughts of suicide. In words that would not have disgraced the heroine of a novel by Rousseau, she described her own feelings of love: "Sublime and all-devouring passion, by exalting the energetic soul that conceived it, it leads that soul to conquer itself. . . . I love for the first and only time, with the ecstasy of an ardent and virtuous heart. . . . 'He has never loved like me,' I tell myself bitterly." (Manon conveniently overlooked her feelings for La Blancherie.) Roland, she thought, seemed scarcely moved by her "love in despair . . . a tragic *grande passion*."[28] It was at this low point that, with financial assistance from Sophie, she withdrew to a rented room in the convent where she had been so happy as a girl (the convent being the recognized place of refuge for respectable women in distress). It was her strategy for bringing Roland to his knees, for she was convinced that he really loved her in his way. They continued to write to each other. Eventually Roland was drawn to visit her in the convent. He was vanquished. They were married on February 4, 1780.

Their daughter Eudora—who in character and talent would prove such a great disappointment to her mother—was born in 1781. Indeed, after Eudora's failure to live up to Manon's high standards, the girl was kept in the background until the moving words written at the end. Manon took to referring to her husband as Cato, with herself as Cato's wife, but this may have been slightly ironical and not quite the Roman compliment it might at first appear. For in a letter to Sophie where she had discussed Cicero's letters to Atticus, Manon had observed that Cicero thought Cato a true citizen but stiff and with little tact. She was to feel the same about her husband.

If the terms of the love letters to Roland are compared with her references to her husband in her memoirs, the picture of Roland that emerges in 1793 is unembellished by flattery or even mere consideration. There is a reason for this change that will soon become apparent. In the memoirs there is no mention of any *"grande passion"* for Roland which, when disappointed, must end in death. On the contrary, she now declared that she had married him "without any illusions"—which may well have been the case, given his dithering and insensitivity. Roland, at fifty-seven or fifty-eight, is described as prematurely aged and "venerable."[29] He may be disinterested, hardworking, a man of learning and integrity, but he is also opinionated. Caustic in his dealings with others, he makes enemies with his sharp tongue. He is easily taken in—and she lists a number of people from Louis XVI to Danton and Dumouriez—who succeeded in pulling the wool over his eyes, whereas she is far more perspicacious in seeing through their schemes and wiles. As for her, she has never trusted the king, whatever fine words he might utter. It is she who remedies such shortcomings of Roland's with her charm and grace. To add insult to injury, she proposes in her memoirs that Roland is "so to speak sexless."[30] For someone who was supposedly trying to preserve Roland's image for posterity, this is not a very attractive picture of a man she once said she loved to desperation. Did she realize how unprepossessing a portrait she was painting of her husband's character? Perhaps she did.

From the beginning of their life together, Manon served as unofficial secretary to her husband, helping him with his writings, including the volumes of his important Dictionary of Manufactures, Arts, and Trades, part of the additions to the celebrated *Encyclopédie* edited by Diderot and d'Alembert. Her literary skill was invaluable and, as she later expressed it, Roland came to think that he had written some of her stylish compositions himself. Since Roland was always busy, it was she who often corresponded with friends he had made through his writings, like Jacques-Pierre Brissot who was to emerge as the revolutionary leader of the Brissotins, better known as the Girondins. After all, she had had plenty of practice in her years of writing letters to the Cannet sisters and to Roland, as well as on her father's behalf.

Through her husband's connections in the worlds of learning, commerce, law, and politics, her own horizon began to expand. She visited England for the first time, meeting among others the naturalist Sir Joseph Banks, who had journeyed with Captain Cook to the South Seas. She noted, too, "the happy results" of the English constitution that she had admired when reading Delolme. In Switzerland she was introduced to the philosopher-poet Johann Kaspar Lavater, influential analyst of physiognomy, who turned out to be surprisingly informed about painting. They were to write to each other in the years ahead.

As was perfectly common in the ancien régime where women were often employed to exert their charm and wit in order to seek advancement for their men folk, Roland sent his wife to Versailles to try to obtain a patent of nobility. It was always easier to win preferment with this in hand. This démarche would seem to contradict all her principles, of which the first was that one's conduct should be in harmony with one's values. Regardless of her anti-monarchical and republican views, however, Manon threw herself with her customary energy into the effort to gain access to influential personages at court. She made four trips to the palace between March and May 1784, seeking the intervention of the duchesse de Polignac (the much reviled favorite of Manon's *bête noire*, Marie-Antoinette) and also applying to Louis XVI's aunt, Madame Adélaïde, and to various duchesses. She did not succeed in acquiring the desired patent of nobility, but she did obtain Roland's promotion to Lyons, his home ground.

It was not the first time she had visited Versailles. Ten years earlier she had been taken there on an excursion with her mother, staying in a borrowed apartment in the upper regions of the palace, close by no less a personage than the archbishop of Paris. Ever the advocate of bourgeois cleanliness and order, she remembered the vile stench from the privy on the floor they shared with this strict cleric, who like the rest was prepared to live in squalor so as to be able to "crawl" before the high and mighty. She surprised her mother then by the vehemence of her "hatred" for members of the court with their haughty airs, and she raged against the sheer injustice and absurdity of it all. Together with her sense of her own worth and her cult of "virtue," it was indignation and resentment that would play a large part in firing Manon's revolutionary ardor.

Nor should the weighty impact of class humiliation be overlooked. Manon never forgot the bitter moments of wounded pride when her estimable grandmother, filled with delight at the girl's talents, had taken her to show them off to the offensively condescending lady, actually a distant relative, whom she had long served loyally as governess. On another equally galling occasion, on a visit to the mansion of a parvenue, Manon and her worthy great-aunt, invited to stay for luncheon, were relegated to the servants' table, where members of the staff could be observed ludicrously aping the manners of their betters. These instances of treatment as an inferior left Manon smarting at such insulting behavior.

To return to her life with Roland after her interlude of soliciting preferment at Versailles: promoted to Lyons, he soon aroused the wrath of the local reactionaries by his enthusiasm for change, enthusiasm passionately shared by his wife. She was much moved by the sufferings of what she called "*la classe malheureuse*," the poor in the Lyons region during the hard recession of the 1780s. Her letters to friends like Bosc, for instance, reveal her frustration at what is going on in Paris, known to her only from correspondents and from the *papiers publics* that she read assiduously with her husband. Nothing fulfilled her dream of action. Her language grew ever more intransigent. "You are nothing but children," she wrote to Bosc shortly after the fall of the Bastille on July 14, 1789. "Your enthusiasm is a flash in the pan, and if the National Assembly does not put on trial two illustrious heads [presumably Louis XVI and Marie-Antoinette], or if some magnanimous Decius does not slay them, you are all f——."[31] This note of forceful vulgarity—struck by a person so responsive to the romantic poetry of landscape and moonlight, and so sensitive to womanly charm and grace—takes one by surprise.

In her correspondence now the tone of redemptive violence becomes increasingly strident. In order to "whip" one's fellow citizens into action, what was needed was for them to prove their mettle in a civil war. It was impossible for a corrupt society to rise to liberty without dangerous upheavals. These were simply the "salutary crises" of a grave political fever. Here, already fully shaped, was the specious revolutionary argument, the vehement rhetoric that was to echo down the centuries. Her dark bloodstained vision was inspired not only by internecine conflicts in ancient Rome but also by more recent civil strife in France and England in the seventeenth century: the Fronde, when for the last time the great nobles rose against the king, and the civil war in England that gave birth to Cromwell's commonwealth.

Apart from preaching and teaching, Manon declared, one must inspire fear. Patriotic writers should denounce corrupt political figures, advice later followed (with little regard for truth) by her enemies. Complete your work or be ready to water it with your blood, she ardently proclaimed. "When the public safety is at stake the citizen should not even spare his father."[32] Was she thinking of the Brutus who slew Julius Caesar (whom some thought to be his father) in order to preserve the Roman republic? Or did she also have in her mind that somber Brutus, depicted so powerfully by David and now on everyone's lips, the legendary founder of republican Rome, who had his two sons put to death because they fought to restore the monarchy? Manon had longed to be born a Spartan or Roman, and now Brissot, sometimes fancifully called "the double Brutus" after these two patriotic murderers, was publishing some of her inflammatory rhetoric in his *Le Patriote Français* as "Letters from a Roman Lady."

WHEN ROLAND was sent to Paris in 1791 to try to settle the debts of the Lyons municipality, Manon accompanied him. She had been eagerly following events in the capital, trying to separate truth from rumormongering. For instance, she had heard the tale that Madame de Staël had been seen throwing notes to her admirers from the gallery of the National Assembly and had been reproved by her father, Necker. Manon dismissed the allegation. Eager to see for herself what was going on, she hastened to attend sessions of the Constituent Assembly (as it was now called). The wordy debates infuriated her to such a degree that she could not bear to return there. Her impatience had been growing in intensity at least since 1782 when the inhabitants of Geneva had aroused her ire and contempt by failing to fight and die for liberty amid the ruins of their city. It seemed to her perfectly obvious that everything was moving much too slowly.

Four times a week, in her salon, Brissot and his associates, together with Robespierre (whom she then admired), were frugally entertained. She sat busy with her sewing or writing letters, listening intently, absorbing all, and remembering the fine details. But, she averred, she did not join in the discussions. Sometimes she had to bite her tongue to stop herself from speaking. Was this entirely true? Could she have been seen as "the Egeria of the Girondins," as their secret adviser, their *éminence grise*, if she always stayed silent? Or in all likelihood in her memoirs—and at a time when her life was in serious danger—was she not intent on trying to preserve the image of a perfectly conventional womanly woman who did not intervene in political affairs? It was the public image to which all intelligent and politically aware women felt it was necessary and safer to conform at times—from Alexandrine de Tencin onward, and including Germaine de Staël and Félicité de Genlis.

With Roland's mission successfully concluded, the couple returned to the provinces. A few months later they were back in Paris but no longer quite so much in demand as before. Thoroughly depressed, Manon was contemplating defeat when suddenly a vital new opportunity presented itself. It was Brissot who approached her first to inquire whether Roland would accept the office of minister of the interior. So she was expected to persuade her husband, and presumably she did not find the task too difficult. An eyewitness has described how Manon was transfigured. For this unexpected appointment (due to the constitutional exclusion of representatives who had already served) Roland was entirely indebted to Brissot and his friends. In Manon's view, Brissot remained the true patriot, despite what she regarded as his lack of gravity, his slapdash way of dealing with serious matters. She appears to have known nothing about his period of gutter journalism or his shady past as a police spy. Nor did she seem aware of the fact that Brissot's wife was a protégée of Madame de Genlis (whom Manon cordially disliked) and that formerly he had had close links to the party of the duc d'Orléans (which she thoroughly distrusted). The historian Pierre-Edmond Lemontey, who knew Madame Roland at this period, remarked that she spoke of nothing but political affairs. She informed him—in a way that now seems profoundly ironic—that she was ready to die on the scaffold. Lemontey said that she seemed to pity his moderation.[33]

In the splendid residence once occupied by Necker and his wife, for whom she had little regard, Manon gave dinners twice a week, attended mostly by political allies. Her comments on the best part of the Girondins are tart. Eloquent lawyers as many of them were, they were incapable of action, they lacked judgment and character, and moreover they were "lazy." As for their associate, the distinguished mathematician and liberal *philosophe* Condorcet, however estimable, he should never have left his study. The minister of the navy, Gaspard Monge, another leading mathematician and an eminent scientist, in ministerial debates had never occupied anything but his chair. She met Thomas Paine, whose writings she thought preferable to the man in person. The revolutionary leaders who would be idolized as role models down the ages were all "pygmies."

No women were ever present at her dinners for she did not have a high opinion of their sense or discretion.

Many people who sought access to Roland approached his wife first and had to pass through her selection process. As his unofficial secretary (and private adviser), she wrote circulars, directives, important public documents. This left her husband greater freedom for his administrative tasks. After all, she insisted, they shared the same values and had collaborated closely for many years on research for his published works as well as on his writings in general. Why shouldn't a woman be her husband's secretary? she asked, adding that this was better than the accepted custom under the ancien régime that allowed women to solicit favors and engage in intrigue. She was to compose the letter to the pope urging the release of two French artists, a sculptor and an architect, both imprisoned in Rome as revolutionaries. It was she who wrote the celebrated letter to Louis XVI, whom she never trusted to keep his word, where she told the king some home truths in her husband's name. In a situation increasingly compromising for the Girondins, her action was decisive. Unsurprisingly, Roland was dismissed together with the other two Girondin ministers.

The "second revolution," the popular insurrection of August 10, 1792, brought Danton to power as minister of justice while restoring Roland to his post. But the scene had changed radically. Manon could not abide Danton, with his large appetites and his questionable financial dealings. Some have suggested that her hostility to him carried a sexual undertone, others that she simply resented the way he ineluctably cast her husband into the shade. Certainly her refusal to consider any accommodation with Danton when he contemplated an alliance with the Girondins was not politic.

Manon attributed to Danton and his faction (wrongly, historians believe) the responsibility for the ghastly massacres of September 1792. Onetime advocate of spilling blood, Manon viewed this savagery with horror. It was one thing to urge bloodletting in rhetoric and another to have to face the grisly reality. The fact was that despite all her protestations on his behalf, Roland's silence was deafening. He was all too ready to wipe the slate clean and pass on. As minister of the interior Roland, along with the rest of the Girondins, had failed to act decisively to prevent the atrocities from taking place. Both Roland and his wife were now left behind as ever more ruthless figures took command, and both came under fierce attack from demagogues. "That Roland woman is running affairs . . . ", clamored Marat.[34]

Manon had always been keen to teach. Privately, Roland appears to have left her in charge of the Bureau d'Esprit Public, possibly an idea of her own, and a sort of propaganda office for educating the people in the proper revolutionary sentiments. "You do not have to be a profound politician to know that public opinion creates the strength of governments," wrote Manon, asserting that here lay the difference between a just government and tyranny.[35] All the same, amid the fear and suspicion fostered by enemy invasion, it was easy to suggest that the Bureau d'Esprit Public concealed a source of sedition—yet another conspiracy theory that could be added to the rest and to the calumnies and obscene innuendos that the demagogues leveled against her. The "austere" Roland himself was castigated and his integrity impugned because of his serious tactical error in opening the king's "iron safe" without first obtaining the authorization of his colleagues. On January 22, 1793, the very day after Louis XVI died by the guillotine, Roland submitted a letter of resignation. It was written by his wife. Her activity was no secret. In the National Convention, Danton had remarked sarcastically that any proposal made to Roland should be put to Madame Roland as well, "for everyone knows that Roland was not alone in his ministerial office."[36]

Husband and wife were now in serious danger in a world that came to seem to her far worse than the ancien régime. Robespierre had embarked on removing all those who stood in his way. With the fall of the Girondins, Roland went into hiding. Why did she not go with him? Serious differences had arisen between the couple. Toward the end of the previous year Manon had fallen deeply in love with a member of her political circle. This was the Normandy-born lawyer François Buzot, already married, who shared her melancholy temperament and her lofty Roman principles. She had flirted with admirers on occasion, but this was indeed romantic passion in the grand manner, the real thing as distinct from what she had once professed for Roland before their marriage. She and Buzot sublimated their love, she insisted in her memoirs, declaring that it never overstepped "the bounds of virtue." Intoxicated by literature and in accord with the religion of feeling, she had confessed all to her husband, following Madame de La Fayette's heroine the Princesse de Clèves and Rousseau's Julie. It was a serious misjudgment on the part of one who prided herself on her psychological acumen. Roland did not behave like a husband in a romantic novel, with noble sorrow or compassionate understanding. He turned bitter and resentful. She had to persuade him to destroy his vengeful memoirs so as not to damage their own image in the eyes of posterity.

Manon was arrested at the same time as the Girondin leaders, on May 11, 1793, and she spent some five months in various prisons: the Abbaye (from which she was freed only to be swiftly rearrested, a sadistic measure favored by oppressors in general); in Sainte-Pélagie; and finally in the Conciergerie. According to eyewitnesses, she behaved with exemplary courage. She showed herself to be a paragon of bourgeois domesticity, cleaning her cell and making it habitable. She kept busy with drawing, reading, and composing her memoirs under pressure and in haste.

Paradoxically, in prison she felt for a while strangely content and free—free to think about her beloved Buzot in a way that Stendhal (who revered her) possibly recalled when having Fabrice, imprisoned in the tower, dream happily of Clélia in La Chartreuse de Parme. Meanwhile, through her friends, Manon was able to correspond with Buzot, who was trying to raise an army in Normandy to march on Paris. When her correspondence with the rebels became known it was enough to seal her fate. With Girondin allies she was a federalist after the American model, at a time when Robespierre and the Jacobins stood for *la France une et indivisible*. Her high hopes for insurrection in Normandy and the South and her rescue by Buzot were short-lived. To her despair, Buzot and his companions fled to Bordeaux instead of to the United States as she had urged. She contemplated suicide in the high Roman fashion—her husband would take his own life and so would Buzot—but she decided to die with the rest of the Girondin leaders.

She was accused of fomenting civil war and of plotting against the unity of the country. It was true. As she wrote secretly to Buzot, she was regarded as one who had sought to "pervert public opinion" through the Bureau d'Esprit Public.[37] Defiantly, she refused to name names at her interrogation. She was not permitted to speak at her "trial" on November 8, 1793, and was hurried to the guillotine on the very same day. Courageous to the last, she had also contrived to arrange her final moments with the skill of a consummate actress. For she aimed to be remembered along with her favorite models of heroic integrity, men wrongfully condemned to death, from Socrates to the seventeenth-century English republican Algernon Sidney. A good friend of hers, Sophie Grandchamp, acceded to her request and stood at a prearranged spot so that she could bear witness to Manon's steadfast and heroic demeanor in the tumbril on the way to the guillotine. Manon had been ready in imagination to die on the scaffold, and here she was, her destiny fulfilled, a martyr to the Revolution that devoured its children.

∽

WHAT WAS HER ROLE? Is it possible to separate it from that of her husband, without whom presumably she would have played no part? Was it she who persuaded Roland to return to Paris in 1791, thus placing him at the center of affairs, making him available for high office, and ultimately by her actions helping to cause his destruction as well as her own? Would Roland have entered the historical stage if she had not propelled him? In her memoirs she speaks of their collaboration while insisting that Roland did not need her to make his mark. Yet it is plain that she was more than a secretary—or a mere copyist, as she sometimes pretended. Together they discussed matters of state. She was his adviser and confidante. She had ideas that he, the workaholic, adopted as his own. Hers was the unstoppable energy, the drive, and the ambition. And it is she (rather than her husband) whom historians and novelists have endowed with the heroic role. Carlyle was quite besotted with the "queenly" and "sublime" heroine; Stendhal, who called her "divine," would have liked to have her as his ideal reader.[38] Given the years she had devoted to the study of history and politics, she felt that she was better equipped intellectually and morally than many of the political leaders of her day. For her the Revolution was a touchstone that few attained. It spelled regeneration, the opportunity to destroy the poverty of "la classe malheureuse."[39] She paid a heavy price for her passionate urge to "regenerate" her fellow citizens who—in the manner of humankind—were singularly reluctant to be regenerated.

For, in the end, the people proved a bitter disappointment to her. When they failed to respond to her attempts to educate them in proper revolutionary principles, they were transmuted into "the vulgar," "the idiotic people," "a debased people that we believed we could regenerate through enlightenment."[40] How all this anger contrasts with the view she held in December 1790 when she told Bosc, "It is not our representatives who made the revolution; apart from a dozen or so, the remainder are beneath it. It is public opinion, it is the people, who always behave well when this opinion is directed rightly."[41] Manon Roland, the revolutionary voice of la moyenne classe—the new middling class of intellectuals, artisans, and artists, of whom so much would be heard in the years ahead—recognized the importance of public opinion in reinforcing democratic government. Where liberal political thinkers like the marquis de Condorcet and the baronne de Staël were trying to measure the vital but elusive new movement of public opinion, Manon Roland already perceived that it could be harnessed to promote the right principles (that is, one's own). That she was not successful in her enterprise does not prevent her from appearing as a precursor of those who would try to manipulate this potent propaganda force in the future.

THREE

Claire de Duras

Dilemmas of a Liberal Royalist

You were made to rule the world . . . —FRANÇOIS-RENÉ
DE CHATEAUBRIAND to Claire de Duras

It is perhaps as rare to find a standpoint founded on the
study of political concerns as it is to find religious faith
grounded in the study of theology. Each person's judgment is prompted by private passions, tastes, vani-
ties. . . . —CLAIRE DE DURAS, *Les Mémoires de Sophie*

In 1786, three years before the outbreak of the Revolution, the
chevalier de Boufflers, then governor of the French territory of
Senegal in West Africa, the highly profitable center of the French
slave trade, brought back for his aunt, the princesse de Beauvau, a
black girl known as Ourika, some two years old. She was about to
be put on a slave ship. This was by no means his only act of largesse.
He made presents of other small black children, along with para-
keets and monkeys, to various members of the French aristocracy.
Around the same time the duchesse de Chartres was enchanted with
"a little Negro" called Scipion whom she petted and spoiled, allowing him to do more or less as he pleased. Yet when he was about
seven years old Scipion had already sensed that his privileged term

was limited, observed Félicité de Genlis in her memoirs, and that when he turned thirteen, like his predecessor Narcisse he would be relegated to the antechambers as a mere servant. That great lady the princesse de Beauvau was not so frivolous and unfeeling, however: she claimed to have loved her protégée Ourika as her own daughter and was deeply saddened when the girl died young, aged about sixteen.

On a few facts like these concerning Ourika's fate, Claire-Louise-Rose-Bonne de Kersaint, duchesse de Duras (1777–1828)—one of the prominent and influential political figures of the Bourbon Restoration—constructed a delicate and moving tale. Her *Ourika* was the great best-seller of 1824. Goethe much preferred it to novels by Sir Walter Scott—and not just because it was shorter. Talleyrand told her he was lost in admiration for her art. Félicité de Genlis who, being fixated on the *Grand Siècle* of Louis XIV, rarely lauded her literary contemporaries, spoke highly of its originality, naturalness, elegant simplicity, and qualities of the first order. In her opinion, a commonplace author would have made Ourika declaim loudly against slavery and the slave trade, whereas Madame de Duras attained her effects far more skillfully by sobriety and restraint. Félicité de Genlis was composing her memoirs around the time the novella appeared, and she clearly perceived a political undertone in the work of fiction. There were numerous editions of *Ourika*, including one printed in Saint Petersburg. Translations in English and Spanish appeared, and one was published in America in 1829. Plays and poems were based on the story. The subject inspired a painting by Gérard and various engravings. Such was the craze that "ourika" collarettes and "ourika" bonnets became the height of fashion.[1]

Claire de Duras knew personally about Ourika's unhappy fate because she moved in high aristocratic circles quite close to those of the princesse de Beauvau, to whom she was distantly connected through her marriage. As a girl she had attended one of the most prestigious convent schools for daughters of the aristocracy. An intimate school friend of Claire's was Lucy Dillon, a descendant of the "Wild Geese," the Catholic Irish who served with distinction for generations in the French royal armies. On her marriage to the marquis de La Tour du Pin, Lucy became a maid of honor to Queen Marie-Antoinette. But as emigrés in the revolutionary 1790s, the marquis and marquise de La Tour du Pin were reduced to farming near Albany with slaves (whom they freed on their departure for home). In her memoirs Madame de La Tour du Pin would recall how as a girl she had disliked having the original Ourika place "ebony" arms around her own "white" neck to please the princesse de Beauvau.

The young Ourika of Madame de Duras's story—privileged, well educated, and accomplished—at first appears thoroughly at ease. This tranquil state lasts until she overhears a conversation that totally destroys her unthinking sense of security. A friend of her benefactress reproves that lady for treating Ourika as a pet and as a cherished member of her family circle when there is no possibility for the girl to have a normal life in French society. For who will marry her? Ourika suffers torments of existential angst and self-hatred when she understands her true position. To add to her pain, her sadness is attributed to "guilty" love for the young man she has always regarded as her brother.

Claire de Duras was writing when the question of the survival of slavery and the slave trade in the colonies, on which so much of French economic prosperity depended, had been in the public mind with varying degrees of intensity for more than thirty years. The battles to and fro between entrenched colonists and their supporters fighting to preserve their commercial interests on the one hand and, on the other, liberal emancipators and abolitionists defending humane principles and rights; the fine declarations, the ambiguities and equivocations—these were all familiar to her through her family circumstances and associations. The chronology of the life of the fictional Ourika is moved forward, differing from that of the real person on whom she is modeled. This is so that the Revolution of

Claire de Duras (Portrait by baron François Gérard)

1789 can raise Ourika's hopes of justice and equality that are not fulfilled. When she turns toward those of her own color she learns with horror about the massacres perpetrated by slaves in revolt in the French colony of Saint-Domingue in 1791, events that did much to turn sentiment away from projects of emancipation. There is no way out for her. She retires to a convent where, despite the consolation of religion, she declines and dies. The tale exposes the frivolity and thoughtlessness of the aristocracy of the ancien régime, the distinction between ideal and reality, but underlying it there is a deeper sense of injustice in life itself to which Claire de Duras has no answer except the bitterness of grief.

✍

WHO WAS THE AUTHOR of this powerful and resonant tale of a happy childhood illusion that is shattered forever? At sixteen Claire de Kersaint was in Bordeaux, one of the five major French slave-trading ports, when she learned from the shouts of a street news vendor that her adored father, the comte de Kersaint, the great naval hero and reformer, had perished by the guillotine on December 5, 1793 (just a month after Manon Roland). She was in Bordeaux with her mother, who was born in the French colony of Martinique, because they were preparing to flee the country and take ship for the New World.

Many years later, in *Les Mémoires de Sophie*, she wrote: "Those who witnessed the Terror in their youth have never experienced the gaiety of their forebears, and will carry to the tomb the premature melancholy that gripped their spirit."[2] She herself would never manage to escape for long from feelings of sorrow and disillusion fostered by her penetrating insight into the darker aspects of human character and conduct. She knew for herself the sense of isolation and estrangement, even of uselessness, that she gave to Ourika. Alluding to society, Claire de Duras once declared (long before Camus), " . . . I do not know what I am doing in that place where I feel so deeply that I am an outsider [*étrangère*]."[3] The questions she raises so powerfully in her original and controversial tales—questions of race, color, identity, and alienation in *Ourika*, of social inequality and injustice in *Édouard*, of impotence in *Olivier ou le Secret*—these are as alive today (if in different form) as they were in French society before and during the Revolution and after the Restoration of the Bourbons in 1814–1815.

It was in an astonishing burst of literary creativity in 1820–1824 that Claire de Duras produced her fictional works. This fount, which sprang forth when she was in her early forties, seems to have dried up as suddenly as it had first appeared. By April 1824 she admitted to her friend Rosalie de Constant, "I am not busy writing, which seizes hold of me on and off. I am as though possessed by something. I am thinking about it constantly. . . . Then, suddenly, everything moves away, nothing remains, and if I want to write nothing at all comes to me."[4] In May 1824 she listed what she had been writing the previous year, including *Olivier ou le Secret*: "At the moment I am engaged in writing Memoirs, a woman's life recounted by herself. It is half complete; I am no longer working on it. All that fine enthusiasm is over. I am not sure I shall finish it."[5] (The work to which she alludes—presumably *Les Mémoires de Sophie*—is incomplete and is known today only through extracts.) It may be supposed that this intense creative flowering fulfilled some vital need and that she could express her innermost feelings in a more subtly complex and contradictory manner in fiction than in her confessional letters to a distant confidante like Rosalie de Constant who remained in Switzerland.

Originally none of her works was intended for publication. Claire de Duras related the tragic story of the alienated black girl to her friends, who urged her to write it down. It was then read to members of her circle. A few copies were printed for them and for charity. Other novels of hers were also read aloud to habitués of her salon or communicated to a select few through a small private printing, through offprints or extracts—on condition of the strictest secrecy, not always obeyed. Usually her hand was forced by pirated

versions, satires, travesties, and unauthorized theatrical perform-
ances. The first two editions of *Ourika* appeared anonymously, but
the third bore Madame de Duras's name. She may have been dis-
couraged from writing by scandal and notoriety when word of the
theme of sexual impotence in *Olivier ou le Secret* became public
knowledge in literary circles. To be talked about and criticized by all
and sundry was one of the main reasons for women being advised
(at least since Jean-Jacques Rousseau) to avoid the literary life. All
this publicity cannot have been pleasant for a woman of the
duchesse de Duras's sensibility and grand social position, but she
survived it.

Did the unwelcome brouhaha ultimately detract from her pleasure in continuing to write fiction? Or was her gift stilled by increasing physical pain and by those deadly *"maladies de l'âme"* or
forms of psychological-cum-spiritual sickness that her protagonist,
Olivier de Sancerre, speaks of in *Olivier ou le Secret*, a type of mal-
ady from which she herself suffered and about which she wrote so
convincingly and so movingly?[6] Such an all-devouring kind of de-
pression could eventually prove fatal. It drew upon regrets about actions that could have been performed and were not, upon feelings
of remorse and guilt, and memories of the past that refused to fade.
It could not be explained to others, for it created "walls of crystal"
between oneself and one's uncomprehending fellow creatures. As
mysterious and elusive as any secret professed by Byron's despairing
heroes, it may well have contributed in the end to undermine the
author herself.

Claire de Duras preserved an aristocratic attitude to writing for
the public, and she did not wish to see herself or to be seen as a professional writer. Although she must have been gratified by the immense success of *Ourika*, she was quick to note any sign of authorial
vanity in herself. Having yielded to the persistent urging of Armande de Richelieu, marquise de Montcalm, the chief minister's influential sister, who wished to read *Édouard*, Claire de Duras was so
irritated by what she considered that lady's foolish comments on the

novel that she pointed them out to her friends, reproaching herself afterward for such an act of literary vengeance and betrayal. She lacked confidence about her work, sought after as it was. "I have great doubts about whether it [*Édouard*] is of any merit," she owned. "I should never have believed before in having this kind of timidity as an author. All the writers I see are so thoroughly convinced that what they produce is superb. . . . "[7] *Édouard* was a novel admired (along with *Ourika*) by none other than Goethe, whose words of praise were communicated to her by a shared friend, Alexander von Humboldt. Her small output contrasts with that of Félicité de Genlis who wrote prolifically, often with didactic intent, and later in order to survive. As Claire de Duras once wittily remarked, Madame de Genlis wrote "like an inkwell to which water has been added."[8] Both Madame de Genlis and Madame de Staël may be considered professional writers, since they wrote unambiguously for publication. Germaine de Staël was a born writer who began writing when she was little more than a child, and who never stopped because she had so much to analyze and to communicate to the world at large. Claire de Duras was not like that at all. She was beset by inhibitions—but, surprisingly, as a writer of fiction she sometimes appears more modern than either of her celebrated contemporaries.

Yet it is not only for her claims as a talented writer, seized by a relatively brief upsurge of artistic creativity, that she deserves to be better known, but also for her vital part in promoting the political career of François-René de Chateaubriand. He and Germaine de Staël shone as the two major literary luminaries of the age. In his gripping autobiography, *Mémoires d'outre-tombe* (nowadays frequently qualified as the best of his novels on account of its numerous departures from strict accuracy), Chateaubriand acknowledged the unique role of Claire de Duras in furthering his political ambitions. He observed complacently that "she alone first recognized what valuable qualities I could bring to politics."[9] Her contribution, however, would not be achieved without her suffering a good deal of anguish that does not really percolate through Chateaubriand's beautifully eloquent phrases of admiration, self-accusation, and easy regret, written after her death.

As regards political principle, throughout her life this gifted woman remained loyal to the memory of her highly cultivated, liberal-minded father. Scion of an ancient noble family of Brittany, Vice Admiral Armand-Guy de Coëtnempren, comte de Kersaint, not only helped to keep open the sea lanes for commerce with France during the American War of Independence, he also became deeply involved in French revolutionary politics. While engaged in the defense of Martinique he had married the governor's first cousin, a lady of considerable wealth that largely derived from the sugar plantations of the colony. From his stay there he had firsthand knowledge of slavery and the slave trade upon which his wife's—and his own—fortune depended. Later Kersaint would be found pleading the cause of the blacks. His liberal outlook may well be regarded as relative today, but it was certainly a vast improvement on the attitude of diehard slaveholders.

An ardent polemicist, the idealistic Kersaint attacked privileges in a pamphlet entitled—possibly after Tom Paine's—Le Bon Sens (Common Sense). When elected député to the Legislative Assembly he asserted that he was happy to be associated with the Girondins, with men like Brissot and Roland. But the massacres of September 1792 left him horrified, and he could not bear the proximity of "men of blood." He was among the courageous few who opposed the death penalty for Louis XVI. Claire de Kersaint inherited her father's courage and strong independence of mind. She saw that there was no possibility of returning to the ancien régime with all its abuses as the ultras proposed. Like him, she would remain a convinced liberal constitutional monarchist, though unsparing in her criticism of royalist folly and error.

Once in the New World in 1794–1795, Claire accompanied her mother first to Philadelphia, then to Martinique, where she would have seen for herself the condition of the slaves who were laboring on the sugar plantations. Since her mother was apparently completely overcome by her experiences and quite incapable of coping with practical affairs, the girl took charge and dealt with matters concerning the recovery of family property on the island. In 1795 they traveled to Switzerland and then to London where they joined the community of French emigrés whose frivolity and foolish optimism she later depicted with a cool eye. Some viewed her askance as the daughter of a Girondin. Unlike her, many of them were living in very reduced circumstances. Among these emigrés was Amédée, duc de Durfort, afterward duc de Duras, who (it is widely hinted) married her for her fortune in 1797. Claire de Duras had great dark eyes and dark hair. In an age that worshiped pale classical beauties like Pauline Borghese, Napoleon's sister, who posed nude for Canova's statue of Venus, and Juliette Récamier, who reclined enticingly yet remote, draped in diaphanous white, for her portrait by David, Claire de Duras believed she was ugly. One of her sharp-tongued contemporaries, the comtesse de Boigne, author of penetrating memoirs, thought such feelings on the subject of her appearance to be exaggerated. Yet this disquiet about her looks goes some way to explain her profound empathy with the sensibility of a black girl like Ourika, brought up in a society where all too often blackness could be equated with ugliness.

Claire's husband, the duc de Duras, issued from one of the most illustrious Breton aristocratic families. By tradition it occupied the coveted post of *Premier Gentilhomme de la Chambre* (or first chamberlain), one of four highly privileged officials of the court who were closest to the king, saw him every day, and ushered into the royal presence those individuals who were granted an audience. The duc de Duras, intensely loyal to the martyred king's brother, Louis XVIII, in his long exile at Mittau and at Hartwell House near Aylesbury, naturally acted in this capacity on the Bourbon monarch's return to Paris in 1814. Unlike many French aristocrats, he had declined to serve at the court of the Emperor Napoleon and had preferred to live quietly at the beautiful château of Ussé, purchased partly from his wife's funds. During the Hundred Days of Napoleon's astonishing escape from Elba and return to power, he and his wife loyally followed Louis XVIII into exile at Ghent where, to her great sorrow mingled with guilt, her mother died. "I was the sole interest of her life," grieved Claire de Duras.[10]

The duc de Duras was said to be "more of a duke" than the egregious duc de Saint-Simon himself (famed through his memoirs as a fanatical stickler for niceties of rank).[11] His liberal-minded wife, to her misfortune (observed her friend Madame de La Tour du Pin), fell in love with him. Claire de Duras, in a letter to her husband in England, written from Paris where she had traveled on family business in 1800, raised timorously the question of their addressing each other by the familiar "*tu,*" while she wrote to him still using the more formal "*vous.*" "Will you forgive me, my dear Amédée, for speaking to you with such familiarity? I know you do not care for it, but I need it . . . . it reminds me of our tête-à-tête when I ventured to use it."[12] By then they were the parents of two daughters, Félicie and Clara. The duc de Duras's model was possibly the king himself, for Louis XVIII (who had no offspring) scarcely ever employed the familiar form even to his brother, the future Charles X, and other members of his family. When the monarch did use it—in private letters—to his favorite, Decazes, the minister of police whom he treated as his son, it was a mark of the most singular regard.

It was obvious to all who met the couple that they were not compatible and that Claire de Duras was her husband's superior in sensibility and intellect. Rosalie de Constant, who was to correspond with her for many years, knew them well when they were staying in Lausanne in 1805 in what was for Claire a never-to-be-forgotten little white house with green shutters. Benjamin Constant's disabled, unmarried, and highly intelligent cousin noted in her diary that while Madame de Duras loved botanizing (like herself) and thrilled to mountain scenery, her husband left her to her own devices and spent all his time hunting. It dawned on Claire de Duras, with her passionate and demanding nature, that her more formal husband was not a kindred spirit. And so she concentrated her affections on her daughters, doting especially on Félicie. (This would prove to be an unfortunate choice, because Félicie de La Rochejaquelein would prefer her second husband's family—famous for its heroic leadership of the counterrevolutionary uprising in the Vendée—to her own. She became a convinced and active *ultra*, much to the grief of her liberal mother.) Eventually, though, in a perfectly amicable manner, the duc and duchesse de Duras would follow their separate inclinations. Through increasing ill health she would be allowed to withdraw from the tedious obligations of social life at court, his favored milieu. All the same, she could exert political influence through her husband, who was in daily contact with the king.

The society of the Bourbon Restoration was highly politicized. This was the era when the foundations of modern French parliamentary life under the *Charte* of 1814 were being precariously established. According to the future liberal leader, the poet Lamartine, in 1823, "nowadays only the subject of politics arouses interest."[13] It was also the age of great political salons, each with its own recognized particular loyalty and nuance. Anyone with pretensions to thought was passionately concerned with the Revolution that had overturned everything and whose consequences—for good or ill—could not be eluded. In an era of dazzling salons (like those governed by Germaine de Staël or Juliette Récamier), the salon of Claire de Duras was seen as both brilliant and powerful. So important was it that she merited a polite rebuke from the chief minister, the duc de Richelieu, who once advised her to moderate the opposition to his policies expressed in her salon.

Her gatherings could be found either in her mansion in the rue de Varenne in the faubourg Saint-Germain, or in palaces like the Tuileries or Saint-Cloud, where the duc de Duras enjoyed grace-and-favor apartments, bestowed at the king's pleasure. Among its habitués were princes, diplomats, political leaders, savants, and writers. At that time foreigners among the victorious Allies—like the Duke of Wellington; the Corsican-born Russian ambassador,

Pozzo di Borgo (Bonaparte's lifelong enemy); and Lord Charles Stuart, the English ambassador—were highly influential in Paris and could be found in her salon. Apart from Talleyrand, *éminence grise* of the Restoration, her guests included the famous naturalist and explorer of South America Alexander von Humboldt, and another ground-breaking scientist, the eminent paleontologist Georges Cuvier. The arts were represented by the poet Delphine Gay and by François Villemain, distinguished professor at the Sorbonne and writer of important works on literature. With his acute sensitivity to current social minutiae, Stendhal keenly followed from a distance Madame de Duras's trajectory, proposing to send her a copy of his *De l'Amour*—though without the chapter on *fiascos* or masculine sexual failures. He listed her quite unjustly with "*les catins à la mode*" ("fashionable trollops"), perhaps because as a well-known Bonapartist he was unlikely to gain access to so elevated a royalist salon.[14] They were liberals of a different stripe.

Claire de Duras, familiar with English literature, was extremely well read—there were nearly two thousand volumes in her library at Ussé. She was curious about everything, judging with discrimination the latest publications and talents. She admired Germaine de Staël, whom she had met briefly in Lausanne, and was distressed by Napoleon's persecution of the author of *Corinne*. After returning to Paris in 1814, Germaine de Staël became a warm friend, and she was to be found expressing esteem for what she called Claire de Duras's singular "naturalness in an artificial society."[15] It was through the duc de Duras that Madame de Staël's letter to Louis XVIII—with its request for the return of the 2.4 million *livres* that her father, Jacques Necker, had lent to the Royal Treasury in 1778—was delivered to the king. As the sum was urgently required for her daughter Albertine's dowry, her gratitude knew no bounds on the success of this démarche.

The two friends corresponded (keeping an eye on the censorship) mostly on current political affairs, the dire state of the nation, and its prospects, until Germaine de Staël's death at fifty-one in

1817. Claire de Duras gives the impression of showing her elder a kind of deference at times. It was said that she took up the gauntlet dropped by Madame de Staël. They were often compared, not least by Chateaubriand himself. Both were seen as more imaginative and intelligent than beautiful. Both women were passionate, possessive, and of an intensely melancholy disposition. Their liberal views, their idealization of English constitutional monarchy, their conviction that many changes made by the Revolution were irreversible, their hatred of the fanaticism and extremism of left and right were held in common. Both were critical of the Bourbons, but Claire de Duras remained loyal to the throne and never enjoyed a republican phase as did Germaine de Staël. Full of energy and enthusiasm, Madame de Staël was the more active figure, more obviously in the public eye with her varied political commitments, obliged to pay the price for them with persecution and exile, more notorious for her numerous liaisons.

More than a novelist, too, Germaine de Staël wrote a great deal on the principles of literature, politics, and society, whereas Claire de Duras's opinions on these themes are subsumed in what is known of her reported observations in her salon, her correspondence, and her fiction. Curiously, both writers touched on slavery and the slave trade via the same source. In Madame de Staël's early tale set in Senegal, *Mirza, ou Lettre d'un voyageur*, written in 1786 when she was about twenty, the black Prince Ximéo's betrothed, whom he betrays, is named Ourika. The young author would have heard the name in 1786 from the governor of Senegal, the chevalier de Boufflers himself, on his return visit home, for he was a friend of her father's. Claire de Duras could have seen a manuscript copy of *Mirza* or read it while she was in London when it first appeared in a collection in 1795, or more probably when it was published in Madame de Staël's complete works in 1820. But apart from touching on the cruelty of slavery and the slave trade, the story of *Mirza* has little in common with *Ourika*.

৩

AMONG THE CONTEMPORARY WRITERS Claire de Duras most admired was Chateaubriand, influential author of an essay on revolutions, of *René* and *Atala* extracted from his *Génie du christianisme*. He was a fellow Breton, nine years her senior (whose somber father had once commanded a slave ship). One summer evening, seated with her friends on the magnificent terrace of the château of Saint-Germain, overlooking the Seine and the great forest, Claire de Duras spoke passionately in defence of *Les Martyrs, ou le triomphe de la religion chrétienne*, much criticized by his contemporaries. This was Chateaubriand's epic novel on the clash of Christianity and paganism under Imperial Rome, with the poetic tale of Eudore, an officer in the Roman armies, and the impassioned Druidess Velléda so fascinating to those who thrilled to the romance of vestal virgins in that era. According to Villemain, who was present, Claire de Duras perceived how Chateaubriand's work was relevant to her own experiences and those of many people she knew. She declared that Chateaubriand "evokes our misfortunes, our bereavements, the martyrs of our own day . . ." as well as the faith and heroic fortitude shown on the scaffold in the face of the pagan executioners. "Are not these the same virtues as those of our brothers, our fathers, put to death in the public square for their God and their king?" Villemain recalled her forceful tone of grief, which moved her hearers "like the very names of Malesherbes and Kersaint," as he underlined her meaning.[16]

She had become acquainted with Chateaubriand in 1808 (though both of them had been emigrés in London, they did not meet there) through Nathalie, duchesse de Noailles, her husband's beautiful and gifted cousin by marriage, who was then Chateaubriand's mistress. Nathalie de Noailles was the daughter of a wealthy, ennobled tax farmer, and if her dowry was acceptable to her highborn in-laws, her own newly rich mother and father were not made welcome. It was Nathalie de Noailles who would collapse into madness like Louise de Nangis, the heroine of Claire de Duras's *Olivier ou le Secret*, surviving for many years in oblivion. On hearing the news of his onetime lover's tragic decline, Chateaubriand wrote to Claire de Duras, "What an ill fate pursues me!"[17] This cry is typical of the self-regarding writer, fond of striking poses, who was as much an example of "the Egotistical Sublime" as Wordsworth, his close contemporary. As Madame de Boigne sharply observed: "He believes in nothing except his own talent, but then that is an altar before which he lies forever prostrate."[18]

Soon Chateaubriand and Claire de Duras were addressing each other as "dear brother" and "dear sister." They went for long walks together along tree-lined boulevards. He would call on her for private talks, appearing only rarely in her salon. Tongues began to wag. Her candid friend, Madame de La Tour du Pin, pointed out to her that what she was feeling for Chateaubriand, with his notorious "seraglio," was not friendship as she deluded herself, but love. Hurt and outraged, Claire de Duras broke with the marquise de La Tour du Pin (who became ever more closely attached to her estranged daughter, Félicie). They were not to be reconciled until Madame de Duras's last illness. According to Stendhal, who claimed that he wanted a plain style in conformity with the Napoleonic Code, Chateaubriand was "an arch hypocrite and maker of sonorous phrases."[19] But what phrases were shaped by that superlative rhetorician! Who can forget his picture of the corrupt Talleyrand and Fouché the regicide as "Vice leaning on the arm of Crime"? The poetic musicality of his prose, those sensuous depictions of moonlit nights in distant or exotic climes, proved irresistibly hypnotic to many—especially his female readers, much to the sardonic amusement of his long-suffering wife. How often he told each of his adoring women in turn that he was hers forever, assuring her that he would give his life for her! Although surviving portraits of Chateaubriand do not show him as particularly prepossessing, he was known as "*l'Enchanteur*," the irresistible charmer. According to Villemain, his first biographer, he was also a man of glacial pride, and at times when in society totally withdrawn into his own thoughts.

After years of intense literary fame, Chateaubriand (who had once served as secretary to the French legation in Rome) decided that he wished to pursue a serious political career. He would then prove to everyone that a man of letters could be just as successful in politics as all those he considered his intellectual and moral inferiors. Chateaubriand was to become the role model of the writer-as-politician for Lamartine, Victor Hugo, and the rest—an outcome for which Claire de Duras might bear some responsibility. In the early days of their association, Chateaubriand discussed his ambitions with her. He was not well-to-do, and he lacked the essential contacts with the powerful that she could readily provide. She lent him money to settle his debts, knowing well that she would never see it returned. With her knowledge and experience of the court, where small things counted for much, she advised him how to conduct himself with patient discretion, and how to flatter Louis XVIII, who disapproved of men of letters in political life. She urged Chateaubriand when he was in England to visit Hartwell House, once the residence of the royal exile, and to write to the king about it, with a quotation or two from Horace, the monarch's favorite poet. The duc de Duras would see that this missive came into the king's hands.

It was Claire who managed to have Chateaubriand restored to his position of minister of state (which he had lost along with its invaluable emoluments when he had offended the monarch). Through her he was elevated to the rank of *pair de France* (a peer in the Upper Legislative Assembly). She passionately argued his merits and suitability for office with leading ministers like Talleyrand, Blacas, and Pasquier. She besieged Villèle, then chief minister, putting Chateaubriand's interests before those of her own family. Through her interventions on his behalf, she contrived to have Chateaubriand appointed minister plenipotentiary to Berlin (he was not satisfied with the Swedish embassy when it was proposed) and then ambassador to London (where he could savor the contrast between his present eminence and his former obscurity as an emigré). It was largely through her considerable efforts that he was sent as French representative to the Congress of Verona, where he impressed Tsar Alexander I, Metternich, and other leading influential notabilities on the European scene. When he rose to be minister of foreign affairs in 1822, she uttered a cry of triumph. "My dream for you is fulfilled," she assured him.[20]

What is extraordinary is Chateaubriand's tone whenever things do not seem to him to be going to his liking. It is not at all the accent of customary elegant French *politesse*, and it does not accord with the noble loftiness that characterizes his stance in his writings. On the contrary, it is the pressing urgency of his demands, the unjust accusations (for instance, the suspicion that Claire is lukewarm and failing to devote her full attention to his cause), and the intemperate reproaches that astonish by their violence. Addressing her he can be peremptory: "See to negotiations," "Intervene with Talleyrand," "Stick to your guns," "Settle everything with Villèle."[21] When he was posted abroad, her letters to him were filled with details about political events at home so that he could continue to keep abreast of affairs in France.

If Claire de Duras ever expected gratitude for the many years of preferring his interests to her own, she did not find it. Nor did he show her any real sympathy or understanding when she was gravely unwell. "M. de Chateaubriand will only believe that I am ill when I am dead . . . ," she told Rosalie de Constant bitterly.[22] By the time she had succeeded in her many struggles on his behalf, Chateaubriand was no longer as ingratiating as when she first knew him. She reminded him—rather tactlessly—that she preferred him when his blue frock coat was threadbare, when he had been "poor and persecuted."[23] In those days, when he needed her, he was a man of simple tastes who professed to wish to retire to the country to enjoy a quiet life (a favorite refrain of his). Somehow he had grown convinced that he alone had accomplished his rise. As he coolly wrote to her from his London embassy, "Yet I am not without some vanity at having created this destiny myself. I have owed it to what I carried within me when I passed through here. I did not know you then. That is something at least that cannot be taken from me."[24] When in Paris he no longer accompanied her on delightful walks or paid his eagerly awaited morning call. On occasional brief visits to her he would sometimes pace the room in silence, frowning, so that she felt afraid of offending him.

It did not take long, though, before she discovered that he was now assiduously attending the salon of Juliette Récamier. He had met her again, after many years, at Germaine de Staël's in 1817, and would remain at least publicly faithful to her—in his fashion—to the end of his life in 1848. This new liaison he had tried in vain to keep secret from Claire de Duras. Her passionate reproaches and snide allusions to his new commitment did not serve her well. He told Juliette Récamier, who was also using her influence on his behalf, that the lady was "half mad," and he spoke of her "cries of jealousy" and her "rages." To add insult to injury, he informed his "dear sister" that it was "only on political matters" that she appeared reasonable.[25]

Claire de Duras was shattered by his betrayal. She had fed on the illusion that their friendship was as unique in his life as it was in hers. This disillusion completed the earlier disappointment she had felt through her husband's indifference and Félicie's disloyalty. She went for walks alone. Missing his morning visits, she even stopped the clocks in her drawing room. Yet she continued to serve Chateaubriand's interests devotedly as a faithful friend whereas doubtless it was ambition that made him endure her words of warning and her criticism.

Meanwhile serious political differences arose between them. Claire de Duras always urged patience and moderation. "I loathe exaggerated and violent opinions," she once declared.[26] She detested most *ultras* and especially their political use of religion. It seemed to her that Chateaubriand was veering ever more to the right, and she did not want him to become the leader of an extremist party. One grave source of contention occurred when Chateaubriand favored intervention in Spain to subdue the liberal uprising and reinstate the Bourbon king. She could not fail to recall how in 1808 Napoleon's invasion of Spain had cost France dear. Certainly she did not think it was wise to risk such casualties again in order to restore a "horrible" absolutist monarch like Ferdinand VII, "so despicable and so despised."[27] Besides, she was sure that the French people were against such a course.

Chateaubriand, however, was eager for honor and glory. In his opinion, her heart was ruling her head. He condescended to assure her that war and peace presented considerations of advantage and disadvantage that only a statesman could weigh. His primary concern (anticipating that of General de Gaulle) lay with France's military standing in Europe and with the country's rank as a first class power, especially after the bitter humiliation of defeat at Waterloo and costly occupation by the Allies. Victory in Spain would restore France to her rightful place. Besides, with the crushing of the Spanish revolt, "we shall be finished with Jacobinism for ever," he informed her.[28] It seems unlikely that she shared this vain hope.

∽

IN PRINCIPLE Claire de Duras was deeply touched by social as well as political developments brought about by the French Revolution. She expressed heartfelt sympathy for the "poor people," sympathy that was not at all common in those of her rank. To her husband, for instance, the lower orders were still "*la canaille*," the rabble.[29] Her particular dream was that one day the government would seek the means of making the "poor people" happy instead of treating them as being of little importance. Sensitive farmers and loyal retainers appear in her fiction. She disliked the way some liberal politicians were merely using words like "the people" when they claimed that the poor were ardent adherents of the *Charte*; for as she well knew, the indigent were far more interested in finding bread than in discussing constitutional details.

Yet whatever her own liberal views, she herself preserved a strong sense of the immutability of rank as well as of the profound suffering caused by this inflexibility. She felt strongly that people are probably better off if they can stay in their place. Did she conceive that her own family origin was not quite as elevated as that of her husband? From Compiègne, where she had witnessed shabby examples of blatant *arrivisme* on the part of aristocrats fighting for position and power when Louis XVIII returned to France in 1814, she had written to her daughter Clara: "My dear child, whatever your position in life, adopt the firm resolve to remain in your station, neither above nor below. . . ."[30] The bourgeois hero's mother in *Édouard* expresses the same sentiment. Moreover, with her husband Claire de Duras would not accept a respectable young lawyer as Clara's suitor.

In her remarkable novel *Édouard* (1825), Claire de Duras elaborates this very theme. She liked to place her fiction at a remove, in the ancien régime, and to leave it to the reader to make connections with the present. Noble-hearted but bourgeois Édouard, son of an eminent lawyer, falls in love with the daughter of his magnanimous aristocratic protector, a love that is reciprocated. A nobleman thoughtlessly voices the belief that she is Édouard's mistress. Outraged, Édouard challenges him to a duel, but to his intense distress the challenge is refused because the nobleman claims he cannot fight with a bourgeois. Unable to restore his beloved's reputation, Édouard in despair seeks death by leaving France to fight for American independence. The marquise de La Tour du Pin, who never forgot that she had been maid of honor to Queen Marie-Antoinette, resentfully criticized both novelist and subject matter, declaring that "nothing is so ill-considered as to say all of that at the present time. She belittles the aristocracy and inflames the other class."[31] The novel's relevance to the inequality and social injustice of the author's own day is manifest.

Claire de Duras had plainly struck a nerve with her yearning for meritocracy, which she thought existed in England and the United States. That desire is evident throughout the book. Her cousin, the duc de Lévis, author of works on finance, of maxims and memoirs, who had flourished in the grand social milieu of the ancien régime that she depicts in the novel, queried the scene of the ball attended by the queen, where the aristocratic heroine chooses to dance with Édouard. This scene was quite impossible, averred the duc de Lévis, because at such an event graced by royalty the nobles would have been dressed in regulation courtly finery (*habit habillé*) whereas Édouard would have been recognized at once by his very clothes as a mere bourgeois, condemned by "the original sin of the inequality of rank."[32] The duc de Lévis, though questioning the detail, nonetheless confirms with this strikingly potent phrase the author's main contention in her novel: the gross injustice of the social inequality that had been attacked by her father.

Still, Claire de Duras was the victim of her own social circumstances and her own contradictions. For instance, she was writing less about slavery in *Ourika*—although the debate about the slave trade had been renewed in the 1820s—than about its consequences in human damage and about individual estrangement that she shared viscerally with her black heroine. Certainly the novella delivers a severe rebuke to an unthinking aristocracy and a selfish and self-indulgent society. Moreover it portrays a black girl who is no less human than those who surround her, who shows deeper moral sensitivity than they do, when in Claire's lifetime there had been debates about whether freed mulattoes—to say nothing of slaves— were to be seen as included in the Declaration of the Rights of Man.

Doubtless Claire de Duras sympathized with the abolitionist stance of Germaine de Staël, who was on friendly terms with William Wilberforce. Her own circle embraced ardent opponents of the slave trade like Alexander von Humboldt, who had been profoundly shocked by the inhuman conduct of the traders he had witnessed on his travels in Latin America. In 1821 he sent Claire de

Duras an English pamphlet, "probably by Wilter Force" (which is how he transcribed the name of the famous abolitionist), and an excerpt from papers from Sierra Leone, adding ironically, "It is surely time to send French ships to these coasts to stop the blacks being thrown into the sea to cure them of conjunctivitis." A few years later, in 1825, he told her about a letter he had received from a French naval officer in Martinique, which revealed how "The clandestine trade in human flesh continues to flourish." Apparently the colonists there were furious with Madame de Duras for choosing as the sympathetic heroine of her "detestable novel" *Ourika* "a black female who had not even the advantage of being a black Creole"— a view whose petty idiocy aroused Humboldt's mockery.[33] Where did generous-hearted Claire de Duras stand between the ideals and sympathies her enlightened friends took for granted that she shared (as she doubtless did), and the source of her own wealth derived from slave plantations in Martinique? Was this unresolved conflict yet another source of the moral pain that undermined her health?

Whatever her intense detestation of social inequality and her awareness of its deleterious consequences, she certainly could not permit her daughter to marry beneath her, given not only her own and her husband's position in society but also the rigid attitudes of her class. Some idea of that social rigidity and snobbery can be gleaned from young Madame Aurore Dudevant (later George Sand), who in 1825 paid a visit to one of her convent school friends, Louise de La Rochejaquelein, only to be scorned by the flunky at the door because she had arrived in a hackney coach instead of in her own carriage. In the same year Henri Beyle, not yet the famous Stendhal of *Le Rouge et le Noir*, was grumbling that he was not regarded as an equal if he traveled by hackney cab to attend a gathering in a salon.

Claire de Duras chose themes that were bold for a woman of her era. For instance, in *Olivier ou le Secret*—which was not published until 1971, by which time part of it was lost—she deliberately selected the "challenge" of an "impossible" subject: sexual impotence.[34] The novel was read only to a few habitués of her salon, but inevitably word of it seeped out. Stendhal, obsessed with the sexual misfortune he liked to call the *"fiasco,"* took up the "challenge" with his first novel, *Armance*. Claire de Duras's delicate hints pale before Stendhal's more obvious clues to sexual impotence in *Armance*, just as his scabrous remarks on the subject (with advice on a homemade dildo) addressed to his good-time companion Prosper Mérimée, far exceed anything she could have written as a woman of refinement.[35] Ultimately, though, sexual impotence in *Olivier ou le Secret* serves as a metaphor, leaving an impression of impotence in general that culminates in the suicide of the hero and the insanity of his beloved.

Claire de Duras had the imagination and daring to challenge in her writings the boundaries of her day within which she felt herself to be confined. "Alas, this world is woven of chains, and the strongest and most independent character is bound by countless immovable considerations . . . ," she complained to Germaine de Staël (who rarely let anything stand in *her* way).[36] An overwhelming sense of powerlessness marks the resonant fiction of Claire de Duras, who nonetheless quite openly—and without any dispute among the leading masculine figures of the day—successfully exerted political influence and power. She did not have to suffer the opprobrium of being called an *intrigante* like Alexandrine de Tencin, either because of her high social position and her husband's elevated place at court, or because the political climate had changed radically, at least for a time. Would Chateaubriand have achieved such political as distinct from diplomatic eminence without her? At last minister of foreign affairs in 1822 through her triumphant efforts, he fell from power in 1824, just a few years before her painful death. He never again attained a cabinet post.

❧ F O U R ❧

Félicité de Genlis

The Cover-up

The true friends of letters and arts will never be dis-
united by that absurd misunderstanding and those
pedantic arguments called *political opinions* in society
today.—MADAME DE GENLIS, Dedicatory Epistle to Anatole de Montesquiou, *Les Battuécas*, 1816

... the political roles that she adopted one after the
other ... she was the patron saint of the revolutionary
clubs before she became a Mother of the Church.—
CHARLES-AUGUSTIN SAINTE-BEUVE on Madame de Genlis,
1825

I was in love only once in my life," owned Louis-Philippe, the citizen king, long married and the father of a family, to Victor Hugo.
"And with whom, Sire?" inquired the poet and peer of the realm, intrigued. "With Madame de Genlis." "But she was your tutor!" cried
Victor Hugo in astonishment. The king laughed, and went on to describe her tough methods as a teacher, including hard manual labor
of a kind never imposed on princes of the blood. "When I was small
I was afraid of her: I was weak as a boy, lazy and cowardly; I was
afraid of a mouse. She made me into a fairly bold and courageous

· 118 ·

fellow. As I grew up I noticed that she was extremely pretty. I didn't know what was wrong with me when I was near her. I was in love but I didn't realize it. She, who knew all about it, understood, guessing at once. She treated me very severely." Victor Hugo, who recorded this conversation in his compelling diaries, added that to some extent Louis-Philippe was her creation. He was not alone: others said as much. Even Louis XVIII considered Louis-Philippe to be "the masterpiece of Madame de Genlis."[1]

When Louis-Philippe ascended the throne after the Revolution of July 1830, just a few months before the death of Madame de Genlis, she had been one of the most famous literary figures in Europe at least since the 1780s. Renowned as a playwright, novelist, and educationist, as the author of works for the young as well as for adults, she was one of the most prolific writers of the age. When she visited England in 1785 and 1788 she was feted by royalty, aristocracy, and celebrities in the world of literature, art, and politics, from Fanny Burney, the author of *Evelina* and *Cecilia* and lady-in-waiting to Queen Charlotte, to Sir Joshua Reynolds, president of the Royal Academy of Arts, and the political orator Edmund Burke, philosopher of the sublime.

In 1815 Jane Austen slyly alluded to Madame de Genlis's *Adèle et Théodore* (1782) in *Emma.* The comte de Las Cases, faithfully sharing Napoleon's exile on Saint Helena, admitted that he was deeply touched by passages in her novels that acted upon him as a stimulus to memories of people and places in his earlier life. In Russia, Alexander Pushkin, ill-fated poet and teller of tales, wrote to his brother, "If you can, send me the latest work by Genlis"—her "latest" being the numerous volumes of her disjointed memoirs published in 1825. George Sand had sixteen of Madame de Genlis's books in her library. As a child she had listened with rapt attention when her mother read to her from the moral tales of *Les Veillées du château* (1784). As a girl she read Madame de Genlis's novels while keeping watch by the bedside of her sick grandmother. And—surprising as it may seem, given Félicité de Genlis's political trajectory from radical chic to ultra conservatism—George Sand suggested in her autobiography that one of the novels, the fable *Les Battuécas* (1816), about a remote and isolated village in Spain where goods were held in common, had helped to shape her own later socialist views.[2]

The elevation of Félicité de Genlis from somewhat dubious and unpromising circumstances to a position of eminence in the fields of education and literature, and a place of important political influence, was due in part to her passion for reading (a passion she shared with Manon Roland). She preferred studying books to most other pastimes, admitting that "at all times, to learn has been my dominant passion," followed closely by her pleasure in teaching.[3] Bring her to a great house with a fine library and she was happy to be left alone reading tomes of ancient and modern history, the great works of seventeenth-century French literature and devotion, not forgetting the memoirs of the Cardinal de Retz, that Machiavellian intriguer during the complex alliances and betrayals of the Fronde, and accounts of notable conspiracies in Sweden and Venice. Her rise was also attributable to talent, single-minded ambition, the self-assurance often to be found in the autodidact, a certain deviousness, chance—and the system of patronage under the ancien régime. Moreover, in her younger days she was extremely attractive (always a help), full of life, impetuous, eyes sparkling with wit and mischief, and her hair was a lovely shade of chestnut, even if she did say so herself. As for the charm of her conversation, it used to enchant her hearers who often commented on its piquancy.

On this apparently slender foundation she came to advise and influence the prince who was at first the most adulated and then among the most hated figures of the French Revolution of 1789: Louis-Philippe-Joseph, duc de Chartres and later duc d'Orléans, to be notorious as Philippe Égalité. Some French historians still regard him (rather excessively) as the Revolution's patron, instigator, and evil genius. Madame de Genlis was to take an active and sometimes a decisive role in his destiny, and even in the course of revolution-

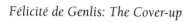

Félicité de Genlis (Portrait by Antoine Vestier)

ary events. Her association with him and her involvement in revolutionary politics led to her being thoroughly reviled by adherents of both left and right. She would have a long life, times would change, and it would not be easy to live down what she had said and done during those tempestuous years.

What experiences, what ideas and ideals propelled Félicité de Genlis into political affairs? Was she originally aiming to be a sort of kingmaker and the power behind the ruler? What exactly were her intentions regarding the future of her pupil, Louis-Philippe? With the hasty and much condemned departure from France of Louis XVI's two younger brothers (the future Louis XVIII and Charles X) in the early days of the Revolution, and other revolutionary eventualities that damaged the monarchy, together with doubts about the vulnerable young heir to the throne, the prospects for the regency of the duc d'Orléans seemed to fall within the realms of possibility. In spite of her vast outpouring of words, in later life she would remain evasive and elusive on the theme of power. Indeed, the novelist Madame de Montolieu, author of *Caroline de Lichtfield*, who met Félicité de Genlis and who corresponded with her for many years, considered her character to be an enigma. How to probe the mystery of a woman writer who, despite her fame and her vast output, was determined to keep her secrets and her counsel? Besides, disconcertingly, she often seemed to do the very opposite of what might have been expected, given the aim for which she appeared to be striving in her eventful career.

✑

CAROLINE-STÉPHANIE-FÉLICITÉ DU CREST DE SAINT-AUBIN, later comtesse de Genlis, then promoted to marquise de Sillery, and also at one time *la citoyenne Bruslart*, was born in 1746 into the *noblesse d'épée*, into an ancient Burgundian family whose menfolk traditionally served in the military. Her father was therefore often absent from home. Fallen on hard times and unable to settle his debts, he spent some time in prison. His wife struggled to bring up their two children, Félicité and Charles-Louis. For a while Madame du Crest enjoyed the protection of a wealthy tax farmer, Le Normant d'Etiolles (whose wife had notoriously left him to become the *maîtresse en titre*, or official mistress—and unofficial minister of state, of Louis XV as the marquise de Pompadour). When Le Normant d'Etiolles wearied of supporting the du Crest family, Félicité's mother moved to the mansion (and possibly the bed) of another opulent tax farmer and a generous patron of the arts, La Popelinière, who famously kept open house with his own orchestra on the premises. At thirteen Félicité was encouraged to pursue her passion for music: in particular her proficiency on the harp was much admired. In this way she became acquainted with many of the leading musicians and composers of the day, from Philidor to Rameau. She was to be a keen supporter of Gluck, whom she knew well, in the celebrated battle between his adherents and those of Piccinni.

The period of relative security *chez* La Popelinière was short-lived. In desperation Madame du Crest tried to profit from her daughter's musical gift by taking her into gatherings of the upper crust, where the girl performed on the harp after supper. Félicité was never invited to sit at table, never treated as a fellow guest. After all, although of gentle birth, she was just another musician, a kind of superior servant. A fee was discreetly passed to her mother. Sometimes charity took the form of cast-off apparel. The humiliation cut deep: it rankled so much that years later Félicité was to give offense to one condescending benefactress whom she satirized in *Adèle et Théodore, ou Lettres sur l'éducation*, a novel that made her literary reputation. This lady recalled that the now elevated educationist Madame de Genlis had once been an impoverished if respectable female (*une demoiselle démunie*) who played the harp in great houses and who had accepted the gowns offered to her.

Félicité might have continued as a professional musician, thoroughly *déclassée*, but she was saved from this dismal fate. Her father, returning from an expedition to the French island colony of Saint-

Domingue, had been taken prisoner by the English. According to her highly colored and romantic account in her memoirs, he showed his daughter's portrait to a fellow prisoner, a young naval hero who—like Tamino in Mozart's *Magic Flute*—promptly fell in love with the model. This was Charles-Alexis Bruslart, comte de Genlis, scion of the younger branch of a powerful and richly endowed family. He was descended from Nicolas Bruslart de Sillery, chancellor of Henri IV and owner of the great château de Sillery in Champagne, long famed for its magnificent vineyards. Charles-Alexis was to inherit the title of marquis de Sillery. He married Félicité in secret in 1763. The leading members of his family were opposed to the match with a penniless girl of the lesser gentry, and relented only after the birth of Caroline in 1765.

Through her husband's relatives Félicité entered a different world. She moved from modest means to comfort and even prodigality. For instance, once, for a lark she and her young sister-in-law dressed up as peasant women and bought all the milk from the local peasantry in order to see what it was like to bathe in it. Evidently it was a much grander world than she had known in the households of tax farmers. The head of the senior branch of the family, Louis-Philoxène Bruslart de Sillery, marquis de Puysieulx, had been successively Louis XV's minister of foreign affairs and minister of state from 1747 to 1756. His wife was the granddaughter of Louis XIV's great minister Louvois, and her circle included a number of survivors of the Sun King's reign and that of the regent, among them the notorious libertine the duc de Richelieu, the onetime ally of Alexandrine de Tencin. Richelieu's early youth had been spent in the last declining years of the Sun King when that powerful monarch was under the dominance of Madame de Maintenon, his morganatic wife. The reminiscences of these men and women who had actually known the *Grand Siècle* enthralled Félicité. Here was a living link with people and events familiar to her only through books. She plied these witnesses with questions, taking notes (a perennial habit), gathering firsthand information that she was to use throughout her life in her stories and biographical novels, or novelistic biographies.

The age of Louis XIV appeared to her as the period when France and French language, literature, and culture had reached the zenith of civilization. This opinion was hardly a novelty, but few would cling to it so tenaciously during the turbulent rise of Romanticism in the late eighteenth and early nineteenth centuries. This was a theme from which she would never deviate. While in many ways she came to hold advanced views, she appeared backward looking or conservative in others. She would prove to be one of the most consistent (and nowadays overlooked) opponents of what she called "false philosophy" and "false philosophers." These included all the leading writers and thinkers of the Enlightenment with, at their head, Voltaire, the anti-clerical author par excellence. (On her travels she visited him once—as who in those days with pretensions to wit did not?) Equally odious in her eyes would be the new writers of the Romantic movement, with their "Germanic" (that is, non-French) airs of melancholy, the leaders of the "modern" literature of her own era, so inferior to those of her idolized age of Louis XIV.

In the company of her new relatives and their friends Félicité found, too, her role model (and the subject of one of her later popular historical biographies) in Françoise d'Aubigné, marquise de Maintenon. Everyone was then as now bemused by that lady's phenomenal rise to power from relative obscurity, and by the extent of her influence on state affairs. Françoise d'Aubigné was the granddaughter of Henri IV's companion-in-arms, the great Protestant poet of *Les Tragiques*, Agrippa d'Aubigné. She was also the daughter of a thoroughly disreputable father, and the modest widow of the disabled bohemian satirist Paul Scarron—a woman who had led an extremely checkered existence. How did Madame Scarron come to be the morganatic wife of Louis XIV, the most powerful, formal, and remote absolute monarch in Europe? Here was the key: chosen to be governess to the numerous illegitimate offspring of Louis XIV and the imperious marquise de Montespan, the widowed Madame Scarron charmed and touched the aging king by her unswerving devotion to his children. Gradually the quiet governess contrived to supplant the king's extravagant and demanding mistress.

What profoundly impressed Félicité was the way that Madame de Maintenon (who had long since converted to Catholicism) laid stress on piety and convinced the elderly king to take his religious duties far more seriously. Religion as the fount of morality would always count with Félicité in her writings. Then there was Madame de Maintenon's conduct, her strict austerity and, above all, her concentration on matters of education. For the one serious subject on which women could expatiate without being criticized for moving outside their proper sphere was the education of the young. This was the area where women felt they could legitimately contribute to the future well-being of the community and the country without being harassed for political meddling. Félicité noted the powerful social influence of education on morals and behavior, "and consequently on public happiness."[4] Apparently the political and social implications of women's involvement in education do not seem to have registered with the conventional public in general. Madame de Maintenon was allowed to establish her school for impoverished young girls of the nobility at Saint-Cyr, controlling its rules, studies, and finances; writing plays (as well as commissioning Racine) for her pupils to perform; and setting down instructions for her collaborators. From time to time Madame de Maintenon, who always dressed soberly in black to distinguish herself from the worldly courtiers at Versailles adorned in costly finery, would withdraw from the court to Saint-Cyr, enhancing her reputation for dignity, gravity, and good works. She was to be found at the king's side during the deliberations of the Royal Council, where she gave her opinion and advice, and helped to shape policy in his last years. Power through a high moral tone and through educating the young—here was a pattern and a lesson to follow that Félicité took seriously to heart.

Presented at the court of Louis XV and launched into *le grand monde* through the good offices of Monsieur de Puysieulx and his wife, Félicité was on her way. Her aunt Charlotte, marquise de Montesson, her mother's half-sister, began to take an interest in Félicité after her marriage into high society. Soon she was receiving lessons in the art of manipulation from Madame de Montesson (who was only eight years Félicité's senior). Charlotte had conceived the plan of marrying the duc d'Orléans, grandson of the regent and father of Louis-Philippe-Joseph. She enlisted Félicité as confidante and ally. Through Madame de Montesson, Félicité was invited to the lavish house parties given by the elegant Prince de Conti at his summer residence at l'Isle-Adam. The immense wealth of such great princes (and members of the high aristocracy in general) was enhanced by the fact that their rank precluded them from paying taxes. The scale of the entertainment proffered by the Prince de Conti was such that each of his lady guests was allotted a carriage and horses for her private use during her stay. There at l'Isle-Adam, where visitors ceremoniously drank English tea, Félicité encountered the elderly Monsieur de Pont-de-Veyle, nephew of the predecessor she called "the famous Madame de Tencin." She also listened attentively to the great authority on niceties of social conduct, the maréchale de Luxembourg, absorbing that lady's dictates on how to behave correctly in society, dictates that she retained for the rest of her life and would pass on to her pupils and her readers.

Félicité accompanied her aunt Charlotte to Villers-Cotterets, one of the numerous grand estates of the duc d'Orléans, where they performed to great acclaim in his private theatre alongside professional actors and actresses. It was the moment when the *théâtre de société* was the height of fashion. That mordant *moraliste* Chamfort counted Madame de Montesson and her niece among the great actresses of the day, "actress" being a word that might have more than one meaning as suggesting, along with dramatic talent, a certain familiarity with the mask. After several years of persistent effort, Madame de Montesson at last achieved her aim and became the morganatic wife of the duc d'Orléans. She might not be received at court, but her new husband saw to it that she had all the appurtenances and the status due the wife of a prince of the blood. She had triumphed. Perhaps Charlotte now felt that Félicité knew rather too much about her and her machinations. They grew more distant, or at least that is the impression conveyed by Félicité's memoirs, where she appears far from charitable to Charlotte, portraying her as avid for money and mean-spirited. In her memoirs she insinuated that her aunt, who was in possession of a vast income, a grand Parisian mansion, and jewels beyond the dreams of avarice—and who happened to survive virtually unscathed through all the upheavals of Revolution and empire—did not do all that she might have done to help her in her long years of exile and pressing need.

Yet it was Charlotte who would make the match between her long-standing lover, Cyrus de Valence, and Félicité's younger daughter, Pulchérie. This gave the seventeen-year old girl a position guaranteed by Charlotte's wealth, but it was hardly the most moral arrangement. In her memoirs Félicité pretends ignorance of the true state of affairs between Charlotte and Cyrus de Valence, engaging there in some embarrassed casuistry. It is one of the rare moments where she expresses scruples about her own conduct, especially as Valence remained her aunt's lover. No amount of quibbling can conceal the fact that this was a shady deal for personal advantage: it did not do honor to the teacher of right conduct that Félicité would profess to be in her writings as well as in her public stance.

◈

IT WAS largely through her husband's influential relatives that Félicité's destiny was changed forever. The marquis de Puysieulx, who happened to be a great friend of the duc de Bourbon-Penthièvre, was instrumental in arranging a marriage between his friend's only daughter, believed to be the greatest heiress in the kingdom, and Louis-Philippe-Joseph, duc de Chartres, heir to the duc d'Orléans. Extremely gratified, the duc d'Orléans saw to it that as a reward for Monsieur de Puysieulx's contribution to the match, positions were made available to members of his family. Félicité entered the handsome Palais-Royal, the Parisian mansion of the Orléans dynasty, as *dame d'honneur*, or lady-in-waiting, to the young duchesse de Chartres, a position that could be inherited by her daughters. Her husband became captain of the guards, with similar privileges for male descendants. Their joint salary was considerable; moreover, they had the opportunity to solicit positions for members of their family. Later Félicité's brother, Charles-Louis du Crest, would be appointed *chancelier*, or treasurer, to the duc de Chartres.

Félicité had occupied her new post only a short time when, as it were by *droit de seigneur*, the duc de Chartres made her his mistress. There is not a word of this in her memoirs, of course. But there is a very revealing passage on "opinion" in its relation to a woman's reputation. "Whoever speaks of *opinion* speaks of a belief without proof positive. If such proofs existed it would no longer be an *opinion* but a formal, irrevocable judgment. Only such a judgment has the power to bring dishonor upon a person's head." Opinion is not irrevocable, she claimed, and it is possible to regain one's position in decent society later on by a change in behavior. "A woman can be ruined for one single flagrant affair, if she cannot deny it; whereas another need not be after a multitude of departures from the straight and narrow, and can regain her position, if there is only hearsay and opinion against her."[5] If opinion had the power to inflict dishonor, wickedness and calumny would know no limits, she asserted. This kind of casuistry indicates her belief in the efficacy of denial, a belief that was long lasting. But the censors of Louis XV's *cabinet noir* knew of her liaison with Louis-Philippe-Joseph from reading their love letters. As for the guileless and devout duchesse de Chartres, whose trust Félicité had won, she did not learn of their affair until very much later.

In those days, when still young, Louis-Philippe-Joseph was a seductive figure of great elegance and charm—"seductive" was the word Félicité would use to describe him. He was also indolent, frivolous, self-indulgent, and dissolute. A close friend and boon companion of the Prince of Wales (future regent and George IV), whom he resembled in many ways, he was famed for his Anglomania. He kept a great residence in Portman Square for his private use when he stayed in London. A regular visitor to Newmarket, it was he who introduced into France the English style of horse racing. Indeed, he favored English fashions and manners at a time when these, along with ideas about the English constitution, toleration, and parliamentary debate, were all the rage in enlightened circles in Paris.

Like all great aristocrats, and especially princes of the blood, Louis-Philippe-Joseph was mindful of his lineage. One cause of intense resentment was the fact that the present house of Orléans took its descent from an illegitimate daughter of Madame de Montespan and Louis XIV. Madame de Maintenon, the former governess keen on the establishment of her favorite charges, had urged this alliance upon the Sun King, who was not to be disobeyed. That absolute monarch had legitimized his illegitimate offspring with Madame de Montespan, princes who were known with a tinge of distaste in some quarters as *les légitimés*. The leading members of the house of Orléans, the younger branch of the Bourbons, were usually bitter about something; above all, about their ill treatment and the slights (real and/or imagined) they received at the hands of the distrustful senior branch, whose issue occupied the throne.

Louis-Philippe-Joseph in particular felt unjustly excluded from the naval or military career he desired. On inheriting the title of duc d'Orléans in 1785, he continued to pursue the traditional Orléans role he had adopted, that of being as difficult as he could whenever possible and notably siding with the *parlement* in its ever more acrimonious conflict with the king. The Paris *parlement*, not to be confused with the Parliament in London, largely consisted of lawyers who enjoyed the right to remonstrate that had been restored by Louis-Philippe-Joseph's forebear the regent—a right they now urged with ever greater enthusiasm and tenacity as the century progressed. A thorn in the flesh of Louis XVI, who ascended the throne in 1774, the duc d'Orléans—along with his circle of brilliant if dissolute aristocrats and dissidents of every degree—had no love for Marie-Antoinette either. The queen was widely detested for her extravagance and her alleged debauchery. Many even maintained that the heir to the throne was not the king's son, and this widespread calumny or "opinion" would underpin some of the later political writings of Madame de Genlis.

Félicité was far too intelligent to imagine that she could hold Louis-Philippe-Joseph's attention for long simply as his mistress. She was soon superseded in that role. But they continued to address each other as "dear friend" in English. She perceived that she could be the Egeria of a prince who was only too conscious of his lack of formal education, and who might even become regent one day, if circumstances were propitious. After all, his licentious great-grandfather had ruled as regent after the death of Louis XIV and during the minority of Louis XV. Moreover, remembering the egregious example of Madame de Maintenon's role in education at Saint-Cyr, Félicité could exercise influence over the next generation. This was a scheme to be evolved gradually.

To please Félicité, whose powers of persuasion must have been considerable, Louis-Philippe-Joseph had a house built for her in the vast park of the convent of Bellechasse (quite close to where the musée d'Orsay stands today). It was to become a kind of eighteenth-century version of Madame de Maintenon's school at Saint-Cyr. Félicité retired there with his little twin daughters. In due course his heir, Louis-Philippe, his daughter Adélaïde, and the two younger sons followed. Her own daughters, Caroline and Pulchérie de Genlis, joined them (her only son having died at the age of five), followed by her niece and nephew. Later two "English girls," Paméla and Hermine, arrived. Naturally, scandalmongers assumed that they were the offspring of Félicité and Louis-Philippe-Joseph. Today it is believed they were adopted, though their true origins have never been satisfactorily determined.

Madame de Genlis was now graced with the very high official title of *Gouverneur*, or official tutor, to the Orléans princes—not governess. This was seen as quite out of the ordinary, and it aroused considerable controversy. She was the first woman to be given such a title and to occupy so important an office, one usually allotted to a distinguished and experienced military man of a certain age. She displaced a predecessor of this sort, whom she belittled. Her appointment gave rise to much savage satirical comment. She riposted with spirit. "Is it because I am a woman?" she asked rhetorically. Could not women succeed just as well as men, and even better, in every sphere? "There are women who have commanded armies, there are some who have reigned, who are still reigning gloriously."[6] She could have been thinking of the duchesse de Longueville in the seventeenth century, who was famed as the moving spirit of the Fronde and who led armies, as well as of her own inimitable contemporary, Catherine the Great, empress of Russia. Clearly Félicité's thoughts were running on command, thrones, and glory.

At Bellechasse she reigned supreme over her private kingdom, having complete control over the plan of education, keeping careful records of expenditure and of the daily conduct of her pupils, and—like Madame de Maintenon—accepting no remuneration herself. Although she was partly indebted to *Télémaque* by the quietist bishop Fénelon, tutor to Louis XIV's grandson, for her view of the moral and religious instruction suitable for a good prince, and to Rousseau's *Émile* for her stress on physical activity and the outdoor life, her methods were innovative. Her favored pupil, Louis-Philippe, when "King of the French," would tell Victor Hugo how as a boy he had had to sleep on bare boards, engage in strenuous physical exercise in all weathers, and learn to turn his hand to manual labor as carpenter, blacksmith, and groom. Such practical activities were combined, for instance, with the study of modern languages, including English, and all this was to stand him in good stead during his years of exile in the United States. There were visits to see how goods were made, meetings with craftsmen, and generous displays of charity and largesse to win popularity. A hint of egalitarianism underlay these teachings. "He had lost everything he owed to the mere chance of birth and fortune; there only remained what he inherits from nature and myself," Félicité was later to claim, with no little self-satisfaction.[7]

Above all, Félicité encouraged young Louis-Philippe to despise the extravagance of the court, to scorn titles and privileges. Here, perhaps, was a faint echo of her youth, her revenge for her period of humiliation as an impoverished musician, an object of condescension because she was seen merely as *une demoiselle démunie*. She taught him to "seek the people's love which alone builds the reputation of princes," as she once expressed it.[8] Consequently, when he ascended the throne in 1830, "the Citizen King" dismantled the royal household, much to the loathing of aristocrats who lost their sinecures, and he sought to give the impression of living as much as possible like his fellow citizens. The upstart Napoleon Bonaparte understood them far better when in 1804 he had established a brilliant imperial court with resonant titles, rewards, and dazzling uniforms. In general, people were to be displeased with Louis-Philippe because what they really desired was a monarchy of splendor and glory, not one that appeared to be headed by someone like them. In this sense Félicité's educational principles and methods also contributed to mold Louis-Philippe for his ultimate downfall and hasty flight to England as "Mr. Smith" in 1848.

∾

IN FRANCE, in an age before the formation of coherent political parties (which were to emerge out of the Revolution of 1789), and when the word *parti* meant little more than faction, the main center of discontent in the years 1787 to 1789 was to be found at the Palais-Royal. For much of that time Félicité remained, if no longer the lover, the confidante of Louis-Philippe-Joseph, duc d'Orléans. He employed his wealth, the notoriously semi-mythical "Orléans gold," source of many a conspiracy theory, in buying popularity (after the manner of Cardinal de Retz during the Fronde). Around the prince, who was then regarded as "the savior of the people," there flocked genuine idealists as well as those eager for power and place, serious aristocratic and other reformers together with the disgruntled and the resentful of all ranks and colors. Many of those who were later to be well-known figures in the Revolution moved in the circles at the Palais-Royal in those days of intellectual ferment. It was a time for the discussion and propagation of the "new ideas." Among this motley crowd were not only Félicité's husband and her brother but also Talleyrand (whom she had known since she was a girl), Mirabeau (who claimed to be her lover), Lafayette, Sieyès, Danton, Robespierre.

One of Félicité's protégés was Brissot, onetime scurrilous journalist, now a committed radical activist, whom she managed to rescue from imprisonment in the Bastille and who was therefore in her debt. He married one of young princess Adélaïde's attendants, a helper in the educational projects at Bellechasse. The future leader of the Brissotins (or Girondins, to use their more familiar name), the ambitious correspondent of fellow radicals in Lyons like Jean-Marie Roland and his wife Manon, wrote an important note for Félicité's brother, Charles-Louis du Crest, about the creation of a party against royal power: "Since the end of the civil war known as the Fronde, there has been only one triumphant party in France, that of the court. The great art of leading a party, an art that the Cardinal de Retz understood so well and used so ill, has been lost through want of practice, and in France all intrigues have been limited to a change of ministers." Henceforward, said Brissot, a party of defenders of the people against ministerial despotism should be created on the English model. "The head of this party should be the house of Orléans," Brissot proposed.[9]

Did this "party" ever exist? On this subject there has been much spilling of ink, and even Félicité's contemporaries were not always quite sure that it did. But the baron de Staël, Germaine Necker's husband, who was then Swedish ambassador in Paris, wrote frequently to his sovereign in the autumn of 1789 about the faction or *"parti d'Orléans."* Clearly there was no doubt in *his* mind that such a party had been formed and was very active in making trouble. Another witness, Merlin de Thionville, firmly declared: "In 1788 I heard people speak of an Orléans faction, in 1789, in 1790, in 1791, still talk of an Orléans faction. Nowadays the name of Orléans is a ferment of trouble among us. . . ."[10] One contemporary insisted that if it did exist, Louis-Philippe-Joseph did not know what was being done in his name. The "Orléans party" appeared as a threat (real or imaginary); something difficult to grasp and therefore sinister and all the more to be feared; a weapon in the hands of demagogues who could make use of it—or the thought of it—for their own advantage. Like much of the inner detail of the Revolution, it remained and remains a matter for speculation. The important thing is that there were people who believed or chose to believe in its existence and who regarded it as a dangerous element in an ever more uncontrollable and fearful crisis.

Félicité tended to spend more of her time at Bellechasse than at the Palais-Royal. Much to her fury, she saw her position of private influential confidante undermined when the reserved, saturnine, frustrated army officer Choderlos de Laclos, author of the sensational novel *Les Liaisons dangereuses*, was appointed private secretary to the duc d'Orléans. She regarded this penetrating study of the corrupt manners of the society that Laclos knew in Grenoble as "an unworthy work: a woman should not admit publicly that she had read it."[11] (The use of the word "publicly" is a nice touch.) Besides, she claimed, she had never met its author and barely knew him by sight. The rivalry of the two writers and their mutual hatred knew no bounds. Laclos painted in vitriol a portrait of the woman he saw as a canting pedant; she, with Cassandra-like warnings, did her best to have this "immoral" character dismissed. Louis-Philippe-Joseph took no notice: "You deserve to be consulted on questions of history and literature," he told her airily, "but you do not understand anything about politics." He also wounded her by suggesting that she could not rise to "the height of the new ideas."[12] All the same, a great ditherer, without any really firm principles of his own, he continued to ask her advice without always following it.

Félicité was hoping that the States-General, which met in May 1789 for the fist time since 1614, would culminate in the reform of many abuses. She was present at the *séance royale*, or gathering in the king's presence, and she listened to the speeches delivered by the king and by Jacques Necker, declaring that she was unimpressed by either of them. She subscribed to the notion that something ought to be done, particularly in the field of education, to improve the lot of the people, something loosely embraced by the word *égalité*. She hated all forms of despotism. High on her list of matters for reform were surviving feudal rights like the *droit de chasse* that allowed the hunting parties of the nobility to ride roughshod over farmland and destroy the crops and the livelihood of the peasants. Presumably she had witnessed such mayhem when she had been a guest on the country estates of great aristocrats like the Prince de Conti. Another grave abuse that she wished to see abolished was the *lettre de cachet*, the document obtained with royal seal against which there was no legal recourse. Dire in all its applications, it could be particularly cruel when used against women. For instance, by *lettre de cachet* a husband could have his erring wife immured without appeal in a convent for the rest of her days. Félicité was to quote an example of this form of tyranny in her memoirs. Madame de La Tour du Pin, in hers, alludes to the similar fate of her mother-in-law, banished to seclusion in a convent for forty-five years.

Despite her claims of living in retirement at Bellechasse with her pupils, Félicité must have known a good deal about what was being discussed at the Palais-Royal and elsewhere. That retirement was not total if she could attend the opening of the States-General. In her salon at Bellechasse she welcomed writers and musicians on Saturdays, and the political world on Sundays. Madame Necker came with her daughter Germaine de Staël, whom Félicité criticized for being badly brought up and talking too much. Among the habitués could be found great aristocrats keen to resign their privileges, like

Mathieu de Montmorency or that supreme opportunist Talleyrand, along with many of lesser degree like Brissot, eager to create a new party, and the constitution-maker, abbé Sieyès, author of "What Is the Third Estate?" She heard the latest views and projects and assimilated many of them with enthusiasm.

In July 1789, hearing that people were tearing down the walls of the Bastille, stone by stone, Félicité hastened to witness the scene with her pupils, the young Orléans princes. They watched from the terrace of the house owned by Beaumarchais, secret agent, entrepreneur, and creator of that subversive barber, Figaro. As an early example of radical chic, Félicité took to wearing a medallion made of polished stone from the Bastille, set with jewels: in the center was the word *"Liberté"* in diamonds, surrounded by a garland of laurel leaves made of emeralds. She also liked to wear a skirt and ribbons in the fashionable red, white, and blue of the new tricolore that replaced the white flag and cockade of the Bourbon kings.

Soon she was visiting the revolutionary clubs, the Cordeliers and also the Jacobins (not yet endowed with its later reputation for extremism). At the Club des Cordeliers she listened to orators who were cobblers and street porters, and their wives who loudly inveighed against the nobles, the priests, and the rich. One *poissarde*, or "fishwife," amused her by being opposed to "mobiliary prejudices" instead of nobiliary ones. Whatever Félicité's ideal wishes for the betterment of the lower orders, which she saw as the interesting class, she could not conceal her prejudices about the vulgar rabble. She appears confused and contradictory on the theme of class. She not only witnessed lively sessions in the clubs, she also attended debates in the National Assembly with young Louis-Philippe. Her patriotic enthusiasm was communicated to him. Before long her pupil could be found crossing out his title of duc de Chartres and signing letters and documents as "French prince in expiation of his sins and Jacobin to his fingertips." Brissot was later to say of Madame de Genlis that in those heady days of the glorious dawn she held views "more republican perhaps than those of many republicans who are slandering her to-day."[13] Her enemies knew her as "*la jacobine*," or "that Jacobin woman."

Conspiracy theories were rife: any upheaval was attributed to "Orléans gold." The march of women of the lower orders to Versailles in October 1789, which Félicité witnessed with her pupils from the balcony of a house on the route, and which resulted in the humiliating forced return of Louis XVI and the royal family to Paris, was widely ascribed to an Orléans plot. People believed that it aimed to establish Louis-Philippe-Joseph as regent. In diplomatic reports to the king of Sweden, the baron de Staël not only expressed his conviction that such a plot existed but also asserted that if the duc d'Orléans had dared, he could have seized power then, when he was at the height of his popularity. "A moment of boldness would have made him master of the kingdom."[14] Instead, to the surprise and displeasure of his friends, he agreed to leave on some vague royal mission, departing hastily with the taciturn Laclos for England (where he was to remain until July 1790). Mirabeau, hitherto one of his keenest supporters, was disgusted, deciding that the prince was nothing but a weak reed. Félicité professed to be thoroughly mystified by the strange conduct of her former lover, and she appears to have drawn a similar conclusion to that of Mirabeau. She published two addresses that caused a sensation. By implication both of them turned attention towards her teenage pupil, Louis-Philippe. One, concerning the proper education of the heir to the throne, suggested the appointment of a suitably superior person (herself?) as tutor. The other favored adoption: the supposedly questionable heir apparent could thus be replaced by a more meritorious candidate— doubtless her own pupil, Louis-Philippe. It looks as if she had transferred her hopes from father to son. "She should be advised in her own interest to leave political matters alone," declared one angry critic, La Harpe.[15]

Yet this was not the limit of her revolutionary advocacy: Madame de Genlis, the well-known proponent of religion, in 1791 published a discourse on the suppression of convents. These were to be replaced by boarding schools for girls with professional teachers instead of nuns. Each girl was to be taught at public expense such practical subjects as finance, law, and the chief articles of the constitution, so that she could be independent, run her affairs, cope with a trade or a farm, and "replace a citizen, that is to say, become a citizen herself." At the same time, in contrast to this bold political project, each girl was to learn to be submissive to her parents and her future husband. It seems odd that the author of this plan did not perceive any contradiction between female independence and submissiveness—or perhaps she did, and this conventional addition was intended to sugar the radical pill.

The question of an Orléans regency would arise once again, but in very different circumstances, after the abortive flight of Louis XVI and his family and their capture at Varennes in June 1791. By this time Louis-Philippe-Joseph's coffers were depleted; he was no longer regarded as the "savior of the people" who had walked in procession with representatives of the Third Estate to the States-General. His great-grandfather had not waited in 1715 for the regency to fall into his lap but had worked hard for it behind the scenes. Louis-Philippe-Joseph could not now decide whether to make a move. Notwithstanding his earlier remarks on Félicité's lack of competence in political affairs, he consulted her. She said she was against his promotion to regent, believing him to lack the character essential for the high position. Besides, her thoughts were presumably running on the future of his heir. Louis-Philippe-Joseph asked her to compose his formal deed of renunciation, which he signed and published. This document was not written by a woman as uninvolved and unconcerned with politics as she would like to maintain in and out of season.

Then something very odd happened in which Félicité played a crucial part. Laclos, in despair at his patron's decision to withdraw, lived up to his reputation as a conspirator. By surreptitiously changing the text of a petition he had agreed to with Brissot, he apparently intended to leave room for Louis-Philippe-Joseph to be proclaimed regent in spite of himself. Félicité saw her chance to outmaneuver Laclos at last. She sent her husband in haste to Bailly, the mayor of Paris, to denounce the plot. If it was the end of Louis-Philippe-Joseph's aspirations to the regency, it was also the end of her rival Laclos at the Palais-Royal. Did she act on principle to right a wrong in political procedure? That does not seem very likely. Was she seeking to eliminate from the possibility of power a loser in the person of Louis-Philippe-Joseph so as to leave the field open for his son? Was she moved simply by detestation of Laclos to seize the opportunity to be rid of him? Whatever her motives, doubtless mixed, Félicité's swift action had the unfortunate consequence that her husband replaced Laclos as Louis-Philippe-Joseph's chief personal adviser and left him open to a fate as disastrous as that of his master.

After the royal fiasco at Varennes, heated debates raged over what to do with the king. They began with the notion of deposing him and moved on to questions about his trial and his ultimate fate, execution. What if, having deposed Louis XVI, put him on trial, and pronounced sentence, there remained the possibility of a plot with the aim of placing his young son or an Orléans prince on the throne? What hope then of getting rid of the Bourbons once and for all, and establishing a republic? This prospect of a Bourbon restoration through the elder or the younger branch was to haunt the leaders of the First Republic. Among the Girondins, François Buzot, Manon Roland's beloved, raised the matter in a passionate tirade in the National Convention once the trial of Louis XVI was afoot. He demanded urgently the exile of all the Bourbons, making no distinctions among them. Jean-Baptiste Louvet, Manon Roland's right hand, seconded his motion. Félicité was stunned: she hurriedly addressed a letter to Louvet in order to try to convince him that through her efforts the Orléans princes had been brought up on "republican principles" and that they were zealous in their republican ideals. Consequently, she claimed, it would be impolitic to sacrifice them to absurd prejudices about their origins.

If Félicité hoped to convince Louvet of her own revolutionary and republican credentials, she was unsuccessful. He replied with polite irony that her royalist principles and the aristocratic prejudices expressed in her works did not reassure him about the convictions of the pupils under her tutelage. Doubtless he was thinking of her famous prerevolutionary writings, like *Adèle et Théodore*, that treated of princely education. Louvet showed Félicité de Genlis's letter to Manon Roland. The Girondins, said Madame Roland, had never seen Louis-Philippe-Joseph as anything but a "dangerous puppet" with his vices, his money, his connections, his popularity—a figure they had always denounced. Louvet said to her: "Here is proof that we are not mistaken and that the Orléans party is not a chimera."[16] The conclusion drawn by Manon Roland, too, was that Madame de Genlis's letter to Louvet confirmed their suspicions and "proved" that the supporters of the duc d'Orléans were up to something sinister.

As the climate worsened, Félicité urged Louis-Philippe-Joseph, as well as her husband, both of whom were elected to the National Convention, to leave for the United States while there was still time. Her pleas were in vain. Charles-Alexis, while adopting the fashionable allusions to Brutus, mistakenly thought he could do some good as a moderating influence. As for Louis-Philippe-Joseph, like many weak people he sought by extremism to give an impression of strength and revolutionary consistency. Now known as Philippe Égalité, he sat with the Jacobins, who simply used him as their tool or, like the Girondins, viciously attacked him. At the same time, with lordly insouciance, he kept his armorial fleurs-de-lys, proscribed by decree, on view in the palace because it would have been "cowardly" to conceal or remove them—a risk that Félicité found difficult to understand. At his behest, in December 1792, she left the country for Tournai with his daughter Adélaïde. When Félicité learned that he had voted for the death of his cousin, the king, she was utterly horrified. Why did he do it? It was an act that sullied his name as well as damaging those who were related to him or associated with him. In contrast, Félicité's husband honorably refused to vote for the king's execution. Charles-Alexis would die by the guillotine only a few days before Philippe Égalité. At his interrogation, her former lover was questioned about that "perfidious intriguer," Madame de Genlis. He declared: "She did not deserve my trust."[17]

∽

IT IS NOT A SIMPLE MATTER to discover Félicité's role because in later life when she wrote her memoirs she did not wish the full extent of her revolutionary and republican commitment to be known. The world was different and so were her political opinions. She was not about to reveal the whole story of her actions. She had to try to preserve the image of the woman of social rectitude, the sensible teacher and moralist, advocate of religion and monarchy, of right and virtuous conduct. Yet Félicité was a revolutionary of the first hour, the exhilarating moment in revolutions that André Malraux was to call "the lyrical illusion." In a letter to her husband, when she wished to summarize the benefits of the Revolution, she declared: "There are two things abolished forever: *lettres de cachet* and the tyranny of classes and of feudal rights. . . . I never thought people went too far, but I always thought they went too fast."[18] The comment that she "never thought the people went too far" makes it sound as if she did not pay much heed to revolutionary excesses, yet elsewhere she told how she was horrified by the atrocities. What is striking is the allusion to the power of class prejudice and her strange belief that it had passed away along with *lettres de cachet* and feudal rights, those patent abuses of the ancien régime. In her memoirs published during the reactionary Bourbon Restoration, she regretfully observed: "My indignation against certain abuses that could easily be reformed inspired me with a kind of enthusiasm for the beginning of a revolution whose consequences I did not foresee."[19] This is a refrain that echoes down to our own day. It is also far from being the whole truth about her involvement.

Given the opprobrium that attached to the name of Philippe

Égalité and to anyone suspected of the "sin" of Orléanism (as it was called), and of seeking to promote an Orléans party, Félicité tried urgently to distance herself as far as she could from any association with her former patron and his family. She had become an exile: her wanderings were to last some seven years and would take her from Tournai in the Low Countries to Bremgarten in Switzerland, and thence to Germany, to Hamburg, Altona, Silk, Hamburg again, and Berlin. Having freed herself from the burden of looking after Adélaïde, finally delivered to the care of a noble relative, Félicité was favored at times by German princes or aristocrats, and she enjoyed the hospitality of cultivated well-to-do Jewish ladies in Berlin, to whom she sometimes gave lessons. Her talent as a musician and her piquant conversation made her welcome in their salons.

Nonetheless it was a precarious existence. In difficult circumstances, often short of funds, she was trying to earn her living and to lead an independent life, writing stories, novels, travel books— ready to turn her hand to anything, even to painting floral designs for textiles. At the same time she felt constantly threatened. "I felt that the factional tendency [*l'esprit de parti*] and the misfortune of having been attached to the house of Orléans would expose me to all kinds of calumny and persecution," she later recalled.[20] There were indeed enemies in hot pursuit who were influential enough to secure her departure from a place of asylum. Portrayed as one who had "made the Revolution" and as a dangerous agitator, she was expelled from Prussia. Principal antagonists were the royalist emigrés who were busy in Hamburg, along with spies, secret agents, and plotters of various shades. The French monarchist emigrés would never forgive Philippe Égalité for voting for the death of the king. Most vocal among the members of "the minor provincial gentry," as she scathingly defined the emigrés in Hamburg, was the sharp-tongued Rivarol. He wrote luridly of her association with Philippe Égalité, calling her with no little exaggeration the "moving spirit of his councils, instigator of his plans, apologist of his evil deeds, and corrupter of his children: a woman who left him only at the scaffold." In this version Philippe Égalité had been merely the "vile instrument of a Fury" who was still living and active.[21]

It would be surprising if Félicité, a vulnerable woman alone for much of the time, did not feel afraid. Henceforward fear seems to prompt many of her political decisions and actions. She had already published several attempts to justify herself, rather as if she sometimes conceived her conduct as that of a public political figure from whom the world demanded a statement or a denial. Now she tried again with her "Summary" of her conduct since the Revolution, and the open "Letter from Silk" published in 1796 and addressed to Louis-Philippe, the very young General Égalité. She maintained there that Louis-Philippe's ideas were far more democratic and radical than hers, that he was ardently republican, and that he held extreme views on equality. It was as if he had somehow acquired such political opinions on his own, as if the tutor he had grown accustomed to call his "mamma" had had nothing to do with it. Her former pupil, who had adoringly absorbed Félicité's tuition, regarded these comments by his onetime revolutionary guide and mentor with no little irony. He had acquired a spirit of independence. They had gone their separate ways after a quarrel.

As for herself, she insisted (none too truthfully), she had always lived quietly in retirement, devoting herself solely to literature, too occupied in writing books to have time for anything else and, above all, submissive to every established government, "for such should be the conduct of a woman and it has always been my own."[22] This declaration from the woman who, in her revolutionary "enthusiasm," had flaunted radical chic, encouraged her favorite pupil publicly to reject his titles, and dared to suggest a replacement for the heir to the throne! Was it not she who had published a controversial discourse on the suppression of convents, composed Philippe Égalité's renunciation of the regency, and intervened to see that it was carried out? Now she was fearful of being tarred with the Orléans brush, eager to distance herself from Louis-Philippe and any possible Orléanist faction. For she was also keen to find a way to ingratiate herself with the Directory, in the hope of being able to return at last to Paris, where her daughter Pulchérie de Valence reigned with other beauties like Juliette Récamier and Joséphine de Beauharnais.

Doubtless deeply worried by her precarious situation as well as by royalist threats, in the "Letter from Silk" Félicité stressed the folly of any desire on Louis-Philippe's part to be the head of an Orléans party and a constitutional monarch at a time when there existed in France a republic founded on morality and justice (odd terms to be applied to the Directory, that byword for licentiousness and illegality). This line of thought concerning the present and future destiny of Louis-Philippe seems to run counter to all she had formulated in her ambitious projects for him. Moreover, she added tactlessly, you have neither the talents nor the qualities necessary for the role. You have many virtues, suited to a domestic life, "but you do not have those required of great kings."[23] Rare were those who believed that she had really parted company from Louis-Philippe: they thought the "Letter from Silk" was part of some devious political maneuver. Its candid assessment of her former pupil's character was to prove a gift to his enemies and would be reprinted at various crucial moments in his career. It was, however, a judgment from which she would never deviate.

∽

THE COUP D'ÉTAT of Napoleon Bonaparte on 18 Brumaire (November 9) 1799 opened the way at last for Félicité's return to Paris. She arrived in 1800 to find everything changed. Street names had been altered, houses of the nobility had been converted into taverns, the very way people behaved was unrecognizable. A new class consisted of people who had profited from the Revolution. Bonaparte's close adviser, her longtime acquaintance Talleyrand, whom she had encountered at least twice in her peregrinations, had been corresponding with her during the years of their dispersal. Whenever he now called on her, she saw him in private. Another helpful friend was the journalist, novelist, and secret agent Joseph Fiévée, who was one of Bonaparte's informants on public opinion. It soon came to Bonaparte's notice that Madame de Genlis and her pen might be useful to him. She was granted a pension and an apartment in the official residential quarters of the Arsénal Library. There she held court, welcoming persons either connected with Bonaparte or favorable to him, while denigrating those—like Germaine de Staël— who were not.

In return for her pension, Félicité was expected to write fortnightly to Napoleon on a subject of her choice. No copies were kept of this correspondence. (Apparently he never received her in audience, though her aunt Charlotte was a friend of his wife Joséphine.) The fact was that the conqueror of Europe never felt secure. He had his paid hacks to uphold his policies in the subsidized press. He employed Fouché, one of the most renowned spymasters of all time, without fully trusting him (rightly, as it turned out). Spies were everywhere, even planted in private homes. Any detail, however trivial, might yield a nugget of information about the true state of public opinion, as distinct from the floods of flattery with which he was deluged. According to Félicité, she wrote to Napoleon solely on nonpolitical matters of religion and morality, on methods for improving trade and providing employment, on the education and well-being of the people. But this is not the whole story.

Talleyrand relates how he read aloud one of her reports to Napoleon soon after the victorious battle of Austerlitz in December 1805: "She spoke of opinion in Paris, quoting several offensive remarks uttered in what was then called the faubourg Saint-Germain [that is, the neighborhood of the old aristocracy]; she named five or six families who, she added, would never support the emperor's government. Certain scathing remarks she reported sent Napoleon into a paroxysm of fury: he swore, he thundered against the faubourg Saint-Germain. . . . When? A few hours after a decisive victory over the Russians and the Austrians."[24] That the "faubourg Saint-Germain" was unfavorable to him could hardly have been news to Napoleon, but that Madame de Genlis actually "named" five or six families when she quoted their offensive words would appear to confirm the view of those contemporaries like Lady Morgan who regarded her as Napoleon's spy.

Meanwhile an endless stream of books renewed her literary fame, which was used politically—like everything else in the First Empire. It served as a counterbalance to that of Germaine de Staël, outspoken in her opposition to the emperor's authoritarian regime. By the early nineteenth century the author of *De la Littérature* was among the most vocal leading advocates of the ideas and values of the *philosophes* of the Enlightenment, many of whom she had met as a girl in her mother's salon. She had reflected deeply on their notions of rational inquiry and freedom of thought, on tolerance and on the possibility and nature of human happiness and progress, and she had produced a number of controversial works that left a powerful impression on her contemporaries as well as on later political thinkers. Félicité de Genlis, on the other hand, regarded herself as the embattled opponent of the Enlightenment, excoriating the "impiety" and destructiveness of some of its best-known representatives. She stressed Voltaire's anti-clericalism, for instance, disregarding his humanitarian campaign to clear the name of the Protestant Calas, tortured and executed on a false charge. She had conceived an odd plan: to "purify" the *Encyclopédie* of Diderot and d'Alembert, and to publish famous works of the *philosophes* "purified" in the same manner. She sought and obtained subsidies to pursue this bizarre task. In this way she can be seen as an important member of the heterogeneous movement of writers and thinkers who battled against the *philosophes*, a movement that flourished from the middle of the eighteenth century and culminated eventually in the counterrevolutionary current of thought of the early nineteenth century and beyond.

Her attacks on Germaine de Staël form part of her general political and ideological campaign against the Enlightenment. Because these attacks were made when a younger fellow author was being persecuted by Napoleon, they do not reflect well on their instigator. Félicité always admitted that Germaine de Staël, whom she satirized in *La Femme philosophe*, was endowed with great talent and was to be counted among the leading literary figures of the age. Nonetheless her judgments on the author of *De l'Allemagne* were severe. Félicité claimed that Madame de Staël attacked morality and religion because she wrote on suicide and divorce. Besides, Germaine had made a grave error: she had never really studied the incomparable French masters of the seventeenth century and adopted them as her models (as Félicité herself had done). That was why Germaine's style and language tended to be so unclear and therefore un-French. As for her major political writings, published posthumously—her thoughts on the French Revolution and on her experience of exile, works that would have a great influence on many liberal thinkers—in Félicité's view they received "exaggerated praise." There can be little doubt that a political intention underlay Félicité's criticism, particularly obvious in her comment that Madame de Staël "made a display of grand liberal principles." What a pity it was, said Madame de Genlis in one of her less sensible comments, that Madame de Staël was not "my daughter or my pupil."[25] Indeed it was her own pupil, Louis-Philippe, who once made a most acute remark about Madame de Genlis. He said she read a great deal and was always taking notes and making extracts, often without thinking deeply about them. "Her ideas arose out of her reading, and only rarely out of her reflections," declared Louis-Philippe.[26] Lack of reflection was never a charge that could be leveled against Germaine de Staël.

Ironically, even Félicité de Genlis herself fell afoul of Napoleon's heavy censorship, though no work of hers was pulped like *De l'Allemagne*. She was not permitted to publish extracts from the memoirs of the marquis de Dangeau (a contemporary of Madame de Maintenon's) that she had discovered in the Arsénal Library. Nor would Napoleon allow her to publish her book on the first Bourbon king, the ever-popular Henri IV, patron of her husband's ancestor. The emperor did not want anything that showed the Bourbons in a good light. Unlike Germaine de Staël, who resisted in public, Félicité de Genlis yielded in private. True, she did not have at her disposal Madame de Staël's considerable means. Besides, she claimed to admire her "benefactor," Napoleon, whose armies were ravaging Europe from Spain to Russia, as the restorer of "religion, order and peace."[27]

By April 1814 and Napoleon's abdication, the tone had changed, and Félicité was bemoaning to Talleyrand "the dénouement of this long tragedy, this pretentious and blood-stained drama," so ill-planned and badly directed.[28] Along with Talleyrand, prime secret mover of the Bourbon Restoration, and countless others, she rallied to the Bourbons, whose virtues she had apparently loved devotedly all the time. Louis XVIII received her at court—as according to ritual he did all *dames présentées*, ladies who had formerly been presented to his predecessors as she had been to Louis XV—but he was disinclined to accept her offer of regular letters. Her book on his remote ancestor Henri IV, adorned with some unfavorable allusions to Bonaparte, was published—with most unfortunate timing—just as the usurper made his extraordinary escape from Elba in March 1815 and swiftly arrived in Paris. All enthusiasm, she began again writing letters to him, but he ignored them and did not restore her pension. After his defeat at Waterloo, and the return of the Bourbons, she was not long in expressing her undying devotion to them.

∽

FÉLICITÉ DE GENLIS was no more opportunistic than most of her masculine contemporaries, from Talleyrand to Benjamin Constant, who turned their coat. How difficult it was to keep on an even and consistent path of principle when faced with that rapid succession of regimes upon which depended one's financial survival, social standing, and possibilities for place, action, and influence! Who could tell for certain whether one's patron and his regime would return to power? Throughout the Bourbon Restoration, however,

Félicité would enjoy the patronage of her erstwhile pupil, Louis-Philippe, with whom she was now reconciled, and who had returned to the Palais-Royal. For a time she acted as hostess for her son-in-law, Cyrus de Valence, who was now a liberal peer of the realm, until his death in 1822. She may have had a hand in some of his speeches. The manners of his liberal associates failed to impress her, since they pointedly did not include her in their discussions. Producing fiction as well as didactic literary works, memoirs, a compendium on etiquette useful for the new class, she remained deeply embroiled in her polemics in favor of religion, continuing to wage war against the *philosophes* until her death in 1830 at the age of eighty-four. She herself had moved from being "la jacobine" and the ardent republican to the enthusiastic Bonapartist, and ultimately to the *ultra*, or extreme royalist. Still, she gradually modified her position as an *ultra*, for she would on no account join those who thought the Revolution was all bad, or who wanted to return completely to the ancien régime as if nothing had happened in the intervening years.

Her trajectory from revolutionary sympathizer and republican activist to embattled royalist and conservative may look familiar, her inconsistencies and her veerings often bizarre. Yet in a cultural climate ostensibly hostile to women's participation in political affairs, she could write in her memoirs: "It would be unfair to include among the class of intriguers all those who engage in public affairs even though they are not directly involved in them: the love of the public good and the wish to help one's friends can lead in that direction quite as much as ambition and greed. I have known decent people and women worthy of respect who had a taste for public affairs, and I approved of them for taking part," because, she added, they had the temperament and the talents essential for success in that field.[29] She did not offer any names, but doubtless she did not mean Germaine de Staël, whom she saw as a political opponent; nor could she have been alluding to Manon Roland, for she disdained the activities and the memoirs of the Egeria of the Girondins—a disdain that was mutual.

As for that farseeing feminist revolutionary, Olympe de Gouges (whom Félicité did not mention), she was—along with other militant radical feminists like Théroigne de Méricourt and the women of the clubs—beyond the pale of society as Madame de Genlis understood it. It was Olympe de Gouges who, in her *Déclaration des droits de la femme et de la citoyenne* of 1790, proposed: "All citizenesses and all citizens should be admitted equally to all dignities, positions and public employment, according to their abilities and without other distinctions but their virtues and talents." She also observed there that "Woman has the right to mount the scaffold, she should equally have the right to mount the tribune."[30] All the same, Félicité's public approval of women's participation in politics in certain unnamed instances, while mild in comparison with Olympe's, was a considerable admission for her day and might have been thought self-referential. On the contrary, it was followed by the usual disclaimers; for she could not possibly be included among such spirits; lacking ambition, too busy writing books, she herself had never engaged in politics, and she certainly had no gifts in that area. If only the lady did not protest so much!

While no militant feminist, Félicité de Genlis had often advocated decent practical education for women, and in particular those of lesser social standing whom she called women of the people. She did not want them to be dependent, nor was she pleased if they played the part of "victims." Moreover, she tried to defend women, above all their liberty to cultivate the arts, to write and publish without being absurdly attacked for neglect of their domestic obligations. She took rather a middle- or upper-class view of these, for she liked to repeat that such duties should not take more than an hour a day in a well-regulated household, after a woman had dealt with her accounts in the morning and given her orders to her servants! Yet Félicité de Genlis had not only held advanced political views as an early republican, she had also ventured to translate them into published work and into action, at some cost to her reputation and even at times to her existence. She could be a penetrating social observer and social satirist. In her later years her interest in political affairs did not decline. In her memoirs she mentions that she questioned the influential counterrevolutionary philosopher Louis de Bonald on politics, and confesses that she enjoyed hearing her old Bonapartist ally Joseph Fiévée, now an *ultra* like herself, discourse on such matters. She even wrote a *Traité politique* for her young friend, Anatole de Montesquiou, where (after Rousseau) she discussed such questions as what constituted the happiness of a nation, whether existing governments had attained this goal, and the quest for the means of attaining it. Apparently this little treatise was not published.

Disconcertingly, though, she veered between impulsive courage and a kind of social timidity or fearfulness, as if constantly reminding herself how, as a woman, she would be perceived in society. This excessive concern with social opinion was a fault that Mary Wollstonecraft—who certainly did not share it—had observed in her long before, choosing to single out for criticism her *"blind* submission . . . to the opinion of the world."[31] As for that acute critic Sainte-Beuve, reviewing her memoirs when they were published in 1825, he felt thoroughly frustrated and charged her with "mystification." Without the burdensome limit that Félicité de Genlis placed on frankness, especially where her political intentions and actions were concerned, she could have revealed much more about what he called with discreet understatement her "complicity" with her age.[32] Her commitment went a good deal further than that.

❧ FIVE ❧

Germaine de Staël
Against the Wind

For me, to talk politics is to be alive.—GERMAINE DE
STAËL to the Duke of Wellington, after the defeat of
Napoleon

She is a machine in motion. . . . Only in France is such a
woman to be feared, and I want nothing to do with
her.—NAPOLEON to Metternich

Yet, Freedom! yet thy banner, torn, but flying,
Streams like the thunderstorm *against* the wind. . . .
      —BYRON, *Childe Harold's Pilgrimage*, Canto 4, xcviii

There were not many in France who took the risk of speaking
out against Napoleon Bonaparte at the height of his power—
and with good reason. In the lead, however, was Germaine de Staël,
his adversary not only in her writings but also increasingly in her
political activities. What inspired this volatile, immensely gifted,
and daring woman of tireless energy and determination to become
the opponent of his regime? And what was the cost to herself?

   In January 1802 General Napoleon Bonaparte, now the first consul, purged the Tribunate established two years earlier, just after he

seized power. Among the members of the moderate opposition whom he excluded was Germaine de Staël's ambitious lover, Benjamin Constant, who was not yet the renowned liberal politician and political thinker that he was to become under her aegis. Napoleon saw Germaine's influence behind the criticism of his regime uttered by the most vocal moderates, and he took the opportunity to send his brothers, Joseph and Lucien, who frequented the gatherings in her salon, to convey a sharp warning: "Advise her not to try to stand in my way, . . . otherwise I shall break her, I shall crush her."[1] The first consul had not been at all gratified by her epoch-making book *De la Littérature* (*On Literature Considered in Its Relations with Social Institutions*), published in 1800, where she observed that what despotic authority must fear most is "the man who preserves his faculty of judgment."[2] She had already told Joseph, when the first consul tried to buy her off as he did with a great many others: "My God, it is not a matter of what I want but of what I think."[3] The expression of independent thought and judgment would never suit the purposes of a military leader intent on personal domination.

At this moment, in the first half of 1802, the conflict became clear and irrevocable. In particular, the Concordat with the papacy, signed in the spring of that year, which restored Catholicism as the state religion, infuriated all those who wished to preserve freedom of conscience and other liberties hard won during the Revolution. It helped to provoke the conspiracy led by General Moreau and less visibly by General Bernadotte, a revolt that was ruthlessly suppressed. Napoleon suspected—rightly or wrongly—that Germaine had played some part in it. Then in December 1802 came her controversial novel *Delphine*, with its arguments in favor of religious liberty, divorce, and other matters that ran counter to his policies. The book was the sensation of the hour: people were said to be too busy reading it to attend Mass or visit the theatre. The preface alone rang with defiance, in a world where, she said, the independent had been silenced and political partisans alone allotted praise or blame. In such a climate writers who wished to express what they believed to be the truth (meaning those like herself) addressed "*la France silencieuse mais éclairée*," the enlightened French public deprived of its voice.[4]

All this defiance was too much for Bonaparte, engaged in laying the foundations of his authoritarian rule, who used his terrible bursts of anger, whether simulated or genuine, as yet another weapon to intimidate his hearers. Germaine received the order to quit Paris. By exiling this sociable being *par excellence* from the capital and from her friends, he had hit upon the most exquisite punishment he could devise for her. Trembling with fear yet really proud at the same time, Germaine drew the conclusion that Bonaparte "fears me. That is my joy, my pride, and my dread. I must own it to you," she told a friend, "I am hurtling towards proscription, and I am ill-prepared to face the troubles of a long exile. It is not my will but my courage that weakens. I am in pain and yet I do not want any remedy that would be degrading. I have fears just like any woman but they shall not turn me into a hypocrite or a slave."[5] Noble words that already described her position and her attitude in the years to come.

Exile is a terrible fate, a source of bitterness and grief since the time of the ancient Hebrews as they sat down by the waters of Babylon and wept. In our own tormented era, a great many people have felt what it means to be forcibly cut off, perhaps forever, from their treasured familiar culture. On this theme Germaine de Staël, the great forerunner of modern literary and political dissidents, still has much of value to communicate. For a woman as highly strung and imaginative as she was, exile figured as grimly as death itself—and she was by no means the first to think of it in that way. She often remembered that nearly a hundred years earlier the statesman and writer Lord Bolingbroke, who had been Alexandrine de Tencin's protector, had associated exile and death. Her thoughts also turned to the poet Ovid, sent into exile by the Emperor Augustus and left to bemoan his fate among the Scythians on the shores of the Black Sea, where he died.

Tradition has it that Ovid was exiled for a poem that gave offense as well as for involvement in a sexual-cum-political scandal. Germaine de Staël's fault in the eyes of the leaders of the Committee of Public Safety in 1795, of the Directory in 1799, and, most potently, of Napoleon Bonaparte from 1802, was not sexual, though her private life and her numerous love affairs were a source of prurient gossip. It was literary and political. Napoleon condemned her to banishment from Paris and to internal exile under constant surveillance and harassment in the French provinces, so that eventually she felt driven to flee abroad. Having grown accustomed to sycophancy of the most blatant kind, he was absolutely furious because she not only failed to praise his mighty military exploits but also omitted to mention them in her books. She was used to the freedom of talk that had flourished under the ancien régime in the days immediately before the Revolution, and so she thought she could criticize his dictatorship in private and in society with similar impunity. Whatever her virtues—and she was certainly courageous—prudence was not among them. For a long time she did not comprehend that in Napoleon she had come face to face with a new phenomenon, one that would prefigure many of the authoritarian tendencies familiar to the modern era. When she grasped fully the nature of his arbitrary regime, she was to analyze it and mount a moral assault upon it that has not lost its power.

Germaine's indiscreet remarks and her defiant actions were perfectly well known to Napoleon. Even when encamped in Boulogne planning the invasion of England, or in Prussia, Austria, or Russia, busily engaged in his ceaseless wars with their thousands of casualties, he took the trouble to be well informed about her sayings and doings. He would find time to write to Joseph Fouché, the supreme spymaster, then minister of police, urging him to tighten measures against "this real bird of ill omen," "this whore, and a dirty one into

Germaine de Staël, 1797 (Portrait by Jean Baptiste Isabey)

the bargain," as Napoleon graciously called her.[6] In his eyes she was a tiresome troublemaker, and he suspected her of actively plotting against him. He said people always left her salon plainly less well disposed toward himself. She had offended him, and that was sufficient cause for punishment. There could be no redress against giving offense to an absolute ruler, she once observed.

She soon came to realize that others did not regard exile—or at least, exile in her case—as so dreadful a fate. As early as 1803 she had written to a friend how "people will get used to my exile and will be surprised at my whim to extricate myself from it."[7] Writers like Félicité de Genlis, who in any event was rarely inclined to speak well of Germaine, or Chateaubriand, both of whom had suffered exile in penury during the Revolution, were not particularly sympathetic to her complaints. Chateaubriand, who visited Germaine at Coppet, her handsome family mansion near the shores of Lake Geneva, expressed astonishment that a person of large means like herself, who resided in a beautiful house, attended by servants and with all the amenities of unspoiled nature around her, could be so unhappy at her banishment from Paris. He was drawn to conclude that whereas he would be well content with the pleasures of solitude in such conditions, there were others of a different temperament who could not be reconciled to it.

Chateaubriand, however, was not primarily a political activist, nor was he the leading and most consistent intellectual opponent of Napoleon Bonaparte. That was the role of Germaine de Staël—with a few rare lapses—almost from the first moment that Napoleon's true colors and his drive toward personal rule and military dictatorship became apparent. Later famously one of "Buonaparte's" most indignant critics, Chateaubriand did not become the object of a Corsican vendetta such as the victor of Rivoli waged against Germaine de Staël. Under the Consulate, the creator of *René* accepted a diplomatic post in Rome in 1803, though he resigned after the notorious abduction and execution of the duc d'Enghien in 1804. As for Germaine's fluctuating companion Benjamin Constant, known to wits as "*Constant l'inconstant,*" he would define in powerful detail the abusive nature of Napoleon's imperial regime, but in a stunning volte-face he was to help the person he had just qualified as a new Attila to put a liberal veneer on his government during the Hundred Days. For years it was Germaine de Staël who found ways to defy Napoleon's military dictatorship: she was the one whose writings and political actions he loathed above all others, and he persecuted her with misogynistic energy for many years through his ubiquitous spies, zealous bureaucrats, and the mean-minded officials of his police.

What was there about Germaine de Staël that so offended Napoleon? After all, he came to hold most of Europe, from Spain to Russia, in his sights or in his grasp. Why did he trouble himself so much about her and try to silence her, a woman whose only force was that of her individual voice and her pen—and, it must be admitted, her connections with influential writers who shaped opinion as well as with powerful rulers and leaders throughout Europe? He took her seriously, treating her as a real threat to his absolute rule. The fact is that just as he represented a new phenomenon, so did she. Both of them were outsiders of genius. He, an obscure officer, born on the wild island of Corsica, long part of the Republic of Genoa, rose like a rocket to dominate the world, crowning himself emperor in 1804, creating an imperial court, a Bonapartist aristocracy, and, in Italian-style family loyalty, establishing his brothers and sisters on the thrones of Europe. She, the daughter of a foreign banker, dazzled her listeners and readers with her intellectual brilliance and penetration, determined as she was to think for herself and to say what she thought in defense of freedom and justice. Eventually she would try to undermine Napoleon's power, regardless of the consequences. At first it may seem that the picture is black and white, but there are subtle tones of grey here and there, equivocal touches that deepen and humanize the conflict between sword and spirit.

The most striking difference between Germaine de Staël and her

predecessors and coevals among women writers is that she stands
out as a coherent political thinker in her own right. She exerted an
immense influence on many fronts, not just on her contemporaries
but also on her successors, women as well as men. A witness of the
events of the blissful dawn in 1789, she also experienced life-
threatening revolutionary moments in the late summer of 1792. She
was acquainted with a good number of the leading participants of
the Revolution, and she was among the earliest French writers to
study seriously its causes and consequences. For her, the Revolution
was not simply an event or series of events: it marked a new era in
human consciousness. Moreover, at a time when "liberal ideas" represented something new in France, she helped to mold political liberalism as a practical force there and to shape its principles and its
direction. She often appears as a militant intellectual (long before
that word was invented) in her reliance on what she saw as the truth
in her struggle against injustice and the arbitrary abuse of power.

Germaine de Staël was certainly not averse to political intrigue
and power brokering when she had the opportunity. But she also reflected deeply on society, analyzed the current situation in light of
the past, formulated her own views, and then disseminated them
through her influential novels, *Delphine* and *Corinne ou l'Italie*, as
well as in her writings both literary and political, *De l'Influence des
passions, De la Littérature, De l'Allemagne*. Each of these works created a profound impression. For her, literature and politics were not
separate spheres. In her view, literature embraced the whole realm
of feelings and ideas, including politics, and she brought to it an
open mind and a passionate curiosity, allied to a gift for analysis that
was second to none. Her mind was the "most comprehensive that
ever belonged to any woman, and perhaps to any man," declared
Benjamin Constant, who knew whereof he spoke.[8] He was then trying to convey something of her intellectual range through the fictional character who embodied some of her traits in his
autobiographical novel, *Cécile*. Germaine de Staël argued always
from experience, unimpressed as she was by theories and systems.

✺

HER EARLY OUTLOOK AND IDEAS were dominated by her deep respect and excessive admiration and love for her father, an esteem that would never waver. She was brought up to know that she was far from ordinary, and she came to believe that she was what she herself would call "*une femme supérieure*," and thus, as a gifted and sensitive woman, estranged and romantically doomed to misunderstanding and misery. The role of suffering genius adopted by male poets, dramatists, and novelists in general, especially those who fell under Byron's spell, was one that she claimed for woman through *Corinne.* Yet while she suffered from her singularity, she could not help rejoicing in it. An immense zest for life, happiness, and fame was the reverse of the fear of nothingness and death and the melancholy temperament she shared with her mother.

Born in Paris in 1766, Anne-Louise-Germaine Necker was the only child of the self-made and highly successful Swiss banker and financier Jacques Necker and his handsome and cultivated wife, formerly a lady's companion, who had settled in the capital. Their daughter did not inherit her mother's good looks—though many remarked on the beauty of her expressive eyes. Her father told her bluntly that she would have to compensate for this shortcoming with her intelligence. The education of Minette, as Germaine was called in her intimate family circle, was widely seen as eccentric. Madame Necker, learned, pious, strict, and demanding, taught her daughter privately. The girl had few companions of her own age. Physical exercise played no part in the curriculum, and excursions were a rare cause for excitement. The devoted couple, Monsieur and Madame Necker, with their talented, susceptible, and imaginative daughter, figured as a strange trio who amazed and exasperated many of the more frivolous or less elevated members of eighteenth-century French society by their inexhaustible mutual admiration, of which they made no secret.

The destiny of Jacques Necker, the father Germaine adored beyond measure, was certainly extraordinary enough. True, he was not the first foreigner to serve as financial adviser to the French crown, having been preceded earlier in the century by the Scottish adventurer John Law, who helped to make Alexandrine de Tencin's fortune. But Necker's contribution and standing were on a different scale, and his intervention in French affairs occurred in tempestuous times. Through banking and speculation of a somewhat dubious kind (though possibly no more questionable than that of many of the financiers and tax farmers of his day), he had amassed a sizable fortune while—unlike Law—he contrived to preserve a reputation for unspotted virtue. As a foreigner and a faithful Protestant, Necker was precluded from enjoying the title of *contrôleur général des finances*, or finance minister, to Louis XVI, a powerful post that embraced home affairs, finance, and public works. Instead, in 1777 he was appointed *directeur général du Trésor Royal*, in effect as royal treasurer fulfilling the same functions. When the king dismissed him in 1781, a procession of aristocratic and other admirers of his financial and administrative genius, among them the rebellious Louis-Philippe-Joseph, then duc de Chartres, visited the fallen minister at his country house at Saint-Ouen.

As virtual minister of finance, Necker made a notably distinct impression by publishing his views not merely to inform others but in order to justify himself and win adherents. In his writings he was an early proponent of the importance of public opinion, convinced as he was of the need to win its support for his policies. He made it clear to all and sundry that he stood for reason, justice, moderation, toleration, and fair treatment for the less fortunate. With his wife and his daughter he had visited England in 1776, and he remained a keen admirer of English liberties and institutions, especially constitutional monarchy. His daughter echoed his Anglomania for the rest of her life, even after she abandoned her trust in constitutional monarchy itself.

As for Madame Necker, she too had her political role. Her Parisian salon was devoted to the cultivation of her husband's image and fame, the dissemination of his financial and political views, and the winning of hearts and minds to his cause. Her Fridays were attended by leading writers and *philosophes* of the Enlightenment, from Marmontel, in his younger days Alexandrine de Tencin's protégé, to Diderot and Raynal. The distinguished elderly habitués of Madame Necker's salon enjoyed nothing so much as engaging her young daughter in discussion on matters—including politics—that some thought to be beyond her years. At fourteen, dressed formally in beribboned finery, with hair stiffly curled and piled high, the vivacious Minette, "all eyes and ears," was the salon's precocious ornament. Unlike her reserved mother who, according to Marmontel, had never acquired the ease and elegance of Parisian conversational style, Germaine's gift for conversation was to be legendary. The art of conversation as practiced with verve and wit in Parisian society would seem as necessary to her as the air she breathed. A number of her later portraits show her with parted lips as if she were in the act of speaking.

Germaine herself would appreciate to the full the importance of public opinion when, on July 16, 1789, the king recalled Necker who, amid scenes of wild rejoicing and adulation, returned in triumph to Paris. He was acclaimed to the skies because the populace, shattered by famine, expected him to put an end to their distress and to save the country from disaster, though in truth it was far too late for that. The surging crowds had carried the garlanded bust of Necker (along with that of another popular savior, Louis-Philippe-Joseph, now duc d'Orléans) through the streets of the capital. Germaine had never witnessed such a consecration of *gloire*, the renown that now formed an aureole about her beloved father's head. Fascinated by its dazzling brilliance, she would never forget it. "My father loved nothing so much as *gloire*. There is something ethereal about *gloire*, it forms as it were the subtle shading between thoughts of Heaven and those of earth," she was to write after her father's death.[9] She herself yearned for *gloire*, and to a large extent this aspiration would dominate her conduct.

What Germaine always believed was that her father, loyal to the king, could have made a difference. But Necker was being undermined by the court party, led by Marie-Antoinette. And besides, Louis XVI was collaborating secretly with forces outside the country that were working to overturn the reforms brought about in the early days of the Revolution. Necker's grand gesture of depositing more than two million *livres* of his private fortune on loan to the Royal Treasury would not help. He was not the only person out of his depth, a vain but well-intentioned moderate who suffered the fate of moderates in a time of growing polarization. When the hollowness of his pretensions to sagacity became apparent, support dwindled away. He resigned in September 1790 and withdrew, "broken-hearted," to the mansion at Coppet, the charming retreat that he had acquired in 1784.

Meanwhile, since 1786 the great heiress Mademoiselle Necker had been married to the impoverished Swedish diplomat Eric Magnus de Staël. Protestant suitors were not numerous, and her parents were determined that whoever married their daughter must be a member of the reformed religion. It was largely a marriage of convenience that took place after long negotiations with Gustavus III of Sweden concerning matters of dowry, status, and the Parisian embassy for the bridegroom. Madame de Staël now enjoyed the title of *baronne*, and wrote entertaining letters to the king of Sweden on topics of the day. It was not long, though, before the newly married couple began to lead separate lives.

Her salon in the Swedish embassy in the rue du Bac, where the principal advocates of a moderate constitutional monarchy gathered to exchange opinions and discuss strategy, became renowned for its brilliance. Madame de Staël "is a woman of wonderful wit, and above prejudices of every kind. Her house is a kind of Temple of Apollo, where the men of wit and fashion are collected . . . ," Gouverneur Morris, the American agent, was to inform George Washington.[10] Among the company could be found not only diplomats like Thomas Jefferson but also liberal-minded members of the

French aristocracy, some from its upper echelons. (It was doubtless the association with persons of such great ancestry that led Stendhal to accuse Germaine of "*ducomanie*," or excessive fondness for people with titles.) Members of the nobility who frequented her salon included Lafayette, hero of the American War of Independence; the liberal *philosophe* Condorcet; Talleyrand, the great charmer, not yet a public figure; and her idealistic friend Mathieu de Montmorency, who was to propose the abolition of privileges of the nobility in the National Assembly. Also to be found among the habitués of her salon was Talleyrand's close friend (and later Napoleon's ally), the handsome and seductive Louis de Narbonne, who was thought to be one of the numerous illegitimate descendants of Louis XV. Much to the disapproval of her parents, Germaine grew enmeshed in a passionate liaison—wildly passionate at least on her side—with Narbonne, the putative father of her two sons, Auguste and Albert.

Another figure who graced her salon was the enigmatic abbé Sieyès, the architect of constitutions (an activity he shared with Condorcet, whom he outlived). Sieyès was on the brink of making his name with his pamphlet entitled "What Is the Third Estate?"—the question to which he gave the now famous reply, "Everything." Germaine thought his writings and opinions would "open a new era in politics like that of Newton in physics."[11] It was partly in her salon that the Constitution of 1791 would be formulated. She was later to recognize its weaknesses, but it embodied many of the improvements she and her friends ardently desired: individual liberty and freedom of the press; the abolition of torture, of *lettres de cachet*, arbitrary exile, and class privileges; freedom of religion and equality for Protestants; and various elements of English law such as trial by jury.

Some idea of what Germaine brought to the discussion may be deduced from one of her early works. It was in 1786, in the same year as her marriage and the opening of her salon as baronne de Staël, that she had begun writing her *Lettres sur les écrits et le car-*

actère de Jean-Jacques Rousseau. She had already written stories and plays, but this was her first work that created a stir when it was published in a limited edition in 1788. It was also the first that sketched her political principles. While criticizing Rousseau—though insufficiently, in Mary Wollstonecraft's opinion—for his treatment of the education of women and his exclusion of them from participating in public affairs and playing an outstanding role, Germaine felt deep sympathy for him, for his despair caused by the dark force of melancholy. The solitary rambler was afraid to be alone, she said. She saw him as tormented by the need to love and the misfortune of not being loved, reflected in the mirror of her own experience and her own dread.

In her discussion of Rousseau's political writings she upheld the view that no government could be established or maintained without the consent of the nation. But she felt that Rousseau was concerned with the power to make the laws rather than with the laws themselves. There is an implied comparison with Necker here. Rousseau's theorizing appears subordinate to the pragmatism of the statesman and reformer, "the greatest administrator of his age," who prefers experience to theory. In her opinion, the best one can achieve is to proceed slowly toward the desired goal, however swiftly that end is attained by thought. Indeed, Germaine's admiration for Rousseau, considerable as it is, falls far short of her admiration for Necker, and it is only gradually that she will move beyond her father's standpoint.

As for her, she proclaims her love of "that liberty which places no other distinction between men but that of nature."[12] Individual liberty remains at the heart of all her writings. Already, in this early work, there is the appeal to reason, the faith in progress attained by enlightenment instead of by violence and bloodshed. At the time the word "democracy" had not acquired the resonance it has today. In a note in her study of the passions, Germaine was to write that as "democracy" had many meanings and did not fit exactly what she wanted to say, she decided not to employ it. Besides, "democracy" still spelled demagoguery and mob rule. As a pragmatist, she recognized that what she called "the most numerous class," inured to hard toil, had not yet been educated for government. She believed therefore that "*la classe éclairée,*" or the enlightened class, was called to govern, and that the rest of the population, then largely illiterate, though equally endowed with powers of imagination, would eventually be raised by means of reforms and through education would be included in the process of government. Although her father was a noted financier, she took little interest in economic matters, her concern being that of politics, and in this she did not differ from many of her most distinguished contemporaries.

When Germaine looked back, years later, on the period from the opening session of the States General in May 1789 (where, like Félicité de Genlis, she was present) to the proclamation of the constitution in September 1791, she saw it as an era of great brilliance for society in general, as indeed it was for herself in particular. It was, she said, "the last time that French wit and intelligence were most dazzlingly displayed."[13] It was certainly one in which she appears to have played a considerable part, though—like Félicité de Genlis—she does not speak of it in her published work, where she presents herself as concerned witness, as commentator and critic, and later as victim, without ever alluding to herself as a woman who had a role in events, a role admired by friends or mocked and detested by enemies. From the snide comments of Queen Marie-Antoinette, for instance, it is plain that Germaine worked to have her lover, Narbonne, appointed minister of war in December 1791. She is thought to have composed or helped him to compose his speeches and reports. He held office for only a few months, until March 1792. With Narbonne she offered to help the royal family escape to England, but largely because of the queen's hostility their plan was rejected. Soon everything changed irrevocably. On August 10, 1792, the First Republic was proclaimed. The armies of Austria and Prussia crossed the frontier. France was at war, and the populace regarded aristocrats, no matter how sympathetic to the Revolution they had proved to be, as a kind of fifth column, in league with the royalist invaders. Germaine managed to hide Narbonne and helped him, along with a considerable number of aristocratic friends, evade capture. She herself, heavily pregnant, narrowly escaped with her life, fleeing to Coppet on September 3 while the massacres raged on.

By January 20, 1793, Germaine was in England, setting up house with Narbonne, Montmorency, and other friends at Juniper Hall near Dorking in Surrey, where she worked on her important study of the passions. Entitled *On the Influence of the Passions upon the Happiness of Individuals and Nations*, it dealt with a subject of the most pressing contemporary political and personal urgency. The book was not ready until the winter of 1795, and it was published in the fall of 1796, by which time circumstances and her thoughts on them had altered radically. The novelist Fanny Burney, whose sister lived near Juniper Hall, became acquainted with Germaine and was deeply impressed at a reading of passages from the early work in progress. Since the American Declaration of Independence, happiness had been claimed a right. Saint-Just memorably announced that it was "a new idea" in France. But was happiness possible?

This was the question that Germaine addressed in the light of her twofold disillusion. On the one hand there was the decline of her love affair with Narbonne, ever more indifferent and resistant to her impassioned and demanding pleas; and on the other the turn of the Revolution away from moderate reform to the appalling massacres of September 1792 and the Reign of Terror that would last until 9 Thermidor (July 27) 1794. In the winter of 1795–1796, too, when the book was nearing publication, there occurred the communist "Conspiracy of Equals" led by "Gracchus" Babeuf, as it were encapsulating the move that the Revolution had taken, in Germaine's view, from liberty to equality, from a real and possible ideal to what she saw as a utopian dream or nightmare. The fear of Babeuf may well have contributed to the appeal of Bonaparte in his early role as the great revolutionary liberator and savior. Indeed, some admirers would never depart from their *idée fixe*: for them he always remained the incarnation of the Revolution and the Republic.

In the introduction to *De l'Influence des passions*, Germaine observed: "What an era I have chosen to write a treatise on the happiness of individuals and nations! . . . Nonetheless it is above all in this age, when the hope or the need of happiness has roused the human race, that one is led to think deeply on the nature of individual and political happiness."[14] Only two years had passed since the end of the Terror in July 1794, and in her judgment it was far too soon to try to examine the origin and nature of such atrocities. All the same, she would remain haunted by the theme. "Even today, reasoning could not possibly approach this immeasurable time. To judge these events . . . is to make them take their place in the order of existing ideas, ideas for which there already are words and expressions."[15] No language as yet existed to cope with such an aberration, she felt. Germaine's response to the Terror was to see it as an event without precedent, "an era outside the course of nature," a throw of the dice that chance could not repeat in thousands of years. Here she was tragically mistaken, for such abominations were to be repeated on a far greater scale in modern times.

Yet, in other respects her analysis of ideological murderers appears prophetic. She noted that the Terror revealed a "systematic method" of killing in cold blood, perpetrated by "reasoning assassins" whose very theories led them into crime.[16] In order to inaugurate their idea of utopia, she observed, these political murderers used guilt by association in their determination to annihilate an entire class. The extraordinary character of fanaticism, she declared, was that it united "the power of crime and the exaltation of virtue." The fanatic "does not believe he is guilty, and he publishes his deeds instead of concealing them." He has decided to lay down his own life for the cause, and this act of self-sacrifice allows him to keep a sense of virtue while committing terrible crimes. "It is this contrast, this double energy that makes fanaticism the most awesome of human forces," she said, as an admirer of energy undeniably fascinated as well as horrified.[17] Later Germaine would return time and again to the subject of the Terror, terrorists, extremists, and political fanatics, trying in vain to probe with the tools of reason and imagination the mystery that obsessed her.

What she yearned for was liberty with order, and while rejecting "*liberté métaphysique*," or abstract liberty, she felt it was still necessary and possible to work toward "*le bonheur réel de tous*," the practical well-being and happiness of all. Her cousin would remark, in an unhappy turn of phrase, that Germaine had "a quite evangelical compassion for the unfortunate members of the lower classes," and that she wished to help those who suffer most from what she called bad "social organization."[18] The lower classes must not be left in physical want—but how this was to be achieved she did not say. In her later years—and not only on her travels—Germaine would become deeply concerned with the question of ameliorating the condition of "the third class," or the suffering lower orders. As for women, to whom she referred as "the disinherited half of humanity," especially those who pursued the passion for *gloire* in politics (doubtless meaning herself), in her experience they were fated to do so at the expense of their personal happiness. This oft-repeated conviction and complaint, however, did not deter her one jot from looking for passionate love and companionship (often in unpromising quarters) or from pursuing *gloire* in politics and literature for the rest of her life.

ꝏ

IT WAS more than two and a half years before Germaine, now in her late twenties, returned to Paris, in May 1795. She was still deeply shaken by the Robespierrist dictatorship and the Terror that seemed to bear no possible relation to all the hopeful principles she had imbibed in her youth from the *philosophes* of the Enlightenment. She engaged at once in communicating her views and in political activity with the aim of creating her ideal of liberty with order through a union of moderates. Such a union seemed to her the only way of countering the advocates and heirs of extremism and unreason. The moment was hardly propitious. Nothing could have been less likely at a time when fear and the passionate intensity of the worst prevailed. This was a period of utter confusion in public life in France and of turmoil in the life of Germaine herself, as she moved—either by compulsion or her own free will—between Paris or its environs and Switzerland, and back again.

The era that followed the fall of Robespierre was one of instability, of corruption and the urge to live for pleasure after the macabre years of the Terror. Jacobins striving to regain their lost domination and royalist counterrevolutionaries working to restore the ancien régime constantly buffeted the government of the National Convention in 1794–1795, and that of the Directory, which followed from 1795 to 1799. In moves that remain complicated and often obscure, the floundering men in power were trying desperately to salvage their authority by resorting to coup d'état and repression. Their chief aim was to put a stop to Jacobins or royalists if either party appeared to be gaining the upper hand. It was not long before they looked to a military savior. And, as it turned out, they cared little for Germaine's libertarian opinions and political activities. They imposed on her the very same punishment without trial—exile—that Bonaparte would use in his efforts to subdue her. When Germaine came to construct her great if broken monument, *Ten Years of Exile*, she counted from the rule of Napoleon, not his predecessors, as she certainly could have done. Perhaps this was because it made for more concentrated drama, but in any case he was then the single antagonist she had in her sights.

Accompanying Germaine to Paris was the Swiss-born Benjamin Constant, onetime court chamberlain in Brunswick, more or less free of his German wife. Despite Constant's extremely eccentric education—even more bizarre than Germaine's—under a series of totally undesirable tutors, he had a passion for learning and was endowed with an analytical mind that mirrored her own. As yet, however, unlike her, he had published no work of note. He had pursued her ardently while she was still immersed in an unsatisfactory attachment to the Swedish republican Count Adolph Ribbing, one of the conspirators involved in the assassination of Gustavus III. When the handsome Swedish regicide turned his attentions elsewhere, to Madame de Genlis's daughter, Pulchérie de Valence, Germaine committed herself to the outwardly less prepossessing Constant. Here indeed was her equal, a brilliant mind, an eloquent and persuasive talker, and she decided to work to promote his political career. They vied with each other in a dazzling tennis match of words that could decline into a slanging match, and that brought out the best—and the worst—in the two of them. Their stormy partnership would be interspersed with dramatic threats of suicide by overdosing on opium, uttered (and sometimes even attempted) by one or the other.

Veering from one extreme interpretation of Germaine's character to another, Constant probed her complexity and contradictoriness. "It is politics, a demanding love as at eighteen, the need for society, the need for *gloire*, melancholy suited to a wilderness, the need for esteem, the need to shine." And he reflected in his diary: "What can others do to counter the agitation of your life, your contradictory desires, your need for a brilliant position?" He could rail against her, showering her with insults, yet at another time he was enchanted by her: "What grace, affection, devotion, intelligence!" He had to admit to himself: "There is nothing on earth as kind, as loving, as witty and devoted as she is."[19] She could infuriate him, but he could not help admiring her qualities. He knew how generous she was and that those who appealed to her for help did not go away without seeing her do her utmost for them.

At the time of Germaine's return, Paris was in an uproar. Famine and paper money had reduced the poor to a distressing state. Riots were still going on in the working-class district of the faubourg Saint-Antoine, and they were being severely repressed. Some people wondered—either with genuine concern or with malice—why Germaine could not stay quietly at Coppet while all this upheaval was taking place, especially as they deplored her volubility and her in-discretion. But inaction led to boredom, melancholy, and somber thoughts, and so Germaine could not bear to remain inactive. Be-sides, Necker's daughter felt she had something to offer in the way of a solution or two to the nation's problems. Above all, she saw pol-itics and public life as her métier, a view that went against the grain of accepted or professed social opinion. And she chose this delicate moment, when everything hung in the balance, to write articles and essays on national and international affairs. These writings analyzed the difficult situation, proposing solutions, and urged an alliance of those of all parties who held moderate opinions.

At the end of 1794 she had published a notable essay, *Thoughts on Peace Addressed to Mr. Pitt and the French*, where, after forcibly ex-pressing her loathing for Robespierre and the Terror, she went on to tell William Pitt, the scrupulous British prime minister, and the Al-lies that their policy of war with France was thoroughly mistaken. This policy was unduly influenced by reactionary royalist emigrés, she declared, and it served only the interests of fanatical Jacobins. Pitt and the Allies should have been promoting the French moder-ates and should have been concerned with the restoration of order and liberty in France. For "one must go forward with one's era." Be-sides, the ruin of France would lead inevitably to the ruin of Europe as a whole. Let the French be allowed to choose their own govern-ment freely; let them establish a constitution that would "reconcile the possible with the desirable" and would preserve the safety of property as well as of the individual.[20] Much that Germaine was to write in the following years was directed to furthering not only her own ideal of the middle way but also Constant's political career. She sought to rescue and preserve the gains brought about by the French Revolution while dissociating it from the Terror that stained it. It is the theme that Byron would later express in his poem *Childe Harold's Pilgrimage* through the image of the banner of freedom, torn by the Terror but still flying.

If Germaine's presence in Paris aroused violent criticism, there

were also many, especially among the talented thinkers and littéra-
teurs, who welcomed her. Once again her salon was regarded as one
of the most brilliant of the day, though it could scarcely be quite as
dazzling as that of 1789–1791, partly because the atmosphere in
Paris no longer inspired heady optimism. Among her friends were
prominent figures of varying political shades as well as leading
moderates like the dramatist Marie-Joseph Chénier (brother of the
elegiac poet and eloquent lover of liberty André Chénier, who died
by the guillotine in the last days of the Terror). There were influential *idéologues*, including their leader, Destutt de Tracy, and the eminent doctor and moralist Cabanis, men whose political views to a
large extent coincided with her own. Joining them were members of
the constitutional committee like Sieyès, Daunou, and Boissy d'An-
glas, with whom she could engage in discussion at a time when they
were framing the Constitution of Year III (1795) which established
the rule of the Directory.

But Germaine, hitherto a supporter of constitutional monarchy,
caused no little surprise by affirming her faith in the Republic, "because it has been made clear to me that, in the present circumstances, republican government alone can give peace and liberty to
France."[21] Her frequent use of the phrase "in the present circumstances" shows how, as a pragmatist, she sought to come to terms
with the new situation. This was in the summer of 1795 when she
produced her essay *Thoughts on Internal Peace*, where she again be-
moaned the way France was being torn apart between two forms of
fanaticism. She realized that in revolutionary times fanaticism
gained adherents with ease, whereas the creation of a moderate
party such as she desired would not be easy and could never inspire
the same kind of single-minded support.

How, then, to counter the forces of extremism? One means with
a long ancestry that she proposed was the possession of property,
eventually to be extended to include the have-nots, because it gave
people a sense of responsibility along with a stake in the stability of
the country. In this way it would guard against extremism and bind

freedom with order. She declared that there must be care to amelio-
rate the physical existence of those without property. At the same
time the means for them to acquire property must be enhanced.
Naturally her so-called "bourgeois" views, though rooted in the
political conditions of the day, found no favor with historians or
critics of a Marxist tinge and their followers during the twentieth
century. Yet she did not have a closed mind on the subject of property. "The men of antiquity did not imagine how we could do without slaves, and we cannot imagine how people could do without
property, but who knows how far the perfecting of the human race
can reach?" she inquired.[22]

By now Germaine was a convenient target for Jacobins as well as
royalist reactionaries. Louis Legendre, formerly her butcher but
now a député who had been a friend of Danton's, openly attacked
her in the National Convention. Like many others of his faction, he
did not make a nice distinction between die-hard royalist emigrés
and the constitutional monarchists who had helped to make the
Revolution in the first place. Besides, people did not really believe
in her conversion to republicanism. Warned that her life was in danger, Germaine hurriedly left Paris. After the abortive royalist uprising of Vendémiaire (October) 1795 against the Convention—a
revolt suppressed with the aid of General Bonaparte—the Committee of Public Safety decreed that Madame de Staël should be sent
into exile. When the decree was withdrawn she returned briefly to
Paris in December before leaving with Constant for Switzerland,
where she spent the greater part of 1796, finishing her study of the
passions and collaborating with him on his political writings.

All the same, the minister of police ordered her arrest should she
venture to set foot in France again, and the Directory even went so
far as to keep her under surveillance at Coppet. In April 1796 appeared an order for her arrest, couched in typically convoluted official jargon: "The executive Directory, informed that the baronne de
Staël, in correspondence with emigrés, conspirators, and the worst
enemies of the Republic, and having participated in all the plots

against the peace of the State, is about to return to France to continue fomenting new disturbances, decrees that the baronne should be arrested if she crosses the frontier, and brought before the Minister of Police to be interrogated, and the report forwarded to the Directory."[23] So much for her declarations of support for the Republic and her moves for peace and reconciliation, to which officialdom gave no credence. Unexpectedly some help came from Barras, known as the strong man of the Directory, with whom she was on friendly terms. Through his good offices she was able to return to France at the end of 1796.

Germaine stayed with Constant at the abbey of Hérivaux, the country estate that, with her financial help, he had recently acquired through the public sale of confiscated national property. In the spring of 1797 she was permitted to stay in Paris where Albertine (presumably Constant's daughter) was born in June. Soon she was engaged in political maneuvers with Constant and other moderate friends who were now seeking to revise the Constitution of 1795 with the aim of placing the Directory on firmer foundations. From Talleyrand, who had sought refuge in the United States, came pathetic calls for help. Thanks to her he was able to return to France, but (he now inquired) how was he to survive without some position? When he threatened to blow out his brains, Germaine hastened to Barras, prevailing on him to come to Talleyrand's assistance. Largely through her efforts, Talleyrand was appointed minister of foreign affairs and took his first step on the upward path to power and profit. He was to prove the most ungrateful of all her protégés. In the years when he served as Napoleon's close adviser, he did nothing to intervene on her behalf.

When the royalists made serious gains, even winning a majority in the Assembly, the personal attacks on Germaine as a woman became increasingly venomous. They were no different in tone from those experienced by Manon Roland or any woman in the public eye. One royalist hack declared that Germaine was "born devoid of grace, with brazen looks and depraved amorous leanings." She was no better than a "prostitute," a "hermaphrodite," and "the busiest and most contemptible female intriguer in Europe."[24] On learning of the projected coup of 18 Fructidor (September 4) 1797, engineered by the Directory in order to put an end to the increasingly successful royalists, Germaine thought at first that the government coup might save the Republic. The purges that followed the very next day horrified her. Royalist députés were imprisoned, executed, or deported in cages to French Guiana (the punishment known as the dry guillotine, since victims were unlikely to survive). Among the prisoners were some of her friends: she hastened to intercede for them, saving one from the firing squad at the last moment, an episode she was to recall in her novel *Delphine*. She had expressed her opposition to the death penalty for political offenses in her *Thoughts on Internal Peace*. Her passionate pleas for the royalist victims did not enhance her claims to republicanism.

The invincible General Bonaparte, the victor of Lodi, Arcole, and Rivoli, who favored the coup of 18 Fructidor, now arrived in Paris. Germaine met him for the first time at a reception given in his honor at Talleyrand's in December 1797. Bonaparte was then in his late twenties, flushed with the glamour of early success, and careful—as he always would be—to present the image he felt necessary for the hour. A man of many faces, he was skilled in the art of manipulating opinion, having crossed the Alps on a mule and not on a fiery steed as depicted romantically in David's magisterial painting. At this moment he was the heir of the Revolution and the savior of the Republic. It appeared that nothing gave him greater pleasure than being regarded as an honored companion of leading contemporary thinkers or *idéologues* when he was elected a member of the recently founded Institut. He displayed ostentatiously at that time his simplicity, his deep love of solitude and philosophy, and his fondness for the poems of Ossian, the Scottish bard—invented by Macpherson—whom Germaine and many of her contemporaries revered as a genuine poetic genius. Admiring letters that Germaine is said to have sent to Bonaparte when he was in Italy have not been found. Doubtless she would have expressed her admiration for him in excessive terms, in the way she had always given voice to her enthusiasms since her childhood. Her father remained far more cautious in his assessment of the hero.

Whatever illusions she may have cherished concerning the admirer of Ossian and the defender of revolutionary and republican liberties, she misjudged her man if she thought of impressing him with her own talents or hoped to draw him into her orbit. Although Germaine was renowned for her fascinating talk and witty repartee, whenever she met Bonaparte she was at a loss for words. She felt so intimidated in the presence of "the most intrepid warrior" (as she called him) that she could hardly breathe. Even if she prepared beforehand what she was going to say, it did not help her in the least. When she heard him speak she was struck by his "superiority." Later she would refer to the fascination he exerted and how she had to resist "the disturbing effect that an extraordinary genius and an awesome destiny produced on the imagination."[25] He was the master of the sightless stare.

Germaine was present at the grand state ceremony when the directors received Bonaparte in the courtyard of the Palais du Luxembourg. His modest attire contrasted with the elaborate finery of their uniforms and their large plumed hats. Talleyrand (who was to aid Bonaparte in establishing his imperial rule) emphasized in his address the austere hero's devotion to the abstract sciences and his love of peace. In fact, Bonaparte had set his mind on conquering Egypt. For this purpose he intended to raise funds by invading Switzerland. Germaine felt deeply the injustice of annexing Geneva to France, for it was a free state though ruled by an oligarchy. During a tête-à-tête with her that lasted nearly an hour, Bonaparte listened to her reasoned arguments, then changed the subject and discoursed on his taste for a quiet country life and the fine arts.

It was during 1798–1799 that Germaine worked on her book *On the Present Circumstances for Ending the French Revolution and the Principles that Should Establish the Republic in France*. This remarkable study has been called a veritable "treatise of political science" and her first great political work. She wanted "all political and moral sciences to be subject to geometric method," holding that by mathematical calculation, the benefit of statistics, it would be possible to reach certainty about great matters in dispute, and that enlightenment would necessarily follow.[26] The role of "writer-philosophers" was to put an end to conflict through the application of analysis to current problems. She had already published, years before, in 1791, an article entitled "By what means can the opinion of the majority of the nation be known?" Her concern now was how to establish what she called "political science" on a sound basis.

In *Des Circonstances actuelles*, Germaine dealt in turn with the state of the parties, the nature of public opinion, the importance of legality, and the role of the press and of writers and intellectuals. She declared her opposition to the military spirit that was gaining ground. This considerable work, an invaluable document on the complex period of the Directory, never saw the light of day in her lifetime. (It was not published until 1979, in an illuminating complete edition.) If it had appeared when it was written, it would surely have established Germaine de Staël's reputation as a significant liberal thinker—something that did not happen until nearly twenty years later with the publication of her momentous *Considérations sur la Révolution française* after her death.

One reason why *Des Circonstances actuelles* was not published in 1799 was perhaps the fear that it might harm Constant's prospects when he hoped to be elected député. In any case, it was hardly the moment for opposing the "military spirit," just when Bonaparte's name was on everyone's lips. Besides, in July 1799 the Directory again decided to expel Germaine de Staël. In effect she had little in common with the men who ruled the country and who were mostly on the make. As one member of her circle declared: "She had no real influence. However liberal and republican her opinions, she could not appeal to such a government. Her aristocratic habits and inclinations, her eagerness to intervene in political affairs and talk about

them indiscreetly, her theoretical, idealistic way of judging everything, her fondness for friends opposed to the regime, made her
troublesome to the Directory. . . ."[27] In short, the powers-that-be did
not regard as an ally a woman with republican opinions and royalist friends, however distinguished and renowned Necker's daughter
might be. They certainly did not want this dubious creature concerning herself tactlessly with matters of moment.

Germaine was at Coppet when she learned from Constant and
Sieyès about the Directory's imminent demise. She arrived in Paris
on the evening of 18 Brumaire (November 9) 1799, when Bonaparte, having returned victorious from Egypt, overthrew the Directory. The part played in the coup by the constitution maker Sieyès
led her and her friends to think that this was somehow a victory for
them. After all, it was through Sieyès that Constant was appointed
a member of the newly established Tribunate. Germaine might well
disapprove of "the military spirit" in her writings, but she felt (and
would always feel) nothing but admiration for the military genius of
the first consul, whose brothers, Joseph and Lucien, could be found
in her salon. Her friendship with them would endure through all the
vicissitudes that followed from her dissensions with Bonaparte himself. It is one of the stranger aspects of the story.

ALTHOUGH Napoleon had made such a display of his attachment to
the Institut and to intellectuals and thinkers in 1799–1800, in fact
he nurtured an extremely low opinion of idéologues—unless they
served his purposes, like the scholars who accompanied him to
Egypt. He railed against the men in the Tribunate who disagreed
with him: "Here we have two dozen metaphysicians who deserve to
be drowned. They are vermin on my clothes. Do they think they can
treat me as they did Louis XVI?"[28] The change from his show of deference to thinkers that he had made in his rise to absolute power
serves as a fine example of his favorite cynical Italian proverb, "Pas-
sato il pericolo, gabbato il santo." He knew from his study of his fel-

low men as well as of himself that the vow made to a saint in the hour of danger is not likely to be fulfilled once the peril is past, and that the saint will be cheated. This was a saying he liked to repeat whenever Germaine's many friends interceded for her and made promises about her intention to keep quiet. When they advised her to be more discreet, she replied, "It is the truth, it is what I think and I shall say so."[29] That was her real position, as he well knew.

Moreover Napoleon particularly disliked women who took an active interest in politics, whereas that subject was meat and drink to Germaine. As she once said, "To be involved in politics is religion, morality, and poetry combined."[30] Napoleon also loathed people who harped on their principles. He harbored no illusions about human goodness. Nor was he concerned like her with the relationship between politics and morality and the perfectibility of the human race. "Why do people talk to me about goodness, abstract justice, natural laws?" he snapped. "The first law is necessity; the first justice is that of public safety."[31] In contrast, she could express the exact opposite of Napoleon's creed: "When, at the bloodiest period of the Revolution, they wanted to sanction every crime, they called the government 'the Committee of Public Safety,' thereby proclaiming the well-known maxim that the welfare of the people is the supreme law. The supreme law is justice," she declared.[32]

Familiar with each person's weakness, Napoleon had no trouble in finding hers. Most people he could win over by their desire for preferment, by awarding them lucrative posts and high-sounding titles. In that way Germaine could not be corrupted. Her real weakness, though, was her susceptibility to boredom and melancholy that made her long for the company of her friends, for discourse and discussion. By condemning her to live forty leagues from Paris, in some provincial town like Auxerre that she called a veritable Scythia, Napoleon found exactly how to make her suffer. Whenever she ventured to ignore the order and moved nearer to the capital than the set limit of forty leagues, an officer would arrive to enforce it. She had to depart with her children within twenty-four hours.

Once she managed to slip briefly into Paris, but Napoleon got wind of the escapade. This constricting existence would encourage her to leave for Germany and Italy in 1803–1805, for Austria in 1807, and for Russia in 1812, and so, paradoxically, would lead her to some of her greatest achievements. The constant surveillance and the harassment she endured are known today down to the last detail from the patient research of scholars into police archives, and Germaine herself did not know the half of it. Byron, who listened to her complaints of ill treatment when he met her in London in 1813, mistakenly declined to believe that the great man would stoop to concern himself with Germaine's affairs.

She was open to attack, too, on the ground of nationality. Born in Paris, naturally she considered herself to be French. Many French people, though, did not regard her as one of themselves, and journalists (who were mostly on Napoleon's payroll) encouraged them in their prejudice. That kind of disinclination to accept certain categories of people born in France as genuine citizens was to persist into the Vichy regime and beyond. Matters were complicated for her when, on her marriage to a Swedish diplomat, she held Swedish nationality. Sometimes, of course, she found it expedient to make use of this when in a tight corner. For instance, it enabled her to help some of her aristocratic friends to escape to Switzerland in 1792 at the outbreak of the massacres. There were even moments when she became quite confused as to where she stood legally on the question of her nationality and her citizenship.

On her husband's death in 1802, as the French-born widow of a foreigner, she should have been able to revert to being French. In her manner and outlook she was French to her fingertips, as writers who met her—like Goethe and Schiller and others in Weimar and Berlin, or Byron in London—were agreed. Yet this Corsican general, born "Buonaparte" in Ajaccio in August 1769 (a mere three months after the French defeated the Corsican patriots and annexed the island), ruled indisputably over France. His enemies might allude to him as a Corsican upstart, but in the light of his victories alone, which covered the country in *gloire*, everyone else regarded him as French. A galling irony here was not lost on her: although born in Paris, she was forced to flee by order of a man "less French than I."[33]

Besides, she could not believe that she, Necker's daughter, celebrated throughout Europe, could be treated in this cruel way. She had mistakenly believed that her fame was her defense. "In seeking *gloire* I always thought that it would make me loved," Corinne, the great artist, admits to the man she loves, Lord Oswald Nelvil, who feebly settles for a more ordinary wife.[34] Germaine was a child of the Enlightenment, after all: she believed in reason and progress, in toleration, in the high ideals of freedom and fairness that had inspired the eighteenth-century movement for reform in France. In light of these values, the authoritarian regime of Napoleon seemed to her an aberration. Surely Napoleon must be amenable to reasoned argument.

Such a notion has endured as the great liberal delusion. There are always those who are not amenable to reason. Following Ovid, who addressed poems of complaint to Rome (and who has been criticized for self-pity as a result), Germaine went on writing embarrassing letters of self-justification, presenting her case—not without a certain casuistry at times—in a manner that seemed eminently reasonable to her. True, the situation was not simple and clear-cut. She engaged some people she knew well in Napoleon's entourage, notably Napoleon's elder brother Joseph, her lifelong friend (who, she says in *Dix années d'exil* in far-fetched partisanship, was forced against his will to be king of Spain), to intercede on her behalf. All such efforts proved vain: the emperor was adamant.

On one occasion, in December 1807, she sent her seventeen-year-old son, Auguste, to appeal to Napoleon. After a long wait the boy was received in audience by the emperor, who treated him severely. Auguste ventured to say that his mother would cease writing on political affairs and would confine herself to literature. "Tell your mother my mind is made up. As long as I live she shall never set foot in Paris again." Napoleon added sharply, "You can make politics by talking literature, morality, fine arts, anything you like. Women should stick to knitting."[35] He knew that she would be unable to keep any promises about avoiding politics once she was in Paris. And then he would have another example of the saint being cheated as soon as the danger was over. He would not be taken for a dupe. In all likelihood he had read and remembered the striking passage in her *De la Littérature*, published seven years before, where she discoursed on the new aspect of literature in the eighteenth century. "It is no longer solely an art," she proclaimed, "it is a means; it becomes a weapon of the human spirit. . . ."[36] Indeed, it looks as if this was the one subject on which she and the emperor agreed: that literature could not be separated from politics. The public, too, had grown adept at perceiving political allusions, the subtext of poems, novels, and plays. People had no difficulty in recognizing the hidden targets of *Delphine*, *Corinne*, or later *De l'Allemagne*.

A woman of penetrating insight, gifted, as she well knew, with the impressive ability to deduce general ideas from her observations, Germaine was also for a long time the victim of blindness where Napoleon and his intentions toward her were concerned. Did she know how much she annoyed him with her novel *Corinne* by lauding the virtues of the English instead of his conquests in Italy, and suggesting that Italian decadence was due to French occupation? The implication was that the Italians should rouse themselves to recover their former glories. When the beautiful and multi-talented Corinne was crowned at the Capitol in Rome, "her chariot had cost nobody any tears," whereas that could hardly be said of Napoleon, crowned king of Italy in 1805.[37] Germaine worried about preserving human life. Napoleon was notoriously careless of it. When thousands of men lay dead on the battlefield, he could coolly say that one night in Paris would make up the numbers. He liked to shock with his brutal remarks, but even at the height of his power he was extremely touchy about criticism of himself and his regime.

Was she aware of how provocative some of her actions appeared to him? For instance, her meetings with the noted journalist Friedrich Gentz, one of the emperor's keenest opponents, when she was in Vienna in 1808, infuriated Napoleon. The emperor was convinced that she was in league with Gentz, though this appears not to have been the case. He forbade his ambassadors to receive her or give her protection. From Bayonne, where he had led the Spanish royal family into an ambush and was maneuvering to seize the throne of Spain for Joseph, he wrote to Fouché: "You will let it be known that up to now she has been regarded merely as a crazy woman, but that now she begins to be placed with a set that is opposed to public order."[38] A barrier had been crossed in Napoleon's calculations about his treatment of Germaine de Staël.

For a long time she went on thinking that the emperor just wanted to frighten her into submission. Not until 1810, when censorship was tightened and Savary, duc de Rovigo, replaced Fouché, duc d'Otrante, as minister of police, did she suffer the full force of Napoleon's ire. It is now known that the emperor personally gave orders for the destruction of all copies of *De l'Allemagne*, her innovative study of German literature, thought, religion, and culture, the fruit of six years' work. Not only did he demand that the book be pulped, he also sent his underlings to Coppet to try to seize all the manuscripts and proofs. But Germaine succeeded in keeping one version concealed while secretly contriving to send the other abroad.

By now there was no possibility of her failing to recognize Napoleon's true designs toward her. Coppet had fallen under French rule when Geneva was annexed some years before. For many months the local préfet had taken to limiting her movements to a few miles from her home, so that she was virtually under house arrest. A few close friends like Juliette Récamier and Mathieu de Montmorency dared to visit her, and in their turn were punished with internal exile. (They were not as apolitical as she averred.) Others warned her that she might well suffer the same fate as Mary Queen of Scots, who had been imprisoned for almost two decades by Queen Elizabeth I, and then beheaded. After all, it was only a few years since the young duc d'Enghien had been kidnapped on foreign soil and executed at Vincennes—a crime sufficiently extraordinary in its day to linger in the collective memory. Indeed, her own arrest was a distinct possibility, and her fears were not illusory. In 1811 the zealous local préfet informed Savary that the order for her arrest had not been issued "for the moment." Clearly the authorities had imprisonment in view. It can readily be imagined how furious Napoleon and his bureaucratic underlings were when they discovered that she had managed to escape their strict surveillance.

In a state of near collapse and terror, on May 23, 1812, Germaine left Coppet, ostensibly for a drive in her carriage with her daughter Albertine. After months of secret planning and diversionary tactics, she was embarking on the momentous roundabout journey that was to take her across war-torn Europe, through Austria, Poland, Russia, and Sweden, to her ultimate goal, freedom in England, Napoleon's bitterest foe.

The persecution of Germaine continued in the realms he had conquered, like Poland, and wherever fears of his displeasure predominated. Her words ring down the ages: "If tyranny had only its direct advocates on its side, it would never prosper. The astounding thing, and one that above all bears witness to the depths of human abasement, is that most mediocre men are at the service of the event. . . ."[39] This inclination she attributed not only to weakness of character but also to the fact that mankind had a sort of need to prove fate right, in order to live at peace with it. She remarked that there were always those who could find philosophical reasons to be content with the powers-that-be.

From the moment that Germaine crossed the Russian frontier at Brody in Galicia shortly after the invading French armies traversed the river Niemen, it was evident that she had moved from being a critic of Napoleon's absolute rule to a militant political activist who was working seriously to destroy it. In Saint Petersburg she conferred with British agents like Admiral William Bentinck, with diplomats like Baron Heinrich von Stein, one of the leading German opponents of Napoleon's regime. John Quincy Adams, future president of the United States, whom she met there, confided to his diary: "She is one of the highest enthusiasts for the English cause that I have ever seen."[40] Tsar Alexander I and his family welcomed her as an honored guest, and he discussed public affairs with her. A former ally of Napoleon, now prominent in the Allied coalition against the emperor, he was in his liberal phase, and he assured her that he intended to improve the condition of the serfs at an opportune moment. Later, in London, when a lady ill advisedly spoke to her about the existence of a free society in Russia, Germaine swiftly countered that she had never known freedom to coexist with serfdom. In *Dix années d'exil*, for the sake of the cause, she is more flattering to Alexander than her true opinions might suggest.

Soon she would find herself at an impasse. France was at war, yet she believed she could now fight against Napoleon while separating him and his followers from the fate of France itself. It was as if, despite all her criticism of their baseness and barbarity, she could ultimately ignore his numerous committed French followers. Napoleon's wholehearted adherents must be "Corsicans" or "Africans" like him, not true Frenchmen. As she saw it, the Allies would defeat the tyrant, and France would return to the body of civilized nations, rather as though the entire Napoleonic era and its wars had not intervened. Germaine was at a lavish entertainment on Prince Naryshkin's country estate overlooking the bay of Finland when a toast was proposed to Anglo-Russian victory over the French, and she suddenly realized that her view was not shared. She protested, and would drink only to the defeat of the Corsican despot. She did not foresee that in victory the Allies would exact an extremely heavy price in reparations, and that France as well as Napoleon would suffer defeat.

Louis XVIII's advisers sent emissaries to her to win her support for their cause, but her distaste for the Bourbons was such that she did not want their return. Instead she ardently promoted the cause of General Bernadotte, now crown prince of Sweden, as the republican leader of integrity to replace Napoleon. She worked devotedly for Bernadotte during the months she spent in Stockholm, then served virtually as his agent in London from 1813. Yet here was in effect another military solution proposed by a person who declared her hatred of the military spirit. There was no secrecy about her propaganda for Bernadotte among English political leaders, the nobility, writers, poets, social thinkers, and reformers. Quite possibly she was the first woman to act in public as political agent for a candidate to restore and head the French Republic. Despite her advocacy, however, few were converted for long to the cause of the procrastinating Bernadotte, and in 1814 the victorious Allies restored the Bourbons to the French throne in the person of Louis XVIII. In a sense, then, her passionate practical activity was to be frustrated, and on her return to France one of the bitterest shocks of her life was to see the Cossacks encamped on the Champs-Elysées.

With Napoleon's astounding escape from Elba, the first Bourbon Restoration was suddenly overturned. Louis XVIII and his court fled hastily to Ghent, and people began to wonder whether Napoleon and his imperial dynasty had returned for good. Some, like Lafayette, chose to join him as the lesser of two evils, especially when Napoleon announced his conversion to liberal ideas. Hitherto united with Germaine in political outlook if no longer in private life or financial matters, Benjamin Constant had been won over to the emperor's new stance and was helping construct the myth of Napoleon the liberal, though it may be supposed that if the emperor had survived in power his newfound liberalism would not have lasted long.

While Napoleon was in exile on Elba, Germaine had learned of a plot against his life and had found a way, through his brother Joseph, to inform him of it. Napoleon now made approaches to her, thanking her for her act of kindness. He pretended to her that he had played no part in the destruction of *De l'Allemagne*, placing all the blame on his underlings. And he assured her that she could speak out freely now that the climate had changed. She wavered, though she says nothing about this in her writings. Mostly she approved of the Additional Act to the Constitution, familiarly known as *la benjamine* after Benjamin Constant's role in framing it. All the same, she had urged Constant to pay more attention to guarantees than to rights.

After Napoleon was finally defeated at Waterloo in 1815, Germaine continued her friendly relations with Joseph Bonaparte. She was always compassionate toward the losers, whoever they might be. She even tried to help Napoleon's brother-in-law, Murat, to remain king of Naples, much to the annoyance of Louis XVIII and his advisers. Germaine de Staël was now an important and active political figure in Paris in the early years of the second Bourbon Restoration, and in the months that remained to her. Like her new friend Claire de Duras, she was a focus of liberal opinion. The leading European notabilities of the age, with the victors Tsar Alexander I and the Duke of Wellington at their head, graced Germaine's Parisian salon. Tirelessly she tried to persuade Wellington to reduce the numbers of the occupying Allied troops and the crippling cost of reparations. To her house at Coppet came men of letters, poets, philosophers, historians, political figures of varying allegiance, to form what Stendhal—who heard tell of it—called "the States General of European thought."[41] She had to be engaged in some cause of the moment. While in England she had become acquainted with the famous abolitionist William Wilberforce, and she was deeply committed to the movement to abolish slavery and the slave trade. At the same time she was working on her major study of the French Revolution and its far-reaching effects, a study greatly pillaged by later historians. A cruel blow put an end to all this activity. In February 1817, as she was leaving a reception at the residence of the king's favorite, Decazes, she was felled by a stroke. It left her partially paralyzed and—most cruel of all for the brilliant talker—unable to speak. She died after much suffering in July of that year.

Could Germaine de Staël ever have been a quiet model citizen under any government of the day? She had irritated Louis XVI as well as annoying his younger brother Louis XVIII; she outraged the Directory as well as infuriating Napoleon. When she looked back on him, the exile on Saint Helena, Germaine tried to be as fair as she could to the emperor in her last writings that were published posthumously, but she did not warm to the task. Clearly no one could deny that the Civil Code had merits. Paradoxically Napoleon's victorious armies carried with them into the lands they conquered the seeds of the libertarian ideas of the Revolution she valued. Her concerns lay elsewhere. What preoccupied her was the abuse of power and its demoralizing and corrupting consequences. She sought to disclose the dangers of such tyranny not only for her contemporaries but for future generations. As soon as it became plain to her that Napoleon was aiming at what she called "*monarchie universelle*," world domination, she tried through her writing and her action to counter his relentless drive toward it.

Napoleon once remarked to his recalcitrant brother Lucien, "I was wrong. Madame de Staël raised more enemies against me during her exile than she would have done in France."[42] It was not often that he admitted a mistake. She provoked the lion. He pushed her beyond endurance. They are like two models of the endlessly repeated struggle between sword and spirit, a struggle for which she paid with her health. Generous, excessive, the contradictory embodiment of energy, imagination, and passion as well as cool reason, Germaine de Staël, the woman writer and outspoken liberal whom Napoleon tried to silence, was never defeated.

SIX

George Sand

The Struggle with Class

...my birth *straddling*, as it were, two classes...
—GEORGE SAND

The bourgeoisie, the property-owning class, there is the
enemy!—PIERRE LEROUX

O ne of the first things George Sand did when, in the spring of
1835, she and Marie d'Agoult moved cautiously toward their
edgy and relatively short-lived friendship was to launch "a pitiless
anathema against the aristocracy."[1] By then, at thirty-one, Aurore
Dupin, Madame Dudevant, had become the famous, not to say notoriously independent, free-living and free-loving George Sand, author of *Indiana, Valentine, Jacques, Lélia,* and many other works that
in a mere four years had established her among the leading and
most influential literary figures of the age. Her questing spirit, as
seeker, as "traveler" on the move looking for the right path, chimed
with that of many of her intelligent contemporaries not only in
France but also in Germany, Russia, England—wherever her often
daring and controversial books were read and discussed. Her writings raised the consciousness of her readers by probing the inner life

of women and their status in a rapidly changing society that she saw as thoroughly unjust to all the underprivileged. Counted among those like Keats to whom the miseries of the world are misery, and will not let them rest, she demonstrates whither and into what strange and perilous seas such generosity of spirit as hers may lead.

Petite, with dark hair, her eyes brimming with intelligence, George Sand could sometimes appear dreamy and withdrawn when in company, or expansive with those she regarded as her intimate friends or her equals in their response to the subjects that interested her. Possessed with excitement over the latest ideas, she was quick to pass them on, always the ready teacher as well as pupil. Marie de Flavigny, comtesse d'Agoult, fair, tall, elegant, and slightly George Sand's junior, enjoyed some notoriety of her own, having left her husband and eloped with Sand's friend, the fascinating Hungarian musician Franz Liszt. But at the time of the early association between the two women, Marie d'Agoult—later the journalist, historian, and none too successful novelist Daniel Stern—was the neophyte to be included among George Sand's numerous half-envious female admirers, one who was moved by an ardent desire to write, though as yet she knew not what.

George Sand was helpful to the aspiring writer, but from the beginning she harped on the fact that Marie was a countess, distinguished for her aristocratic airs and graces. Doubtless George was fully aware of the place that Marie d'Agoult had formerly held with her husband at the court of the reactionary Charles X. Marie tried to rise to George's lighthearted humorous tone that actually covered a good deal of angst and doubt, but she was never at home in it. The author of *Indiana* engaged in endless banter about making an exception for her new friend, who was to be regarded as separate from others in "the patrician sphere." While George said she agreed with Marie's observation that the aristocracy was no more subject to vice and corruption than other sections of society—in short, "the non-superiority of various social classes"—nonetheless she insisted that she herself wished to be with the oppressed and not the oppressors.[2]

George Sand (Portrait by Julien Leopold Boilly)

No little irony attaches to these exchanges because the true social position of both women would have been highly equivocal if regarded by a stickler for degrees of nobility, a type by no means rare in the early nineteenth century. Marie d'Agoult's mother, who had married an impecunious aristocratic French emigré, was a member of the wealthy Bethmann family of Frankfurt, well-established Jewish bankers who had converted to Lutheranism. Germaine de Staël had made use of the Bethmann banking house in her travels. Goethe was to be found making dubious jokes about Rothschild and Bethmann. The Jewish origins and financial connections of the Bethmanns were not matters to which Marie, daughter and wife of French aristocrats, with her refined and elegant manner, chose to allude.

In time the friendship between George and Marie soured. Marie had incautiously made critical remarks about the succession of George's lovers at her country home at Nohant in Berry (where Marie had been a favored guest), and had communicated to a third party her conviction that George's talent was on the wane. All of this was duly reported to George. The gloves were off. Marie would complain about the mixture of bourgeois conventionality and bizarrely unconventional conduct to be found in George, about the vulgarity of some of her sallies and her practical jokes at Nohant, her way of behaving "at her age" like a bohemian student, and in particular about her unforgivable "want of breeding, although she is well-born."[3] Meanwhile George privately gave details of her former friend's declining liaison with Liszt to Balzac, who used them in his novel *Béatrix*, while in her own political novel *Horace* George would take Marie as the model for the pretentious vicomtesse de Chailly, portrayed as artificial in every conceivable way, including her claims to nobility: "descended from a family of financiers . . . she wished to pass for well-born."[4] So this sense of class animosity was what partly underlay George's supposedly lighthearted and exaggerated flattery of "the countess," "the princess," "Mirabella," the woman with whom she would never really be reconciled.

George Sand had not always been a pronounced enemy to aristocracy. Yet if anyone was the very embodiment of class difference it was the author of *Valentine*, whose plot—like that of Claire de Duras's *Édouard*—turned on the problems of an ill-fated love between a well-born girl and a high-souled man of lower social standing. In her autobiography she was to write that through her own mixed ancestry she was born astride two classes—an image that suggests some tension. For she was divided between different sides of her extraordinary inheritance, and this meant that she was often asking herself who she was, and committing to paper widely differing accounts of her origins, her outlook, and her life, according to her standpoint of the moment. Not surprisingly, many of her contemporaries were as puzzled as they were fascinated by George Sand and her infinite variety.

Where indeed did she stand in the social spectrum, as it was then understood? For a novelist to give a fictional character such ancestry as George Sand's would be seen as absurdly far-fetched. Her forebears were a peculiar mixture of high and low. Her great-grandfather was the dashing victor of Fontenoy, Maurice de Saxe, womanizing son of the libertine elector of Saxony, King Augustus II of Poland and his mistress, Aurora von Koenigsmark. George's beloved grandmother, Aurore de Saxe, born in 1748, daughter of Maurice de Saxe from his liaison with a highly cultivated courtesan, took as her second husband a man of ancient lineage but minor nobility, Louis-Claude Dupin de Francueil, then in his sixties, who had been a friend of Rousseau. As a wealthy tax farmer, Dupin de Francueil might figure also as a member of the higher bourgeoisie. That George's charming and spendthrift paternal grandfather, who died in 1786 long before she was born, could have bourgeois associations was not something she would be inclined to recall in later accounts of her ancestry, where he would be criticized for doing nothing for the poor with his money.

Totally different from this royal and aristocratic lineage—mostly on the wrong side of the blanket—was the origin of her mother, Sophie Delaborde, a small-time Parisian actress who had led a very checkered life with various men before her marriage to Maurice Dupin while he was serving in Napoleon's armies. Naturally Aurore de Saxe, Madame Dupin de Francueil, regarded this union of her cherished only son with a woman she believed to be a "camp follower" as a dreadful misalliance. The sudden tragic death of Maurice Dupin, when he was thrown from his horse one night close to Nohant, left his widow Sophie and his mother locked in a bitter conflict over his young daughter, Aurore, then four years old.

This struggle darkened the girl's childhood. Her grandmother, after settling an annuity on Sophie, or paying her off, took sole charge of the child's education from 1809 to 1821, from the age of four or five to that of sixteen or seventeen. Those years were paramount. It was her grandmother who fostered her gifts and encouraged her to write. Young Aurore's affections were divided between her mother—whom she saw from time to time at Nohant or else with her free and easy plebeian relations on rare visits to Sophie's Parisian home—and her devoted and highly talented grandmother, well read, musical, with her elderly circle of "old countesses" and members of her titled family. In the hope of controlling Aurore's growing rebelliousness, particularly as regards *tenue*, or well-bred behavior, her grandmother finally decided to send her to a Parisian convent for girls of the aristocracy. Some of them, like Louise de La Rochejaquelein, who belonged to the celebrated royalist family that had fought heroically against the revolutionaries in the Vendée, became her friends.

When Aurore's grandmother was paralyzed by a stroke, the girl spent long hours with her at Nohant, gaining a deeper appreciation of that lady's rare qualities. Her grandmother was now worried about seeing Aurore settled in a suitable aristocratic marriage before it was too late; she had come to an arrangement with a relative, René Vallet de Villeneuve, that Aurore would be protected and would marry one of her cousins. After her grandmother's death, however, he and his wife appear to have stipulated that the marriage could not take place unless Aurore promised to have no contact with her plebeian mother. Aurore refused, and the marriage was off. It would be surprising if this act of desertion by her aristocratic relations when she was vulnerable did not arouse her resentment. Their betrayal was to contribute to her distaste for the prejudices of the aristocracy, a distaste that would later be reinforced by her links with a powerful movement of social and political unrest, and by the noted reformers, rebels, revolutionaries, and utopian thinkers she was to encounter.

Young Aurore was now thrown back upon her volatile mother, who was also anxious to see her married and off her hands. She was deposited with a somewhat louche family where she met her future husband, Casimir Dudevant, the illegitimate but acknowledged son of minor Gascon gentry. Contented at first with their life at Nohant and the birth of her son Maurice, Aurore soon became bored with Casimir, a rather limited countryman who did not share her wide-ranging interests and her curiosity about everything. On holiday with Casimir in the Pyrenees in 1825, she was attracted to a handsome aristocratic lawyer from Bordeaux. This was Aurélien de Sèze, nephew of the famous defender of Louis XVI when that unfortunate monarch was on trial for his life. To Aurélien, who preserved his family's royalist convictions (and with whom she was involved in a relationship that may or may not have been platonic), Aurore gave an account of herself where the aristocratic side of her origins and her loss of status came to the fore.

There was no sign, then, of the loathing for aristocracy that she would emphasize from the first to Marie d'Agoult nearly ten years later. As she told Aurélien de Sèze in a long inventive letter that could have come from some epistolary novel: "Born of *noble* and highly regarded parentage, brought up by my grandmother, one of the outstanding women of the age, I was destined for a marriage that would raise me to the highest ranks of society. It was forgotten that my father had made a garrison marriage." As for his widow, as she called her mother, she "lived in retirement on a pension paid by my grandmother," who received nothing but hatred and curses in return for her generosity. "My child, what a fate awaits you if you fall into her hands!" warned her grandmother. "You do not know your mother. God preserve you from ever knowing her!" The author of this touching version, which gives a foretaste of her narrative skills, had already told Aurélien how her aristocratic relatives had reneged on their promise to protect her, how they had abandoned her after her grandmother's death to endure the "tyranny" of her mother and her mother's relatives. "I foresaw that all was lost to me and that I would no longer occupy in society the rank for which I had first been destined. It is hard to step down the social ladder," she remarked, remembering to add that she had preserved her reputation and her virtue.[5] It might almost be part of a moral tale by Félicité de Genlis, whose works Aurore much admired in her youth. Indeed, it is a clear statement of her pained response to losing caste, but it is not a version that she would preserve when she decided later to reinstate her plebeian mother in the story of her life.

She was already keenly interested in politics by the mid-1820s, for she questioned Aurélien on the subject, somewhat to his irritation. "You, too, lapse into republicanism?" he asked her, reminding her that she had been scolded by a Parisian they had met "when you wanted to talk politics."[6] With Casimir, who had known the boredom of post-Napoleonic garrison existence, she had moved in a circle frequented by men who had participated in Napoleon's wars, "brave veterans of the old army" (such as her father would have been if he had lived), liberal Bonapartists often with republican inclinations. Her idealization of the father whom she barely knew, and who had fought with the invading armies in Italy and Spain, would have made her feel at ease in such gatherings. Besides, she tried to help Casimir to success in the local elections of 1827. Yet, given certain circumstances and certain people to be mollified and courted, out would come the disclaimers. "I am too much of a woman (I admit it to my shame) to be a very warm partisan of any particular doctrine, but my ignorance of serious matters [that is, politics] does not go so far as to forbid me to honor integrity in politicians where feelings and conduct are concerned. These are details of our current history that my sex is allowed to know and appreciate."[7] (She was employing here the same argument that Alexandrine de Tencin had used many years before, and then more urgently Olympe de Gouges during the Revolution, as well as Sophie de Condorcet when faced with Napoleon. That argument rests on women's right to know what is going on and what affects them often as a matter of life or death.) This particular disclaimer was addressed to François Duris-Dufresne—brother-in law of the celebrated General Henri Bertrand who had loyally accompanied Napoleon into exile on Saint Helena—her district's liberal and republican député since 1827. As the local leader of Casimir's party, Duris-Dufresne was a figure whose prejudices had to be flattered by her modest (and probably tongue-in-cheek) profession of female ignorance.

In spite of George Sand's later political commitment and political writings, there would often appear an undercurrent of discomfort when she spoke of politics. In her mind, for a woman to be able to deal seriously with political matters required a certain sort of intelligence and a degree of "pedantry" that she disliked. From the first she would be regarded as Germaine de Staël's successor, and in her early days as a novelist she was called "the Corinne of the Quai Malaquais," where from 1832 to 1835 she had an apartment by the Seine. This accolade did not appear to give her pleasure. She came to feel that Germaine de Staël—however estimable—as a political thinker and writer on political affairs was "boring" and fell into the category of female pedantry, famously excoriated by Rousseau. And although George would respect the talent of her own somewhat older contemporary, Hortense Allart, who had published in 1824 her *Lettres sur les ouvrages de Madame de Staël*, she condemned her too as a pedant. Hortense Allart, a novelist and historian of repute and a fellow practitioner of free love, hesitated to become the aging Chateaubriand's mistress because she differed from him on politics, being opposed to his policy of war in Spain when he was foreign minister. She wrote widely on political subjects, as indeed did George herself. On this theme of women's political writings George would manifest the contradictory nature in which she took a certain pride. It will become clearer, later on, what exactly lay behind her attitude to what she called "politics."

In her autobiography, begun in 1847 and first published when she was nearing fifty in 1854–1855, George would tentatively claim that she owed her political and social awakening to a novel by Félicité de Genlis. This was *Les Battuécas* (1816). Deeply impressed when she had read it as a girl of sixteen or seventeen, George in middle age regarded it as "socialist in its entirety" (which it certainly is not). Although George said she had never reread it—perhaps wisely, for it declines into conventional romance—on the whole she remembered the most interesting part of its plot fairly well. This concerns a valley in Spain hidden by inaccessible mountains where the inhabitants, the Battuécas, who have no idea of property and hold "all goods in common," have lived in peace and equality cut off from the outside world. According to Madame de Genlis, sheep wander freely, there are no shepherds because there are "no private owners; they are part of public wealth."[8] Gold, money, the products of art are unknown there. Discovered by missionaries in the sixteenth century and converted to Christianity, the Battuécas remain isolated, preserving their simplicity and innocence.

Then one of the young men of this strange community, Placide, a poet, curious to see the world, seizes the opportunity to leave this secret utopia and broaden his mind. He is enchanted with the beauties of civilization but deeply distressed by its injustices. When, horrified, he sees a woman in rags with her two starving children, he seizes a large loaf of bread from a bakery to give to her, and a violent fracas with the baker ensues. Madame de Genlis arranges for Placide's protector to give him a lecture on the realities of the civilized world and the necessity of property, a lecture that George thought feeble when she came to write her autobiography. Indeed, George observed there, "it is weird, but perhaps it is to Madame de Genlis, the teacher and friend of Louis-Philippe, that I owe my first socialist and democratic instincts." It looks as if George was un- aware of the revolutionary activities of Félicité de Genlis. As for George, she was trying to read back into her youth the socialist ten- dencies and views she adopted in her maturity. Strictly, there was no way George could have held socialist views as a girl, for the word "socialism" did not become current until 1831. What she could have experienced were "democratic instincts," as she called them, humanitarian responses and empathy with the sufferings of the un- derdog.

Having inserted an important "perhaps" when acknowledging her political debt to Madame de Genlis for her "first socialist and democratic instincts," George went on to repudiate it: "But I am mistaken, I owe them to my unusual position, to my birth *strad- dling*, as it were, two classes, to my love for my mother, countered and broken by prejudices. . . ." She owed them too, she remarked, to her education and upbringing, and to the contrasts in her life from an early age. "Thus I was a democrat not only through the blood of my mother coursing in my veins, but through the struggles that the blood of the people stirred in my heart and in my existence, and if books impressed me it is because their tenor only strength- ened and sanctioned my own."[9] George spoke of inner "struggles" in her early life due to the clash of classes in her inheritance, strug- gles that occurred long before her socio-political commitment. By the time she wrote her autobiography, George had long reinstated her mother and her mother's class role in versions of the story of her life, but in fact it took her some time to arrive at her "socialist and democratic" stance.

∽

THE MOMENT when Aurore Dudevant first arrived on the Parisian literary scene in the winter of 1831–1832 happened to be marked by a great shift in sensibility. For a long time since the Revolution of 1789 there had been a growing concern with the fate of "the unfortunate class," "the inferior class," as indeed was reflected in their different ways in the writings of Manon Roland, Claire de Duras, or Germaine de Staël. But by the 1830s this concern with the contrast between class privilege and class deprivation had moved center stage. Following the Revolution of July 1830, declared the noted historian François Furet, "The idea of class . . . becomes the epicenter of revolutionary culture, as after the aristocracy the bourgeoisie is henceforward its scapegoat."[10] Whatever its benefits, the new industrial revolution also brought much suffering to workers who barely survived on subsistence wages or who could not even find employment. In the countryside, bad harvests led to famine. The gap was noticeably widening between haves and have-nots, between indigestion and starvation, as George Sand was to put it succinctly. Splendid as they were, the new machines, factories, railways, steamships, and other signs of "progress" could not provide the answer, she would later write in the first of her *Lettres à Marcie*.

The desire was widespread for an all-embracing vision that could transform and "redeem" society. Purely political answers no longer seemed adequate: social and economic solutions were needed. Many—from the followers of comte Henri de Saint-Simon onward—were ready to offer them to a public that hungered for answers capable of promoting spiritual as well as material well-being. Saint-Simonians and the rest were propounding some new religion, New Christianity, with a new Messiah. Various candidates were soon to be put forward as the new Jesus, including the proletariat as a whole. The word *class* began to figure ever more prominently. "Class" may be a fiction, as the distinguished biographer P. N. Furbank proposed in his *Unholy Pleasure or the Idea of Social Class*, but if so it is one of those fictions in which people believe and upon which they act.

Without being committed to any doctrine other than Bonapartism and republicanism, Aurore Dudevant had long been interested and concerned with political matters, the state of society, the prospect or otherwise of social betterment, and the fate of the oppressed and the exploited "*dernières classes.*" And this sociopolitical concern was present even before she became a published writer and before she encountered some of the leading political and social thinkers of the day. Her early novels, from *Indiana* onward, reflected this lively concern to greater or lesser extent. It is possible to trace every twist and turn, every nuance of her enthusiasms, her fluctuations, and her responses in all their passionate variety almost from day to day. They reveal a person who has not yet found a stance that fully satisfies her.

A vital turning point had been reached with *les Trois Glorieuses*, the Three Glorious Days, the Revolution of July 1830 that banished Charles X with his foolish attempt to turn back the clock, establishing Louis-Philippe in his place to the rejoicing of liberals of various shades. These included disciples of Germaine de Staël, members of the *juste-milieu*, or moderates, as well as many who were more obviously on the make, having been invited to "get rich." Aurore Dudevant wrote from Nohant to a bachelor friend, the lawyer Charles Meure, on August 15, 1830, about the new order of things and her fear of the possible return of absolutism. As she made it perfectly clear and would continue to do so, she did not warm to Louis-Philippe. "I am a dyed-in-the-wool republican," she declared roundly, disinclined to praise the idols of the day, especially those liberals who were now in power and whose blatant ambition and greed, she said, disgusted her. She was never a liberal in a sense in which Germaine de Staël or Benjamin Constant would have understood the term. What she especially admired, she assured Meure, was the "wise, steadfast, brave and peaceful behavior of the whole of France and especially those classes, the objects of so much scorn and calumny, who did everything and who will certainly not be given any office or decorations for their trouble." She was looking for the best way "to restore well-being and calm among the inferior classes . . . and as for me, I naturally tend to side with the weak against the strong," she said.[11]

A few weeks later, on September 17, 1830, she was reaffirming the fact that she was a republican. "What does it mean to be a liberal?" she asked Charles Meure. "I am not one for rose water, and even less for water that is lukewarm." Already the note of intransigence, a virtue in some quarters in France, can be heard. "Why do you not accept that a woman may believe that men can become better and more happy by changing the state of an essentially rotten and decrepit society?" she inquired. She was growing increasingly dissatisfied with the outcome of the July Revolution that seemed to her to have changed nothing but the flag. She admitted that she did not like popular uprisings and upheavals, but in the present crisis, when everything had been questioned, why not raise a more solid edifice? What she had in mind was a republic that was not a blood-stained tyranny as in the past but "one more generous and profitable to the *dernières classes*, the lowest classes of society" who were being exploited. And she went on: "If I were a man I should take the trouble to express, after mature reflection, my desire for a republic. I would engage in serious studies, which I have neither done nor need to do. . . . But in the present state of affairs, that is, as long as I haven't got a beard, I can certainly amuse myself without causing any trouble by constructing my little dream in my mind. . . . I am so well known as a creature of no importance, feeble-minded and rather quirky. . . ."[12] This was a facetious and ironic profession of ignorance, uttered by a young woman who had read eighteenth-century political philosophers like Mably, Locke, Condillac, and Montesquieu with her grandmother, and who was familiar from an early age with Rousseau's *Contrat social* and his discourses. More recently she had ordered and read Benjamin Constant's political writings and those of Royer-Collard, among liberal political thinkers of different tendencies.

By October 1830 she was writing to a woman friend to confide her disillusion with the people, whom she found so stupid as to misunderstand those who cherished them. Yielding to force, the populace declined into wild rage. "These are some pretty aristocratic thoughts," she said, while taking care to add that her heart was still in the right place for "it is with kindness that change will be made to the manners of this brutalized class, treated up to now with such scorn that it could not progress." She declared to Charles Meure that it was not a change of dynasty or constitution that was needed but "a great reform in society." After the exaltation she had experienced at the time of the July Revolution, she now felt she had been "a dupe."[13]

Then she began to have closer contact with political affairs and events at the center of things in Paris. By the winter of 1831 she had left her husband Casimir at Nohant and was settled in the capital for part of the year, aiming to establish herself as a writer. She responded to all the new ideas. She attended a "stormy and interesting" session of the Chambre des Députés. The debates in the Chamber did not impress her—they never would. "Politics sucks in everything," she reported to Casimir. "It takes up everyone's attention. . . . I haven't the least enthusiasm for all that."[14] One of the upheavals she witnessed was the sacking of the Archbishopric of Paris on February 14. Her feelings about the revolutionaries were wildly ambivalent: "I saw the people, half grotesque, half terrifying, bedecking itself with ecclesiastical ornaments. . . ." This enraged crowd consisted of coarse, loathsome vandals who were destructive yet at the same time decent and honest, for they were not seeking to profit by pillage. She could well understand, she said, the discontent of those who were counting on better things, and she foresaw a great revolution with results that would be disastrous to the ambitious and the intriguers, one that would be quite different from this "pocket revolution."

Meanwhile, as a budding journalist of limited means, she went everywhere—to meetings, clubs, the cheap seats in the *paradis*, the highest theatre balcony. This was when she adopted masculine garb for convenience, in order to gain access to places where women were not admitted or where they did not venture alone. "I have been everywhere and I have seen everything with my own eyes," she was happy to tell Charles Meure. "I adore the racket, the storm, even the danger, and if I were selfish I should like to see a revolution every morning, it amuses me so much."[15] But by the spring of 1831 she was writing to him from Nohant, "I am thoroughly fed up with politics," and she was ready to forget all about supporters of monarchy and republic and leave them to get on with it. She would insist that she had nothing but contempt and loathing for all men, "whether kings, republicans, absolutists, so-called moderates."[16] But such expressions of disillusion with politics, to be repeated at intervals in the future, did not prevent her continued fascination with everything that was going on.

She could hardly avoid the events of June 5 and 6, 1832, the uprising in the cloître Saint-Merri, the famous failed revolution, for people were fighting in the streets under her window on the Quai Malaquais. She saw the Seine stained with blood and corpses piled high in the morgue. This was the period that she would evoke years later in her controversial political novel *Horace*. At the time the result was that she felt equal hatred for kings and the sanguinary rebels who wanted to proclaim freedom at any price. While taking a humanitarian view, she soon realized that it was impossible to shut out politics, however much she wished to do so when she returned to Nohant, where discussions continued at her fireside.

George had never favored a change in constitution as a solution for the country's ills, as had Germaine de Staël. Instead she had moved toward hopes of impending social change; but when it failed to arrive she had grown disillusioned, convinced that society was hateful and lost. This disappointment with the socio-political impasse of the early 1830s coincided with the "spleen," the skepticism and the deep despair that pervade the Byronic first version of her novel *Lélia* (1833). These were the years when she was involved in all the vicissitudes of her tempestuous affair with Alfred de Musset, the liaison with the Venetian doctor Pietro Pagello, the passionate friendship with the actress Marie Dorval. It was a time she would later regard as one where she had lost her way, a period of egotism when she was preoccupied with introspection and insufficiently concerned with action to improve the condition of those less fortunate than herself.

Then, in April 1835, while engaged in the tortuous negotiations to obtain a legal separation from her husband, George was introduced to an eloquent and charismatic lawyer of peasant stock. He was to leave a deep imprint on her thinking, reinforcing her inclination to intransigence that had already surfaced from time to time. This dominating and domineering figure was Louis-Chrisostome Michel, known as Michel de Bourges. By no means was George the political innocent that she presented in the sixth of her *Lettres d'un voyageur*, which treated of her friendship with Éverard, as she called Michel de Bourges—friendship that soon grew into a stormy love affair. She was already acquainted with the proliferating and differing sects that were propagating social renewal. She had spoken with representatives of all sides of opinion. These included Saint-Simonians (whom she had thought impractical on hearing their preaching in Paris in 1831, when she was embarking on her first attempts to gain a living as a writer). She had also talked with Carlistes (or Legitimists, followers of Charles X and the elder branch of the Bourbons), with disciples of Lamennais before she met the controversial priest himself, with members of the *juste-milieu* supporters of Louis-Philippe, "and yesterday with Robespierre in person," that is, with the fiery Michel de Bourges. At the time she professed to dislike his ideas, but all the same from the first moment his effect on her was intense and disturbing. It seemed to her that "if the extreme Left comes to power my head will be on the block along with many others because I shall say what I think."[17] But would she be able to resist his rhetoric?

Indeed, Michel was then at his most extreme. At a time when she was floundering in doubt and despair, here was a man who knew his own mind and how to express his ideas forcefully. She had once said notably to Charles Meure in September 1831 that she did not care for the lukewarm, and Michel certainly was not that. He was then an outspoken disciple of "Gracchus" Babeuf, guillotined under the Directory in 1797, and of his follower, Filippo Michele Buonarroti, arch-conspirator active in the secret society of the Carbonari, who was still alive. It was Babeuf who with his "Conspiracy of Equals" had advocated the absolute equality that had been opposed by Germaine de Staël in her devotion to individual freedom. Significantly, Babeuf was also an early proponent of the class struggle.

In May 1835 George attended the *procès monstre*, the important mass trial held in the Chambre des Pairs in Paris. Michel was outstanding among the defenders of the 121 men who stood accused of taking part in the workers' uprisings in Lyons and other cities in the preceding year. In her later account of her conversations with Michel, George described vividly an encounter that had made a profound impression on her. It was during an evening stroll close by the palace of the Tuileries when he had passionately expounded his extremist vision. What he wanted, he thundered, striking the balustrade with his cane, was to destroy everything, and that meant not only the palace but all signs of a corrupt civilization, so as to create a clean slate where all could start afresh and the new utopia arise in all its dazzling purity. In her autobiography, written many years later, George lightly gives the impression that she resisted his readiness to do away with civilization and the arts. At the time she said gaily elsewhere, in *Lettres d'un voyageur*, that she was prepared to relinquish all her property as long as she could keep her grandmother's portrait and grave at Nohant. Moreover she expected her children, Maurice and Solange, to be *"égalitaires enragés,"* fierce egalitarians, ready to give up everything for the poor.[18] It was at this time, when George was so stirred by Michel's fanaticism, that she was displaying to Marie d'Agoult the full force of her loathing for aristocracy.

Toward the end of her popular historical novel *Mauprat*, published in 1837 (though it had been in her mind since 1835), George obliquely expressed her feelings about property through her heroine, Edmée. This strong-minded young woman acts throughout the book as the mentor of her cousin Bernard, offspring of the wild Mauprat clan. Now married after many vicissitudes, they experience the upheavals of the Revolution of 1789 with a certain equanimity. As Bernard coolly relates: "We welcomed readily as a just sacrifice the abandonment of a great part of our possessions to the laws of the republic." Moreover Edmée, extremely compassionate though she was, never failed to acknowledge the "holy fanatical grandeur" of the revolutionary age. She remained loyal to her "theories of absolute equality." There were certain names (doubtless including Robespierre's) that made others shudder but that "she venerated with a kind of conviction I have never seen in any other woman."[19] The same might be said of George herself, who thought Robespierre was "the greatest man in modern times." George had adopted the view of the Revolution held by members of the extreme left, by Michel de Bourges and by Buchez and Roux in their influential history of the French Revolution, published in the years between 1834 and 1838, a work that she owned.

In this light Manon Roland, however heroic, and the Girondins in general stand as representatives of the bourgeoisie, for a selfish concern with individual freedom; while Robespierre, together with the violent extremists in the Convention and the supporters of the Terror work for the good of the people and to put an end to poverty. There can be no doubt, then, who are the false and who the true revolutionaries. Some years later the flamboyant Provençal poet Louise Colet, whom George neither esteemed nor trusted, wrote on *Charlotte Corday et Madame Roland* and received a flea in her ear for sympathizing with the Girondins and for failing to "understand" the limitations of their doctrines. Besides, in her defense of Robespierre and the Terror George would assure Louise Colet that "the rage and frenzy of a party do not at all disprove the idea that produced and inaugurated it"—a view that continues to find favor with intellectuals who remain persistent apologists for an ideology that adopts Terror in pursuit of the ideal.[20]

Apart from such radical elements in her novels of the period like *Simon* and *Mauprat*, it is in her intimate letters addressed to friends and associates that George reveals the extent of her extremism colored by Michel's, an influence that lasted into the 1840s. Her views at this time are quite distinct from those she would express in her autobiography, written in shock and disillusion after the failure of the Revolution of 1848. In her correspondence with Adolphe Guéroult, a moderate Saint-Simonian, for instance, this violent note is loud and insistent: "The day will come when . . . we shall arise," George informs him. In the future there will be "a race of ferocious proletarians, proud men ready to seize once again by force all the rights of man." But where are they? They are seduced by talk of toleration and civilization that is only pretense. She finds Guéroult and the Saint-Simonians far too slow, patient, and peaceable, whereas "each person should be a republican in the style of Robespierre," that is, should implement the republican system "swiftly and violently." She assured Guéroult: "I love your proletarians, first because they are proletarians, and then because I believe they carry within them the seed of truth, the grain of future civilization."[21] In a letter addressed to the Saint-Simonians, whose meetings she was attending, she declared that she saw them as builders and her own friends as destroyers. "Besides, loyal to old childhood affections, to old social hatreds, I cannot separate the idea of *republic* from that of *regeneration*, the salvation of the world seems to me to rest on us to destroy and for you to rebuild."[22] The burden of the salvation of the world, no less, was being readily assumed.

At this time, ever the pedagogue, she was lecturing her son Maurice, aged twelve and a half, on class divisions in society, complaining that while the members of the National Guard who defended property with guns were lauded, those who gave their lives for the people, for "*la cause du peuple*," were called revolutionaries, brigands, and murderers. Her intransigence culminated with her impassioned justification of Louis Alibaud, who on June 25, 1836, had attempted to assassinate Louis-Philippe. For George, writing to her publisher, François Buloz, Alibaud was nothing less than a hero. "Many of my friends oppose me and cast me off as a fanatic although I do not busy myself with politics any more than does my cowherd," she told Buloz without flinching. To call Madame de Staël "boring," as she had notoriously suggested in *Lettres d'un voyageur*, had elicited cries of horror, whereas Alibaud could be excoriated as a debauchee and a murderer with impunity. In her opinion, Alibaud's person was "sacred"; he was the only courageous man in France.[23]

Not until January 1837 did George begin to free herself from Michel's domination, telling him that he was not the person she had dreamed of, that he was on the wrong road. By June the liaison was at an end. Their association had lasted some two years. He had prepared the ground for her continued socio-political commitment on the extreme left, a commitment that would increasingly take an active form in the public eye. George Sand's emblematic and controversial novels, stimulating and daring in their challenge to received opinion, were being read everywhere in Europe and beyond, penetrating into countries like Russia where more strictly political writings were banned by the censor. Her feelings and ideas about independence and revolt, about the destiny of women and the need to rescue the insulted and injured, were powerful motors of opinion at a time when literature was seen as important and had fewer competitors in the area of communication. They aroused outrage, opposition, discussion, admiration, imitation. Moreover, it is in the 1830s rather than the 1930s that the leftist mind-set about the class role of the proletarian, the excoriation of the bourgeois, and the fascination with the merits of the working classes take hold. While not confined to her, such notions, filtered though her potent poetic imagination, carried a great many people with her. What George Sand began to feel ever more intensely was social guilt. How could she enjoy her privileged position, her security at her beloved Nohant, and remain happy when so many of her contemporaries had little or nothing and were unhappy?

∽

DURING THE FOLLOWING DECADE George Sand became passionately *engagée* on the left and deeply involved in social and political writing and action. This commitment certainly had profound roots in her personal background and experience, as she liked to explain whenever an opportunity presented itself—an explanation that tended to vary subtly according to her mood and the estimated political stance of her hearer. It was not only in the socio-political elements in her novels and other writings that her response became manifest but also in her activities: her promotion of a working class literature, her fostering of poets and writers among the workers, and her important part in founding influential journals of opinion like *La Revue indépendante* and the local paper, *L'Éclaireur de l'Indre*. The emphasis fell on class, in particular on the working class, the proletariat and proletarians, the masses (words frequently to be found in her vocabulary). She was not alone among writers either in her elevation of the proletarians or in her efforts on their behalf, but by virtue of her literary status and reputation she appeared high among the most prominent and controversial.

It seemed to her that the view expressed by Michel de Bourges— act to destroy everything now and see later what should be done to create a new society—was totally unsatisfactory. She came to prefer the notion that reflection and discussion should precede action. Having detached herself from him, she was drawn to the ideas of a pioneering socialist thinker—long since overshadowed—whom Heinrich Heine called the greatest philosopher of the age and whose opinions held an immense fascination for writers and artists. Many saw him as the poet among philosophers. Pierre Leroux was a master printer, apparently the first member of the Parisian working class to enter George's circle. Poverty had prevented him from pursuing the higher education for which he was fitted, but he had succeeded

in making his mark as a journalist. An adherent of Saint-Simonism, he had left the Saint-Simonian family at the time of the schism of 1832, the year in which, so George said, she had read some of Leroux's writings. She dated their intellectual collaboration from 1837, and by 1840 declared that she was becoming "ever more attached to Pierre Leroux," a spiritual attachment that entailed considerable financial support for the permanently impecunious philosopher and his family.

Profoundly impressed by his *De l'Humanité, de son principe et de son avenir*, George adopted with enthusiasm his "religious and philosophical principle of equality" that was to lead to a moral revolution in humanity. His socio-political-religious preaching did much to help assuage a burning spiritual hunger. The socialism of Leroux was inseparable from metaphysical speculation. Many years later, when more detached, she would refer to his "metaphysical intoxication"—a heady mix in which she had passionately shared.[24] A new form of Christianity, a new Evangel must replace the outworn tenets of a church that had failed because it had upheld despotism. This "good news, the new Gospel" that figured so largely and so tellingly in her novels like *Spiridion* and *Consuelo*, would be formulated not by the sterile bourgeoisie but by "the voice of the people." But who exactly made up "the people"? Eventually even Pierre Leroux himself, to whom she generously acknowledged her debt, would not fit the bill when she later encountered a person who seemed more completely proletarian than he was. Of Leroux she was to say that although he had been "born and brought up as a proletarian," later he had pursued his studies hither and thither, rather like a gypsy, "today a worker, tomorrow a journalist, often bourgeois in deed without ever being one in his heart, and in short, that is not truly a proletarian, whatever he may do to become one again."[25] Such hairsplitting concern with the precise definition of a proletarian shows how important the matter of class was to her.

Two other proletarians entered the scene. She had made the acquaintance of the genuine article, though not a member of the urban proletariat like Leroux, in Agricol Perdiguier, a carpenter from the Avignon region, who was striving to put an end to divisions in the workers' associations, the battles between the various *compagnons*, or journeymen, who engaged in internecine warfare during their travels around the country. (It was to the cause of uniting the workers that Flora Tristan, author of *Union ouvrière*, was tirelessly devoted.) George, much affected on learning of Perdiguier's experiences and his attempts to unify the workers, took him as the model for Pierre Huguenin, the saintly, even Christ-like proletarian hero of her novel *Le Compagnon du Tour de France* (1840)—a novel denigrated by Marie d'Agoult. As George was to say in her preface of 1851, the book sought to convey the manners of the people that were "largely unknown to the other classes."[26] She learned much about these customs from Perdiguier, and she was eager to enlighten the public on a largely disregarded area of contemporary life. Perdiguier also encouraged her interest in the increasing number of worker poets, often disdained by literary critics. To that end she became the patron and sponsor of various poets and writers among the workers: her purse was open to them as it was to Leroux and Perdiguer.

George knew that the exemplary figure of Pierre Huguenin did not exist in reality. As she saw it some years later, "When I drew the character of Pierre Huguenin I knew perfectly well that the bourgeoisie and the nobility would welcome him with a loud burst of laughter because I knew equally well that he had not yet shown himself. But I was sure he had been born, that he existed somewhere. . . ." His arrival on the scene was a matter of a few years, not a question of the remote future. "I considered as certain the possibility of a proletarian equal in intelligence to the men of the privileged classes," she said. She meant, doubtless, that he and his like would be equally well educated and able to hold their own. And this figure would be bringing with him the "virtual force of his kind."[27] This vigor and energy—found in drama and fiction in such lowborn young men as the elder Dumas's Antony or Stendhal's Julien Sorel—

that would seem perennially attractive to those who felt as she did that the other classes were etiolated and in permanent decline.

"I dream, therefore I see," said George Sand, adapting Descartes to convey her sense of herself as a visionary. She dreamed of Huguenin as "the new man," the man of the future. His beloved, the noble Yseult de Villepreux, promises that she will never marry anyone but Huguenin, and she gives her reason. "I decided to marry a man of the people in order to be one with the people," proclaims Yseult.[28] Momentous reasoning: to belong unequivocally to the people, that is George Sand's own dream and desire. In her novels the interclass love affair or interclass marriage, often figuring a lower-class man and a well-born woman—a reversal of the union between her own parents—may strike today's reader as a commonplace of romance, but in the 1830s and '40s this development contained an essential part of George Sand's revolutionary message on the need for equality and reconciliation between the classes. But it is reconciliation between an aristocrat on the one hand and, on the other, a proletarian or a poor peasant or an artist of humble birth. The bourgeois is not part of the equation.

This theme of class reconciliation expressed through fiction does not accord with the continuing violence of George's class animosity in private, especially where the bourgeoisie is concerned (though she is prepared somewhat reluctantly to make a few exceptions for old friends). She herself had decided to play down or reject a good part of her ancestry, the royal and aristocratic connection represented by Augustus II of Poland and Maurice de Saxe. Her maternal grandfather, the bird seller, displaces her paternal grandfather, the affluent tax farmer Dupin de Francueil. All the same, the portraits of her great-great-grandmother Aurora von Koenigmark and of her great-grandfather Maurice de Saxe remained on the walls at Nohant. And even when short of funds she would never sell the seal and snuffbox of Maurice de Saxe.

As for the bourgeois, she agreed with Pierre Leroux in declaring him the enemy. She explained why. (The stereotype is nowadays all too familiar and with the benefit of hindsight has a sinister ring.) The bourgeois did not feel a deep love of humanity, she claimed, nor did he possess the heroic courage to devote himself to it. He was selfish, base, sly, materialistic, and mercenary. He experienced a kind of "shame" vis-à-vis the unfortunates whom he exploited and feared. His advocacy of theories of slow and cautious reform, his indulgence in parliamentary verbiage and political deception and chicanery, and his total absence of social and spiritual vision placed him beyond the pale. "These liberal bourgeois do not have the necessary guts, and their so-called democracy is a system of tutelage and ill-disguised preservation of the past," she roundly declared.[29] Clearly, in the 1840s, George—who had always hated anything "lukewarm"—showed no more respect for liberal parliamentary democracy than she had done in the 1830s when dazzled by the impassioned revolutionary rhetoric of Michel de Bourges. The reign of the bourgeoisie could not last, she was sure of it. The bourgeois would recognize that they must give way to men of the people who were "more proud and strong." This consummation devoutly to be wished was not likely to occur without a revolution—the coming revolution that many besides herself, from the liberal poet Alphonse de Lamartine to the terrorist Auguste Blanqui, foresaw and worked to accomplish.

This diatribe against the bourgeoisie and parliamentary reformism was addressed to the third of her charismatic proletarians with Leroux and Perdiguier. His name was Charles Poncy, a self-educated stonemason from Toulon. In his role as talented worker poet he had much to teach "our corrupt classes," she told him. She saw this rather cautious upholder of artistic values as the incarnation of the strong and energetic proletarians whose destiny she had foretold: "You are the first of these new men," she assured him, "the true bringer of light [*l'éclaireur véritable*], opening a path where no other man of the people in our day has advanced so far. . . ."[30] It was to Charles Poncy that she chose to expatiate upon her plebeian origins and commitment, confiding that although "born apparently in the ranks of the aristocracy, I belong to the people by my blood as well as in my heart. My mother was lower in the social scale than yours. . . . She did not belong to that hardworking class which gives you a title of nobility among the people." On the contrary, George insisted, her mother, who had wandered from the straight and narrow, came from what George called the debased race of "gypsies," a dancer, "less than a dancer," who played walk-on parts on the boards of the lowest theatres on the Parisian boulevards. As for herself, her grandmother had brought her up as a lady (*demoiselle*) and an heiress: "But I never forgot that plebeian blood flowed in my veins. . . ." No great efforts were required "to separate myself from that caste to which I am less intimately attached than to my mother's womb," she said, in her unsolicited candor telling him perhaps more than he wished to learn.[31]

This was a theme to which she continued to revert. "As for me, I have nothing bourgeois in my blood. I am the daughter of a patrician and a gypsy," she reminded a long-standing friend, the lawyer and banker Alphonse Fleury, when they differed on political matters. She took the opportunity to inform the journalist and historian Louis Blanc, author of *L'Organisation du travail*, a militant on the extreme left, about her proletarian credentials, about "*ma mère, la fille du peuple.*" To her aristocratic relative René Vallet de Villeneuve, with whom she was now reconciled, and who after all knew her background perfectly well, she spoke of elements in her origins that she loved, including members of the nobility like her grandmother and the "people" from whom her mother issued. There followed yet another diatribe against the bourgeoisie. As to class, "It matters little to me," she added airily, "for I do not belong to any caste."[32] Could this be true if she urged upon others her visceral links to the working class? It surely did matter to her, or she would not have worried over the subject so often and so long, nor would she have protested so much about her rejection of her royal and aristocratic ancestry while insisting upon her ties to her mother's side of the family and her proletarian essence. There is a genuine struggle in seeking to find some way to accept or reject pieces of the muddled reality of her origins while discreetly maintaining all the while her actual role as a member of the property-owning class, as mistress of the beautiful mansion and country estate at Nohant—a contradiction that was not lost on Marie d'Agoult when writing under her pseudonym Daniel Stern, in her acid comments to the German press. In George's manner of adjusting her life story to hearer or reader, she is expressing a real need to convince herself and them about her desired social class and her genuine commitment to the proletarian cause.

∾

GEORGE WAS NOW ENTERING her "communist" phase. The 1840s witnessed much puzzlement over certain words in the political vocabulary. "Socialism" had entered general use in France in the 1830s, but "communism" soon met with perplexity as well as fear and condemnation in certain circles. In *Horace* (1841), George attempted to portray the Parisian working class of 1832—the sufferings of Marthe at the hands of her drunken father, the idealized young artisan and painter Paul Arsène contrasted with Horace Dumontet, the useless and self-indulgent bourgeois. The word *communisme*, inoffensive in 1832, had since become a bugbear, as George proposed in the course of the novel itself. Her prudent publisher François Buloz, worried about the reactions of the reading public in troubled times, took fright: "You are not a communist, I trust, at least up to *Horace* I never found a trace of it in your writings." He wanted changes to the text. Adopting a lofty literary stance, George refused to change a comma, advising him to reread a few pages of her earlier books like *Jacques* and *Mauprat*, claiming that all her works, even those that might look anodyne, expressed "continual opposition to your bourgeois . . . your governments, your social inequality and an enduring sympathy for the men of the people."[33] She was not particularly worried about the quarrel with Buloz because she could always publish the novel in *La Revue in-*

dépendante, which she had just founded with Pierre Leroux and Louis Viardot.

So George took to calling herself a communist some three years before Karl Marx adopted the term for himself early in 1844—though, as might be expected, her version was rather different from his. At first she was clearly unsure about the word, and she asked Leroux what it meant. None too confident himself, he replied that communism was like Chartism in England (that is, a workers' reform movement), and that personally he preferred "communionism" as signifying "a social doctrine founded on fraternity." But he acknowledged that many people were choosing "communism" to refer to a republic where equality was the rule. As late as January 1848 George was questioning whether communism was indeed the name of her belief, at a time when the socially aware former priest Lamennais could include it among deceptive systems that led to slavery. For George, communism was simply the name she gave to her dream of "ideal fraternity as desired by the early Christians." She did not expect to live to see its day dawn. In her eyes it posed no threat to anyone. She distinguished her own communism from that of any other system. As for herself, she had never been a member of any sect. Besides, she was bored by the makers of systems and utopias: "I've seen so many of them!" she exclaimed.[34] And she would continue to declare that she was a communist, though she knew that the word inspired absurd and irrational terror and enmity, she said, in those who did not understand it.

As a well-known journalist, one of the contributing editors of *La Revue indépendante*, as well as an influential novelist of cultural and socio-political ideas, George Sand crossed paths with that of many of Europe's leading writers, political thinkers, historians, activists, and agitators of the day. Among them was the young Karl Marx. At the time when George was claiming to adhere to communism as a form of ideal fraternity desired by the early Christians, Marx was beginning to formulate his potent concept of the class struggle.

It is held that Marx first mentioned the class struggle in his "Introduction to a Critique of Hegel's Philosophy of Law," published in the extremely short-lived journal the *Deutsch-Französische Jahrbücher*. At that time, in 1843–1844, he was living in Paris. His formulation of the schema of bourgeoisie and proletariat and the class war between them has been dated to the last months of 1843. This was a few years before *The Communist Manifesto* where, as is well known, the class struggle occupies an extremely important place. "What I did that was new," Marx would congratulate himself with particular emphasis in 1852, "was to *prove*: (1) that the existence of classes is only bound up with *particular historic phases in the development of production*; (2) that the class struggle necessarily leads to the *dictatorship of the proletariat*; (3) that this dictatorship itself only constitutes the transition to the *abolition of all classes and to a classless society*."[35] Marx was utterly convinced that he had "proved" the essential role of the class struggle in the threefold course of human history, an idea that was to become an enduring shibboleth down to our own day. His notion of class conflict is offered as a kind of "scientific" instrument, as a key for interpreting all societies, past, present, and future. Yet no documentary evidence is required or indeed adduced to support the claim.

At the time of Marx's stay in Paris in the early 1840s, when he visited members of workers' associations and talked far into the night with Pierre-Joseph Proudhon (famed for his view that property is theft), the place was teeming with writers, intellectuals, conspirators, and agitators. Paris was the refuge of hard-pressed emigrés and exiles from Germany, Russia, Poland, Italy, and elsewhere. For many, France was the almost sanctified place of an apocalyptic event, the French Revolution of 1789, with its larger-than-life protagonists who had shattered the old forms forever. According to the satirist Henri Monnier in 1842, "Never in any age did humanity have as many saviors as at present. Wherever you walk you tread on a messiah; each one has his religion in his pocket, and as regards formulae of perfect happiness you are confronted only with an embarras de choix."[36] In Paris, Marx, then aged twenty-five, could not escape this strange spiritual ambience any more than could George Sand. Like her, he had read Leroux and wanted the "total redemption of humanity" through the proletariat.

It was in Paris, in the midst of this ferment, and influenced considerably by his reading of French writers, that Marx arrived at the formulation of some of his fundamental ideas, including the necessity and inevitability of the class struggle. Nearly ten years later, in 1852, he was to remark: "No credit is due to me for discovering the existence of classes in modern society, nor yet the struggle between them. Long before, the bourgeois historians had described the historical development of the class struggle."[37] Marx was referring to French historians of the Revolution of 1789 whose works he had read, and who interpreted the event in terms of a conflict between the bourgeoisie and the aristocracy, where the former were seen to be victorious. Not only had Marx studied eighteenth-century *philosophes*. He had also read some outstanding women writers on politics. He did not disdain to make extracts from the memoirs of Manon Roland, with her visceral hatred of monarchy and aristocracy, as well as from writings by Germaine de Staël, one of the earliest to attempt to define the nuances between the different sections of society in her subtle reflections on the French Revolution.

Marx also read Sand's paper *La Revue indépendante*. In *The Poverty of Philosophy* he would quote out of context the words "*le combat ou la mort*," the bloody struggle or annihilation, from her *Jean Ziska*, an account of the grim leader of the fifteenth-century heretical sect of the Hussites who had figured in her masterpiece, the historical-cum-metaphysical novel *Consuelo* and its sequel, *La Comtesse de Rudolstadt*. *Jean Ziska* had first appeared in three issues of *La Revue indépendante* in 1843, and Marx could have seen it there. He could have been introduced to her, too, like other members of his circle, and he was to inscribe a copy of his *The Poverty of Philosophy* "To Madame George Sand, from the author."[38] It was in 1844 that the German writer and agitator Arnold Ruge, at that time Marx's collaborator on the *Deutsch-Französische Jahrbücher*, recently founded in Paris, approached George Sand to invite her interest and cooperation in their own journalistic enterprise. Apparently, unlike Heine and many other prominent writers, she did not accept the invitation. But Arnold Ruge met her and introduced to her the Russian revolutionary anarchist Mikhail Bakunin, whom she would ardently defend against accusations of treachery in 1848 in a letter she addressed to Marx himself.[39]

It would be neat to say that while Marx was formulating his "scientific" theory of the class struggle—which would ultimately have such deleterious effects on the lives of millions who would be eliminated solely for their class—George Sand was expressing desires only for class harmony and reconciliation, as in the denouements of many of her novels. But such was not the case; her approach was far more complex and contradictory. Her enmity to the bourgeoisie was scarcely less virulent than his. All the same, in her eyes, Marx—had she paid him much heed—would have figured among the systematizers and sectarians for whom she had no sympathy. She was later to say that there were two kinds of communism, hers and theirs.

᙭

GEORGE WAS ABOUT TO FIND HERSELF in a position that had never been occupied before by any woman in France. It was also a place in which her views on class could have full scope. The Revolution of February 1848 that overthrew her *bête noire*, Louis-Philippe, brought her hastening eagerly to Paris from Nohant. She was welcomed as a person who could be of use to the new regime. She was already well acquainted with many of the radical republican leaders—including Louis Blanc and Ledru-Rollin—who had been in the forefront of the opposition during Louis-Philippe's reign and who were now prominent members of the provisional government of the Second Republic.

Through Ledru-Rollin she was engaged to carry out propaganda—"gratis," as she would later insist—and to serve as political agent on behalf of the ministry of the interior. In fact she occupied a post as unofficial adviser on public relations, cultural affairs, and electoral policy. One of her important tasks was to write for the official *Bulletins de la République* various unsigned articles aimed at informing, warning, and advising the public. On occasion she composed government circulars for the ministry of education as well as for the ministry of the interior. She also wrote articles for the press, and she founded and contributed to the short-lived paper *La Cause du peuple*. On ceremonial occasions like the Fête de la Fraternité in April, she would appear in public with the rest of the government. Her presence and her role were a gift to the often misogynistic caricaturists. Ledru-Rollin, who seemed pleased enough with her efforts at the time, later—when things went wrong —accused her of throwing her weight about (which she naturally denied), while she accused him of being insufficiently supportive and chivalrous in her hour of need.

In the beginning it was the time for euphoria. George's hopes ran high: at last like-minded men, who shared (as she thought) her principles about improving the lot of the workers, now held power, and her egalitarian ideals were about to be realized. Here, for instance, was Louis Blanc, in charge of the *Ateliers Nationaux*, the National Workshops set up to provide employment. Hortense Allart, who favored a more down-to-earth liberal republicanism, was convinced that in the early days George really was dreaming of the imminent arrival of equality and fraternity. The people had proved to be "sublime," George repeated, and there was even an alliance between rich and poor on the barricades (one that she had not actually witnessed). She confided to her son Maurice, who remained at Nohant as the youthful mayor, that she was thrilled to be called upon right and left at all hours, for she was working "like a statesman" (*un homme d'Etat*).[40]

Members of the provisional government—whom George had already summed up as well intentioned but divisive and incompetent, when writing to Charles Poncy on March 8—gathered in her fifth-floor *pied à terre* in the rue de Condé, where they held discussions on policy and were soon engaged in mutually exclusive intrigues. Around this time she became particularly attached to a figure outside the government, the rash, idealistic Armand Barbès, inveterate romantic conspirator, who had already endured many years in prison. She gathered information, making a point of assessing public opinion, listening to people as they talked in the streets. "I know *better than anyone else* what is going on both within the government and in the depths of the working-class districts," she confidently assured the conservative René Vallet de Villeneuve.[41] This was no idle boast, for at a dinner early in May she was to impress so acute an observer and farseeing analyst as the author of *De la Démocratie en Amérique* with her intimate and detailed knowledge of the "situation of the workers in Paris, their organization, numbers, weapons, preparations, their state of mind, their passions, their awesome intentions." At the time Alexis de Tocqueville thought her account was exaggerated, but later he had to admit that its accuracy was confirmed by events. He actually saw her then as a sort of politician, "*une manière d'homme politique*," he owned.[42]

From the very beginning the problem of the forthcoming elections had to be addressed urgently and became part of her sphere of activity. This turned out to be in essence a matter of class. How to be certain that representatives of "the real people" (that is, those who shared one's view as to who constituted "*le vrai peuple*") would be elected? These certainly did not include the bourgeoisie. The subject dominated her thoughts, especially when it became all too clear that a great many workers and peasants were not just illiterate but also seemingly unaware of their true interests, and quite indifferent or hostile to those who had the people's good at heart. It was George who proposed the idea of sending capable workers like Charles Poncy—who proved none too keen to oblige—to convert people in the regions. The aim was that each *département* should select one urban worker and one peasant to serve as representatives in the National Assembly and so provide a counterweight to the power and influence of the bourgeoisie. George did her utmost to carry the revolution into the provinces, but it was an uphill task to judge by her own district in Berry.

In her view not only loyal commitment was required but "fanaticism, if needful," and a readiness to break ties of affection if these were opposed to the advance of a power elected by the people and "truly, *fundamentally* revolutionary." There should be no hesitation in "sweeping away everything that has the bourgeois spirit." Anything rather than members of the bourgeoisie: better even to have men of straw than vain, petty, hairsplitting lawyers as before. As for those "bad députés" who did not have the correct republican socialist views, George told Maurice forcefully that they should be "*chucked* out of the window." She impressed on him that the will of the people "will be shown in the Assembly *inside* or *outside*, and will carry the day" (her emphasis).[43] All this was completely in accord with the extreme opinions she had been expressing in private for the last ten years and more.

So there was really nothing new in the words of the notorious sixteenth *Bulletin de la République* of April 15 that caused such an uproar, words for which she took responsibility while admitting to Maurice that it was "a bit steep." What was challenging was their public utterance and the fact that they could be interpreted as a call to take to the barricades. "If the elections do not bring about the triumph of social truth," she wrote, "if they are the expression of the interests of a caste," it would be a disaster. "There will then be only one path of salvation for the people who fought on the barricades, it would be to demonstrate its will for the second time. . . ."[44] What made matters worse was that this encouragement to take to the streets appeared on the day before the independent leaders on the far left attempted to challenge and overthrow the government.

She was not alone. Even some ministers and high officials wanted to take complete control of the government and were busily engaged in hatching plots, and George was fully aware of the intrigues. Among the different plotters were Ledru-Rollin and Louis Blanc. According to Marie d'Agoult, writing as Daniel Stern in her history of the Revolution of 1848, George sided with Louis Blanc rather than with Ledru-Rollin, and was "one of the prime movers of the conspiracy."[45] Certainly George was close in outlook to Louis Blanc in his wish to bring full employment through the National Workshops, an undertaking that was doomed to failure from the beginning. Indeed, George did not believe that Louis Blanc would succeed on his own. All the same, she herself stood out against any return to the old ways, to the system that had made the worker depend like a slave on work that was measured out or withdrawn at the will of the employer.

On May 15 George was walking in the midst of members of a peaceable crowd who were keen to demonstrate their support for suffering Poland when those in front of the march, including Barbès and Blanqui, burst into the National Assembly in another attempted coup d'état. George knew that both Barbès and Blanqui were conspiring, as was their wont, for she had listed them among the various plotters. Still, she said that her friend Barbès had acted on the spur of the moment, unlike Blanqui and the others. He even told her afterward that if he had not been distracted under the stress of events, he would have included her in his government. Would she have opposed him if he had been successful? When he was arrested she left Paris for Nohant, which actually came under attack from enraged locals. She feared for Maurice and for herself. Well-wishers even urged her to flee abroad, but she stayed home. Thus it was that George did not witness the popular uprising of the June Days. The savagery of the repression that followed upon it filled her with horror and put an end to her high hopes for the working classes.

Despite her enduring hostility to the "blind bourgeoisie" whose victory in June she saw as "the absolutism of an entire class," in her published writings she had said when addressing the middle class in March that "the class struggle must cease when laws secure work for all Frenchmen." She had also declared in March in her *Lettres au peuple* that "the miracle of fraternal union will wipe the very word of classes from the book of humanity," although this dream of reconciliation was being frustrated by the bourgeoisie.[46] So, like Marx, she envisioned ultimately a classless society, but she never embraced the paradox of a necessary class struggle to attain it. A growing fear of class war can be sensed in her words to the liberal Tocqueville in May. It is also present in her letters in June addressed to that tireless fighter for Italian independence and unity, the republican Giuseppe Mazzini. She had wanted social not political revolution, she said. It just seemed to her that unfortunately in the midst of a social revolution, others did not know how to avoid a social war.

∽

ONCE AGAIN George was fed up with politics. What becomes extremely illuminating in the months that follow the débâcle is her attitude to her political role. What role? It had never existed—a line maliciously to be endorsed by Sainte-Beuve in his article on her pastoral novels, in particular *La Mare au diable*, in February 1850. As she had informed the editor of *Le Constitutionnel* just before the Revolution: "I do not engage in politics."[47] Later on, her role as a woman made a notable reappearance: "I do not believe I have the right to meddle in intrigues and electoral maneuvers, I never have done and I never shall. My role as a woman is against it."[48] This was said at a time when she had been working consistently to remove by hook or by crook the power of the bourgeoisie from the National Assembly. The commonplace of her role as a woman could always be invoked as an excuse, even if by now it was not a very convincing one. She was obviously trying to make a clear distinction between what she had felt and done and what was regarded as politics proper.

She had no political passions, she asserted, only passion for the idea, and certainly none in the narrow meaning of the word "politics" that signified replacing one man in power with another—despite her considerable efforts to secure the election of members of the working class and the peasantry to the Assembly. After June

1848 she took to speaking a good deal about politics proper, "*la politique proprement dite.*" She herself was incapable of engaging in anything of the sort, she told none other than Ledru-Rollin. There were similar denials. "I admit that I hate what is called politics today, that is to say, this clumsy art . . . ," based on compromises, on raison d'état, she informed a republican journalist. Never had she been "involved in active politics, which I believe unsuited to my sex," she assured the editors of various political papers.[49] The clear distinction between politics proper and her own activities on behalf of her generous humanitarian and egalitarian beliefs enabled her to feel a little more comfortable, perhaps, and to indicate that she had never dirtied her hands like a politician. She commented acutely on the character faults of political leaders like Ledru-Rollin, Louis Blanc, and the rest of her former associates. They had not been up to the task, they were to blame, and, moreover, the people were not ready, just as they had not been ready in 1830. No blame attached to her. Her hopes were deferred, that was all. The struggle for bread would continue, as it had in the last forty years, but there would be no happiness without the "reconciliation" of all the interests involved. Forgetting conveniently her own earlier readiness to abandon property and to urge others to do so, she now asserted that it would never disappear completely because it was inherent in human nature. Besides, she admitted that she gave thanks to God every day for having Nohant as a refuge from a horrible world. By December 1848, when Napoleon's nephew, Prince Louis Napoleon Bonaparte, was elected president by a large majority, she could say that she was "resigned."[50]

One thing becomes clear. The distinction she now made so often between politics proper and her own doings was one that she may have long sensed, though she had not earlier formulated it in so many words. It helps to explain to some degree the way she had distanced herself from women writers whom she regarded as intellectuals, pedants, and as actively committed to what she saw as politics proper, women she otherwise admired. These included not only liberals like Germaine de Staël and Hortense Allart but also a socialist activist like Flora Tristan. Moreover it goes some way to explain her lofty detachment from Eugénie Niboyet and her friends on *La Voix des Femmes* who wanted her to be the first woman to stand as a candidate for the Assembly. As long ago as her *Lettres à Marcie*, George had claimed that women in Europe did not seek to participate in parliamentary debates. While for many of her enlightened readers, both men and women, George radically changed attitudes toward the position and status of women, nonetheless she would have nothing to do with a direct political agenda that proposed women candidates and participation in the parliamentary politicking that she fundamentally despised.

The same distinction between politics proper and her own attitudes must surely have been in her mind when she solicited an audience of the Prince President Louis Napoleon Bonaparte for the second time on January 20, 1852. After his coup d'état of December 2, 1851, that put an end to the Second Republic, many were being deported to penal servitude in Algeria or Cayenne, sometimes never to return. Her decision to intercede for them and seek an amnesty was a private initiative. None of them had asked her to intervene. She urged them to abstain from opposition. Among the deportees were workers, carpenters, and vine growers she knew personally. Preeminent among those who fled into exile were friends and former associates who had served the Second Republic. Some skeptics thought her magnanimous gesture as "a white-haired woman on her knees"—she was in her late forties—was a canny means of loftily dissociating herself from them, avoiding being tarred with the same brush and even being condemned to exile.

George had had some contact with Louis Napoleon years before when he sent her his reflections on the extinction of poverty. She knew that he had made use of the Republic in order to destroy it. When elected president in December 1848, Louis Napoleon had sworn to uphold the constitution of the Republic and he had seized power in a militaristic coup. The indiscriminate fusillades in the

days that followed were largely unprovoked, for there was little re-
sistance among the population. They left hundreds of corpses.
Nonetheless the majority of voters approved the coup in the
plebiscite. No wonder George was disillusioned with the people.
Now she was treating with a dictator in terms that never cease to astonish: "I am not Madame de Staël," she assured him. "I have neither her genius nor the pride with which she fought against the twin
forces of genius and power. My spirit, more broken or more fearful,
approaches you without show or obstinacy, without secret hostility,
for if such were the case I should exile myself from your presence
and should not be urging you to hear me."[51] What was Germaine de
Staël doing here? What was the meaning of this strange disclaimer,
with its resonant allusion to exile—whether her own potential exile
or the actual exile of her friends and colleagues and the bitter ten-
year exile endured by her predecessor? What message was George
trying to convey to the new man in power, and why?

The prince president knew that she was not Madame de Staël,
just as he was not his mighty uncle. She wanted him to realize how
she was seeking to play a totally different role from that of her illustrious predecessor. The signal being given was that George Sand
did not intend to be the outstanding dissident, the active opponent
of his regime, as Germaine de Staël had been of Napoleon's. The idea
that the creator of *Lélia* lacked the genius or spirit of the author of
Corinne seems ludicrous. Yet many years before, in her *Lettres d'un
voyageur*, George had seen her predecessor as "a mind infinitely
stronger and more intelligent than mine."[52] In short, she was stress-
ing modestly that Germaine de Staël was more of a thinker—and
above all a political thinker—than herself. It must have seemed to
George that her attitude of supplication was apolitical, that it simply continued the compassionate humanitarian stance on behalf of
victims of oppression that she had long adopted and that she wished
to convey.

A number of her contemporaries did not see it in that way, and
they declined her offer to intercede for them. This was the course

followed by Victor Hugo, who had gone into exile protestin
did not want anyone to deal with the odious regime on hi
If some for whom George won remission were deeply thank
ers were ungrateful (just like some friends of Germaine c
when she had managed to save them from being massacı
ways, Louis Napoleon managed to elude George's appeals fc
eral amnesty. Yet she chose to feel sorry for him and to pres
opportunist adventurer with a tear in his eye as the dupe o
visers. The regime was quick to profit from her response.

One of the ungrateful beneficiaries of her intercession
fail to mention Germaine de Staël. This was Marc Dufraisse,
active préfet de l'Indre under the Second Republic, and on
extreme left opponents of Louis Napoleon. He wrote to h
exile in Brussels, and after some patently insincere flattery
this being one of the finest pages in her life, he settled down
was really on his mind: the regime's violation of right and la
haps, he intimated slyly, it was better for George to be hersell
than to play the role of Madame de Staël, "even though sur
her," and so arouse Louis Napoleon's vindictiveness (the ir
tion being that George in all likelihood would then have
exile). Others took up the theme. Louis Blanc, an exile first
gium and then in London, thought she was compromising t
position by her entreaties. He maintained that she was comn
a political mistake. Politics did not come into it, George crie
was simply fulfilling her role as a woman whose prime obli
was compassion for the unfortunate. As for Mazzini, he crit
her attitude of resignation, when in his opinion she should
been protesting against an immoral state of affairs—rath
Madame de Staël had done. When the historian Jules Michele
ited George in March 1852 he confided to his diary that whi
found her "*bonne*," kindness itself as always, nonetheless "p
are not always grateful to her for this kindness. Why? Because
rives partly from a sort of skeptical ease in accepting e
thing. . . ." She did not hide the fact that she could not see r

difference between the victors and the vanquished. "And what of justice, Madame?" inquired Michelet. "Is that nothing between the two camps?" He set the question on what he called the firm territory of what was just and lawful. "Law alone can legitimately employ the means of force," he declared cogently.[53] Michelet did not record her response, if any.

The episode of her intercession for the victims in 1852 marks the beginnings of the legend of "*la bonne dame de Nohant*," a legend she encouraged. The reputation for womanly kindliness and compassion would eventually obscure the long years of her passionate revolutionary activity against the bourgeoisie and on behalf of the extreme left and the working classes. It took a writer with the acuity of Flaubert to appreciate that his fellow "troubadour" possessed special knowledge, and he would apply to her when researching the Revolution of 1848 for his political novel *L'Éducation sentimentale*. To Mazzini she had once candidly admitted, "I do not have a political mind, although I have political feelings and a kind of understanding of social and philosophical ideas."[54] These words might be applied to many writers who have become embroiled in politics and the advocacy of political violence out of generous sympathy for the sufferings of the wretched of the earth when all they had were "political feelings." These, however, could take them a very long way.

A curious anecdote may serve as an intriguing footnote to George Sand's long struggle with the subject of class. It appears that a person who was friendly with the author of *Consuelo* in the last years of her life told Varvara Komarova, the groundbreaking biographer who wrote under the pseudonym of Wladimir Karénine, how it was in vain that George Sand showed herself to be a democrat in her manners and beliefs. For on occasion the aristocrat stood revealed, and "she knew so well how to play the *grande dame*" that she inspired involuntary respect.[55] So her never-to-be-forgotten grandmother, with her insistence on *tenue*, prevailed in the end.

Epilogue

Politics penetrates into the human condition. . . .
—FRANÇOIS MAURIAC, *Bloc-Notes*

It has been said that every evocation of past time stands at the crossroads of the real and the imaginary. That is a salutary reminder of how far the attempt to bring individuals of the past to life—and especially writers, who are notoriously slippery manipulators of the word—rests on troubling ambiguities. Remembered speech that looks so brilliant and convincing on the page—how reliable is it? Private letters offer a unique and fascinating glimpse of candor intermingled with self-presentation and self-preservation. Life stories and memoirs record past events and feelings about them seen through the prism of current relationships and the ideas that the author holds at the moment of writing. Sometimes, when a writer offers a long and detailed transcription of dialogue that was purportedly spoken in actuality, we have to surmise that the minute after he or she left the room the private notebook or diary was readily at hand, so that every word could be jotted down immediately with total recall.

How potent and essential such command of the word once was! How many surviving letters and documents, how many volumes of autobiography and memoirs, and how many novels and stories remain as invaluable sources for an approach undertaken in the earnest desire to recover a particular sensibility and allow the dead voice to be heard again! Indeed, it is because remarkably gifted women from Alexandrine de Tencin to George Sand could write so well that their voice is not lost. In attempting to portray some intriguing French women authors during a very long period of history of roughly 150 years, I have sought to uncover elements of continuity along with their perplexities and certainties, their inner conflicts and decisive actions, and to restore their individual voices to the general ongoing record of social and political life.

What becomes clear is that—over many generations in France and despite misogyny, distrust, insult, exclusion, inadequate formal education, absence of rights, and all the other familiar disabilities endured by members of the female sex—intelligent and talented women participated in political life along with their masculine contemporaries, even though the women were not formally regarded as part of the framework of institutions and the workings of political power. Both before the Revolution of 1789 and after it they still found access to power and exerted influence over those who held it. Although they were denied positions of power themselves, each of these women writers variously had a hand in it: Alexandrine de Tencin in the rise of her brother Pierre to high office; Manon Roland in the appointment of her husband as minister of the interior and in her advice and collaboration in the running of his ministry; Claire de Duras in the political and ministerial career of Chateaubriand; Félicité de Genlis in the destiny of Philippe Égalité and the education and the political shaping of Louis-Philippe; Germaine de Staël in the promotion of Narbonne to minister of war, Talleyrand to minister of foreign affairs, and in the financial and political establishment and advancement of Benjamin Constant; George Sand in her unofficial place and activity in the government of the Second Republic.

Yet none of these aspects of real political influence or role, as customarily understood, does full justice to the truly significant face of the political responses and actions of these women writers. For an appreciation of the changing movement of public opinion and the part they played in it, they offer important insights. Here is the indifference to class distinction shown by Alexandrine de Tencin in a hierarchical society and her utter contempt for the person of an inadequate monarch. Concern about class inequality and injustice figures increasingly, even in a woman as highly and securely placed as Claire de Duras. Awareness of social deprivation and empathy with the poor and unfortunate are to be found in Manon Roland, Félicité de Genlis, and Germaine de Staël until it bursts into the urgent radicalism of George Sand, with her idealization of the proletariat and elevation of the working class. With Claire de Duras there is the deep understanding of the psychological wounds inflicted by conquest and slavery upon even a privileged black fellow human being, and with Germaine de Staël the commitment to working for the abolition of the slave trade.

Here are women involved in the founding of a federal republic (Manon Roland); revolutionary radicalism (Manon Roland, Félicité de Genlis, George Sand); postrevolutionary reactionary conservatism (Madame de Genlis); liberalism under a constitutional monarchy (Claire de Duras, Germaine de Staël); and socialism and communism understood as a spiritual force (George Sand). All too often the revolutionary radicals end in disillusion (Manon Roland, George Sand). Even a liberal republican idealist like Germaine de Staël, who deserted constitutional monarchy for republicanism, and who gave literary form to her liberal ideas and ideals in the days when they were something new, saw her hopes thwarted by events, by the return of the Bourbons. If at certain moments Manon Roland or George Sand embraced revolutionary fanaticism, Germaine de Staël remained its supreme enemy, as she was of despotism. In short, these women writers were connected with a wide and varied range of political movements.

Moreover they could engage publicly and openly in controversy with women whose views they opposed, as Félicité de Genlis does in her loud counterrevolutionary denunciation of Germaine de Staël's role as the self-proclaimed disciple of the Enlightenment and as the propagator of what Madame de Genlis denigrated as the "new" liberal ideas. George Sand, in her distaste for wishy-washy liberalism and the early struggles and vagaries of fledgling French parliamentary democracy, notoriously fastened her criticism upon her predecessor Germaine de Staël's political intelligence and her position as one of liberalism's leading representatives. In effect the creator of *Corinne* and the author of *Lélia* are at opposite poles: Germaine de Staël takes her stand on liberty and the rule of law against the moral depredations caused by Napoleon's ever-expanding tyranny and the widespread acceptance of it. She perceives the hidden kinship between absolute equality and despotism. Long before George Orwell, she insists on the importance of employing words accurately, at a time when those in authority misuse them in order to blind the population with cloudy and dangerous rhetoric. George Sand, in her quest for a spiritual form of socialism and communism, places absolute equality before individual freedom, and before justice and law. The diverse attitudes of these women writers—while naturally affected not only by their female relatives and companions but also by fathers, brothers, lovers, friends—grew from experiences in their youth, developed, matured, changed over time no less than those of their masculine contemporaries with whom they were ineluctably enmeshed in a mutual interchange. They all shared in the same field, that of their society and its socio-political life.

Clearly Alexandrine de Tencin thought engaging in politics was fun and a way of making up for time she had lost in the convent. For Manon Roland there was the thrill of being there at the beginning of the Revolution, determined to change everything for the better by destroying the monarchy and replacing it—as she thought—with a beneficent republic. With Claire de Duras, political activity offered a means of banishing bitter memories, disappointments, betrayals, melancholy thoughts, and all the things that could not be changed in life itself. For Germaine de Staël, equally subject to melancholy and desperate to escape from it, politics spelled something noble and splendid, akin to poetry or religion, and she could not do without it, whatever pain it brought her. It is evident, too, that in the novels of Claire de Duras, Germaine de Staël, and George Sand, for instance, socio-political themes are rarely far from the surface.

In their attitude to politics the women writers portrayed in these pages often faced a dilemma between what they were feeling and thinking and actually doing in the political sphere and what was conventionally expected of them in their "proper sphere" as women. They would be reminded that politics was an accursed topic for women, something they should stay well clear of—especially if they valued their peace of mind and their position and reputation. It did not matter how obvious their involvement in politics was; at the first sign of controversy they would claim in their defense that they had never touched the pitch of politics, for to do so would have been contrary to their feminine role, one (they insisted) they had always scrupulously observed. This mantra, often repeated with wit, malice, or irony, can be heard from Alexandrine de Tencin to George Sand and beyond. It was a form of hypocrisy forced on them by a society that for the most part preferred to maintain its traditional façade rather than acknowledge and face the reality of woman's place in it and her contribution to it.

The distinction that George Sand made between her own kind of politics and "politics proper"—a distinction she embraced in order to distance herself from her words and public actions of the later 1830s and the 1840s—leads in a direction that she doubtless did not intend. For her, politics proper bore the stigma of accursed politics: it meant boring, trivial, and futile parliamentary debates; the delays and compromises of reformism instead of change and action now; disputes about institutions and constitutions and replacing one man in power with another. What really mattered was to do something about the awful conditions and deprivation faced by those at the bottom of the ladder. In this sense she had what she called political ideas and feelings rather than being concerned like Germaine de Staël with the machinery of government, the exercise of power, the making of laws, and the workings of justice—the themes of politics proper.

Claire de Duras once acutely observed that it was as rare to find a political standpoint founded on the study of political matters as it was to find religious faith founded on theology. Each person's judgment was prompted by private passions and tastes, she asserted. Many continued to hold strong political opinions and pursue political ends who had never opened a book on political thought—though this could not be said of Manon Roland, Félicité de Genlis, Germaine de Staël, and George Sand, all of whom were well read in eighteenth-century political philosophy and well versed in current political movements and ideas. Yet there appears to be a good deal to the view: that feelings rather than concern with political institutions do often play a large part in the choice of a political stance, and that these feelings are often inspired in the first place by literature or works of art. There is, for instance, the impact of the memoirs of Manon Roland, incomparable icon of revolutionary heroism and sacrifice; the contribution of *Corinne* to the movement for the emancipation and unification of Italy; the influence of George Sand's novels on rebels and revolutionaries in Russia and elsewhere. In this sense the subject of politics proper takes second place to that of political culture as a whole. Some women writers made a vital and challenging contribution not only to literature but also to political life.

Chronology

1715	Death of Louis XIV. Regency of Philippe III d'Orléans during the minority of Louis XV.
1716	John Law establishes his bank in Paris.
1719	Death of Madame de Maintenon, morganatic wife of Louis XIV.
1723	Death of the regent.
1726–1743	Government of Cardinal Fleury.
1735	Madame de Tencin's *Mémoires du comte de Comminge* published anonymously.
1745	Madame de Pompadour becomes Louis XV's "*maîtresse en titre.*"
1746	Birth of Madame de Genlis.
1747	Birth of Louis-Philippe-Joseph, later Philippe Égalité.
1748	Birth of Aurore de Saxe, George Sand's grandmother.
1749	Death of Madame de Tencin.
1754	Birth of Manon Phlipon, Madame Roland.
1761	Jean-Jacques Rousseau: *Julie, ou la Nouvelle Héloïse.*
1766	Birth of Germaine Necker, Madame de Staël.
1769	Birth of Napoleon Bonaparte.
1773	Birth of Sophie Delaborde, George Sand's mother.
1774	Death of Louis XV; accession of Louis XVI and Marie-Antoinette.
1776–1781	Jacques Necker heads the royal treasury.
1777	Birth of Claire de Kersaint, Madame de Duras.

1782	Madame de Genlis: *Adèle et Théodore*. Choderlos de Laclos: *Les Liaisons dangereuses*.
1788	Necker recalled.
1789	States General convened. Revolution: fall of the Bastille. Necker exiled and recalled.
1791	Flight of Louis XVI and his family: their capture at Varennes. Slave revolt in Saint-Domingue.
1792	Roland appointed minister of the interior. First Republic proclaimed. September massacres.
1793	Louis XVI guillotined. Fall of the Girondins. The Reign of Terror. Madame Roland writes her *Mémoires* in prison; she is guillotined.
1794	Fall of Robespierre, end of the Reign of Terror.
1795–1799	The Directory.
1795–1796	Conspiracy of Equals led by "Gracchus" Babeuf.
1796–1797	General Bonaparte's victories in Italy.
1797	Bonaparte elected to the Institut.
1798–1799	Bonaparte's expedition to Egypt.
1799	Coup d'état of General Bonaparte, who becomes first consul.
1800	Madame de Staël: *De la Littérature*.
1802	Bonaparte is Consul for Life; he dismisses liberal critics from the Tribunate. Slavery is restored in the French colonies. Madame de Staël: *Delphine*.
1804	Bonaparte crowns himself emperor. Execution of the duc d'Enghien. Birth of Aurore Dupin, George Sand.
1805	Napoleon crowned king of Italy.
1807	Madame de Staël: *Corinne*.
1808	French armies invade Spain.
1810	General Bernadotte elected crown prince of Sweden. On Napoleon's orders, Madame de Staël's *De l'Allemagne* is pulped.
1812	Napoleon invades Russia. Retreat from Moscow.
1813	Napoleon defeated at Leipzig.
1814	Allied invasion of France. Napoleon abdicates and is

	banished to Elba. Return of the Bourbons: Louis XVIII, Louis XVI's brother. Promulgation of the *Charte*.
1815	Napoleon escapes from Elba and hastens to Paris. Louis XVIII flees to Ghent. The Hundred Days: birth of liberal Bonapartism. Napoleon is defeated at Waterloo and exiled to Saint Helena. Return of Louis XVIII.
1817	Death of Madame de Staël.
1818	Allied armies of occupation withdraw from France. Madame de Staël: *Considérations sur la Révolution française*.
1821	Death of Napoleon.
1822	Chateaubriand appointed minister of foreign affairs.
1823	Madame de Duras's *Ourika* is first published anonymously.
1824	Death of Louis XVIII; accession of his brother, Charles X.
1825	Madame de Genlis publishes her *Mémoires*. Death of Henri de Saint-Simon: publication of his *Le Nouveau Christianisme*. Development of Saint-Simonism.
1827	Death of Madame de Duras.
1830	July Revolution: the Three Glorious Days. Accession of Louis-Philippe, son of Philippe Égalité. Death of Madame de Genlis.
1832	George Sand: *Indiana*. She witnesses the June insurrection.
1833	First version of George Sand's *Lélia*. Growth of utopian socialism.
1834	Revolt of the workers in Lyons.
1835	George Sand attends the "mammoth trial" of the accused workers.
1836	Louis Alibaud attempts to assassinate Louis-Philippe.
1837	George Sand: *Mauprat*.
1841	George Sand becomes a founder and contributing editor of *La Revue indépendante*.
1842–1844	George Sand: *Consuelo, La Comtesse de Rudolstadt*.

1843–1845	Karl Marx in Paris.
1847	Lamartine: *Histoire des Girondins*.
1848	February Revolution. Abdication of Louis-Philippe. Proclamation of the Second Republic. George Sand's activities as unofficial minister of propaganda. Uprising and repression during the June Days. Prince Louis Napoleon Bonaparte, Napoleon's nephew, elected president of the Republic.
1851	Coup d'état of Louis Napoleon Bonaparte.
1852	He is proclaimed Emperor Napoleon III.

Notes

THE PLACE OF PUBLICATION is Paris unless stated otherwise. In the text, translations from French are my own unless attributed in the Notes. Emphasis in a quotation belongs to the author of it unless declared otherwise.

Prologue: In Search of a Political Voice

1. Jean-Jacques Rousseau, *Julie, ou la Nouvelle Héloïse*, Part 6, letter v (Garnier, 1952), II, 297–298.

2. Ibid., Part 2, letter xiv, I, 271.

3. Madame de Staël, *Considérations sur la Révolution française*, Part 3, chapter xxvi, ed. J. Godechot (Tallandier, 1983), p. 340; *Dix Années d'exil*, ed. S. Balayé and M. V. Bonifacio (Fayard, 1996), pp. 51–52, 321.

4. Sainte-Beuve, *Chateaubriand et son groupe littéraire sous l'Empire*, ed. M. Allem (Garnier, 1948), II, 153.

5. Marc Fumaroli, *La Conversation* in *Trois institutions littéraires* (Gallimard Folio, 1994), pp. 127, 135, 155.

6. Élisabeth Badinter, *Émilie, Émilie, l'ambition féminine au XVIIIe siècle* (Flammarion, 1983), p. 447.

7. Rousseau, *Les Confessions*, ed. B. Gagnebin and M. Raymond (Gallimard, Folio, 1959), Book XI, p. 660; Maurice Cranston, *The Noble Savage: Jean-Jacques Rousseau (1754–1762)* (Chicago: University of Chicago Press, 1991), pp. 280–281, 295.

8. Sainte-Beuve, *Chateaubriand*, II, 134.

9. George Sand, *Histoire de ma vie, Oeuvres autobiographiques*, ed. Georges Lubin (Gallimard, Bibliothèque de la Pléiade, 1970), I, 42–46.

10. Ibid., I, 1248 note.

11. Rousseau, *Confessions*, Book IX, p. 498.

12. Rousseau, *Lettre à d'Alembert, Oeuvres complètes*, ed. B. Gagnebin and M. Raymond (Gallimard, Bibliothèque de la Pléiade, 1995), V, 94–95, 1365.

Notes

13. Sainte-Beuve, *Cahiers I, Le Cahier vert 1834–1847*, ed. R. Molho (Gallimard, 1973), pp. 239, 245.

14. Madame de Staël, *De l'Allemagne*, Part 3, chapter xix (GF Flammarion, 1968), II, 218.

15. Badinter, *Émilie*, p. 149.

16. Béatrice d'Andlau, *La Jeunesse de Mme de Staël (1766–1786)* (Droz, 1970), pp. 109–110.

17. Raymond Trousson, *Préface, Romans de femmes du XVIIIe siècle* (Laffont, 1996), pp. viii–ix; Madame de Genlis, *De l'Influence des femmes sur la littérature française* (Maradan, 1811), p. 364.

18. Jean-Paul Clément, *Chateaubriand: Biographie morale et intellectuelle* (Flammarion, 1998), p. 223.

19. Chateaubriand, *Mémoires d'outre-tombe*, ed. M. Levaillant and G. Moulinier (Gallimard, Bibliothèque de la Pléiade, 1966), I, 904.

20. A. Bardoux, *La Duchesse de Duras* (Calmann-Lévy, 1898), pp. 309–310.

Chapter 1. Alexandrine de Tencin: Scandal, Intrigue, and Politics

1. Pierre-Maurice Masson, *Madame de Tencin* (Hachette, 1909), p. 233.

2. Ibid., pp. 35–36.

3. Madame de Tencin to the duc de Richelieu, *Oeuvres complètes* (D'Hautet, 1812), IV, 169–170.

4. Duc de Castries, *La Scandaleuse Madame de Tencin* (Perrin, 1987), p. 268.

5. Jean Sareil, *Les Tencin* (Geneva: Droz, 1969), p. 235.

6. Ibid., p. 117.

7. Castries, *Scandaleuse*, p. 72.

8. Thomas Macknight, *The Life of Henry St. John, Viscount Bolingbroke* (London: Chapman and Hall, 1863), pp. 469–470.

9. Ibid., pp. 470–471.

10. Duc de Saint-Simon, *Additions au Journal de Dangeau, Mémoires*, ed. Yves Coirault (Gallimard, Bibliothèque de la Pléiade, 1987), VII, 507–509.

11. Castries, *Scandaleuse*, pp. 112–113.

12. Madame de Tencin, *Le Siège de Calais, Oeuvres complètes*, II, 86; *Anecdotes de la cour et du règne d'Édouard II, roi d'Angleterre*, Book 2, IV, 45; *Les Malheurs de l'amour*, II, 147.

13. Marivaux, *La Vie de Marianne*, ed. Michel Gilot (GF Flammarion, 1978), Part 5, p. 215.

14. Masson, *Tencin*, p. 193.

15. Ibid., p. 241.

16. Ibid., p. 190.

17. Castries, *Scandaleuse*, p. 88.

18. Raymond Trousson, *Préface, Romans de femmes*, p. 9.

19. John Lough, *An Introduction to Eighteenth-Century France* (London: Longmans, 1960), p. 268.

20. E. and J. de Goncourt, *La Duchesse de Châteauroux et ses soeurs* (Flammarion and Fasquelle, 1934), p. 260.

21. Madame de La Fayette, *La Princesse de Clèves*, ed. H. Ashton (Cambridge: Cambridge University Press, 1940), pp. 6, 15–16, 33, 35.

22. Madame de Tencin, *Le Siège de Calais, Oeuvres complètes*, I, 218–219.

23. Ibid., II, 20.

24. Madame de Tencin, *Malheurs*, III, 9.

25. Madame de Tencin, *Anecdotes*, Book 2, II, 23.

26. Masson, *Tencin*, p. 133.

27. Sareil, *Tencin*, p. 200.

28. Ibid., pp. 204–205.

29. Castries, *Scandaleuse*, pp. 152–153.

30. Ibid., p. 155.

31. Sareil, *Tencin*, p. 324.

32. Madame de Tencin to Richelieu, *Oeuvres complètes*, IV, 184.

33. To Richelieu, Ibid.

34. To Richelieu, IV, 169.

35. To Richelieu, in Castries, *Scandaleuse*, p. 214.

36. To Richelieu, IV, 170–172.

37. To Richelieu, IV, 181.

38. To Richelieu, IV, 159–160, 168, 183.

39. To Richelieu, IV, 165.

40. E. and J. de Goncourt, *La Femme au XVIIIe siècle*, ed. Élisabeth Badinter (Flammarion, 1982), p. 299.

41. Montesquieu, *Lettres persanes*, ed. Laurent Versini (GF Flammarion, 1995), p. 216.

42. Castries, *Scandaleuse*, p. 201.

43. Masson, *Tencin*, p. 252.

Chapter 2. Manon Roland: The Making of a Revolutionary

1. Madame Roland, *Mémoires*, ed. Paul de Roux (Mercure de France, 1989), p. 270. See also Thomas E. Crow, *Painters and Public Life in Eighteenth-Century Paris* (New Haven and London: Yale University Press, 1985); Robert Darnton, *The Literary Underground of the Old Regime* (Cambridge, Mass., and London: Harvard University Press, 1982).

2. Letter of September 19, 1777, *Lettres de Madame Roland aux Demoiselles Cannet*, ed. C. A. Dauban (Plon, 1867), II, 175.

Notes

3. Madame Roland, *Mémoires*, ed. Roux, p. 215.

4. Ibid., p. 307.

5. Ibid., p. 233.

6. Letter to Varenne de Fénille, March 21, 1789, *Lettres*, ed. C. Perroud (Imprimerie Nationale, 1900–1902, 1913–1915), II, 47.

7. Letter to Jany, October 8, 1793, Letters from Prison, *Mémoires*, ed. C. Perroud (Plon, 1905), II, 395.

8. Letter of March 24, 1776, *Lettres Cannet*, I, 359–360.

9. Ibid., I, 360.

10. Letter of January 23, 1778, Ibid., II, 237.

11. Extract from *Mes Loisirs*, Ibid., II, 483.

12. Letter of October 26, 1776, Ibid., I, 454; letter of August 19, 1777, Ibid., II, 158.

13. Lough, *Eighteenth-Century France*, pp. 144, 291–292; Rousseau, *La Nouvelle Héloïse*, Part 2, letter xvii, II, 250; Letter to Bosc, October 8, 1789, *Lettres Cannet*, II, 572.

14. Sainte-Beuve, *Oeuvres*, ed. M. Leroy (Gallimard, Bibliothèque de la Pléiade, 1960), II, 897.

15. *Mémoires*, ed. Roux, pp. 222, 244, 289.

16. Letter of January 5, 1777, *Lettres Cannet*, II, 7.

17. Letter to Bosc, August 23, 1782, *Lettres*, ed. C. Perroud (1900), I, 200.

18. Letters of September 19 and October 4, 1777, *Lettres Cannet*, II, 173, 187.

19. Letter of July 1, 1777, Ibid., II, 125.

20. *Mémoires*, ed. Roux, p. 284.

21. Letter of January 11, 1776, *Lettres*, ed. C. Perroud (1913), I, 359–360.

22. Letter of July 1, 1777, *Lettres Cannet*, II, 127.

23. Roland and Marie Phlipon, *Lettres d'amour (1777–1780)*, ed. C. Perroud (Picard, 1909), p. 373 note.

24. Ibid., pp. 204–205.

25. Ibid., p. 117.

26. Ibid., p. 282.

27. Ibid., pp. 282, 284.

28. Ibid., pp. 286, 293.

29. *Mémoires*, ed. Roux, pp. 149, 237.

30. Ibid., p. 330.

31. Letter to Bosc, July 26, 1789, *Lettres*, ed. Perroud (1902), II, 53ff.

32. Letter to Bosc, January 29, 1791, Ibid., II, 232.

33. Pierre-Edmond Lemontey, quoted by Jules Michelet, *Les Femmes de la Révolution* (Adolphe Delahays, 1854), p. 171 note.

34. Marat, *L'Ami du people*, September 2, 1792, in Madame Roland, *Mémoires*, ed. C. Perroud, I, 221 note.

35. *Mémoires*, ed. Roux, pp. 92–93.
36. Paul de Roux, Introduction, Ibid., p. 2l.
37. Letter to Buzot, July 6, 1793, *Lettres*, ed. Perroud (1902), II, 499.
38. Thomas Carlyle, *History of the French Revolution* (1837) (London: Chapman and Hall, 1903), Book V, chapter ii, III, 178–179. For Stendhal, see *Vie de Henry Brulard, Oeuvres intimes*, ed. H. Martineau (Gallimard, Bibliothèque de la Pléiade, 1955), p. 275; *Souvenirs d'égotisme*, Ibid., p. 1393; *Correspondance*, ed. H. Martineau and V. Del Litto (Gallimard, Bibliothèque de la Pléiade, 1968), I, 175, 198.
39. *Mémoires*, ed. Roux, p. 336.
40. Ibid., pp. 184, 226–227, 343.
41. Letter to Bosc, December 20, 1790, *Lettres*, ed. Perroud (1902), II, 206–207.

Chapter 3. Claire de Duras: Dilemmas of a Liberal Royalist

1. *Ourika*, ed. Roger Little (Exeter: University of Exeter Press [1993], revised ed. 1998). I am indebted to Professor Little for information about Madame de Duras's visit to Martinique as a girl, and for his article "Le nom et les origines d'*Ourika*" in *Revue d'Histoire Littéraire de la France*, 1998, no. 4, pp. 633–637, which he kindly communicated to me. For Madame de Genlis, see *Mémoires* (Ladvocat, 1825), VII, 292–293, and IX, 308. See also C. L. R. James, *The Black Jacobins* (1938) (London: Penguin, 2001); Hugh Thomas, *The Slave Trade* (London: Papermac, 1998).
2. A. Bardoux, *La Duchesse de Duras* (Calmann-Lévy, 1898), p. 54.
3. Letter to Rosalie de Constant, February 6, 1824, Gabriel Pailhès, *La Duchesse de Duras et Chateaubriand* (Perrin, 1910), pp. 282–283.
4. Letter to Rosalie de Constant, April 6, 1824, Ibid., p. 284.
5. Letter to Rosalie de Constant, May 15, 1824, Ibid., p. 462.
6. *Olivier ou le Secret*, ed. Denise Virieux (Corti, 1971), pp. 147, 216 note 44.
7. Letter to Rosalie de Constant, July 23, 1824, Pailhès, *Duras et Chateaubriand*, p. 467.
8. Letter to Rosalie de Constant, July 24, 1824, Ibid., p. 449.
9. Chateaubriand, *Mémoires d'outre-tombe* (Pléiade), I, 93l.
10. Comte d'Haussonville, "La Baronne de Staël et la Duchesse de Duras," *Femmes d'autrefois, hommes d'aujourdhui* (Perrin, 1912), p. 197.
11. Philip Mansel, *The Court of France, 1789–1830* (Cambridge: Cambridge University Press, 199l), p. 139; Françoise Wagener, *La Comtesse de Boigne* (Flammarion, 1997), p. 273.
12. Letter to Duc de Duras, 2 Frimaire An IX, Bardoux, *Duras*, pp. 82–83; Philip Mansel, *Louis XVIII* (Stroud: Sutton, revised ed. 1999), pp. 294, 330.

Notes

13. Stendhal, *Courrier anglais* (March 6, 1823), ed. H. Martineau (Le Divan, 1935), I, 90.
14. Stendhal, Letter to Adolphe de Mareste, June 12, 1820, *Correspondance* (Pléiade), I, 1026.
15. Madame de Staël, Letter to Madame de Duras, October 1, 1816, d'Haussonville, *Femmes*, p. 211.
16. Pailhès, *Duras et Chateaubriand*, pp. 402–403.
17. Ibid., p. 149.
18. Wagener, *Boigne*, p. 186.
19. Stendhal, *Courrier anglais*, IV, 82.
20. Letter to Chateaubriand, December [?] 1822, Bardoux, *Duras*, p. 435.
21. Ibid., pp. 184, 187, 234, 344.
22. Letter to Rosalie de Constant, June 7, 1826, Pailhès, *Duras et Chateaubriand*, p. 484.
23. Bardoux, *Duras*, pp. 281–282, 376–377.
24. Chateaubriand, Letter to Madame de Duras, April 2, 1822, Bardoux, *Duras*, p. 286.
25. Bardoux, *Duras*, pp. 279, 387; Pailhès, *Duras et Chateaubriand*, pp. 170, 172.
26. Letter to Rosalie de Constant, October 28, 1823, Pailhès, *Duras et Chateaubriand*, pp. 270, 278.
27. Bardoux, *Duras*, pp. 361, 413.
28. Ibid., p. 418.
29. Letter to Madame de Staël, September 1, 1815, d'Haussonville, *Femmes*, p. 204; Bardoux, *Duras*, p. 262; Madame de La Tour du Pin, *Mémoires . . . Correspondance*, ed. C. de Liederkerke Beaufort (Mercure de France, 1989), p. 344.
30. Bardoux, *Duras*, p. 160.
31. Madame de La Tour du Pin, Letter to Félicie de La Rochejaquelein, December 30, 1825, *Mémoires . . . Correspondance*, p. 394. See also Madame de Duras, *Édouard*, in *Romans de Femmes*, ed. Trousson, pp. 1009–1070.
32. Duc de Lévis, Letter to Madame de Duras, November 8, 1825, Pailhès, *Duras et Chateaubriand*, p. 473.
33. Ibid., pp. 429, 463.
34. Letter to Rosalie de Constant, May 15, 1824, Ibid., p. 382.
35. Stendhal, Letter to Prosper Mérimée, December 25, 1826, *Correspondance*, II, 96–98.
36. Letter to Madame de Staël, September 8, 1816, d'Haussonville, *Femmes*, p. 212.

Notes

Chapter 4. Félicité de Genlis: The Cover-up

1. Victor Hugo, *Choses vues*, 1847–1848, ed. Hubert Juin (Gallimard, Folio, 1972), pp. 197–198; Guy Antonetti, *Louis-Philippe* (Fayard, 1994), p. 496.

2. Jane Austen, *Emma*, chapter 53; Las Cases, *Le Mémorial de Sainte-Hélène*, ed. Gérard Walter (Gallimard, Bibliothèque de la Pléiade, 1963), II, 202; Alexander Pushkin, Letter to L. S. Pushkin, May 1825, in *Pushkin on Literature*, trans. and ed. Tatiana Wolff (London: Athlone Press, 1998), p. 145; George Sand, *Oeuvres autobiographiques* (Pléiade), I, 627–630, 1036, 1387 note.

3. Madame de Genlis, *Mémoires inédits sur le dix-huitième siècle et la Révolution française depuis 1756 jusqu'à nos jours* (Ladvocat, 1825), VI, 241, and I, 254.

4. Ibid., VI, 21.

5. Ibid., II, 209–210.

6. Gabriel de Broglie, *Madame de Genlis* (Perrin, 1985), p. 116. See also his *Le Général de Valence* (Perrin, 1972).

7. Madame de Genlis, *Mémoires*, IV, 164.

8. Broglie, *Genlis*, pp. 191, 171; Mansel, *Court of France*, pp. 187, 191–193.

9. Émile Dard, *Le Général Choderlos de Laclos* (Perrin, 1936), p. 163.

10. Hubert La Marle, *Philippe Égalité* (Nouvelles Editions Latines, 1989), p. 723.

11. Madame de Genlis, *Mémoires*, II, 151.

12. Ibid., IV, 98, 116; Broglie, *Genlis*, p. 118.

13. Broglie, *Genlis*, pp. 190, 200.

14. Baron de Staël, in La Marle, *Égalité*, p. 424.

15. Broglie, *Genlis*, p. 197.

16. Madame Roland, *Mémoires*, ed. Roux, pp. 58–59; La Marle, *Égalité*, pp. 721–722.

17. Broglie, *Genlis*, p. 261.

18. Ibid., pp. 226–227.

19. Madame de Genlis, *Mémoires*, IV, 66, 68.

20. Ibid., IV, 148.

21. Broglie, *Genlis*, 278; Jean Harmand, *Madame de Genlis: sa vie intime et politique* (Perrin, 1912), pp. 344–345.

22. Broglie, *Genlis*, p. 282.

23. Ibid., p. 283.

24. Harmand, *Genlis*, p. 395 note 4; Las Cases, *Mémorial*, II, 1044 note.

25. Madame de Genlis, *Mémoires*, V, 353–355.

26. Guy Antonetti, *Louis-Philippe*, p. 116.

27. Madame de Genlis, *Mémoires*, V, 137.

28. Madame de Genlis, Letter to Talleyrand, April 6, 1814, Las Cases, *Mémorial*, II, 1044–1045 note.

Notes

29. Madame de Genlis, *Mémoires*, IV, 69–70.

30. Olympe de Gouges, *Déclaration des droits de la femme et de la citoyenne* (articles 6 and 10) in Georges Poisson, *Choderlos de Laclos* (Grasset, 1985), p. 311.

31. Mary Wollstonecraft, *A Vindication of the Rights of Woman*, 1792 (London: Penguin, 1975), pp. 205–206.

32. Sainte-Beuve, *Oeuvres* (Pléiade), I, 97, 103.

Chapter 5. Germaine de Staël: Against the Wind

1. Simone Balayé, *Madame de Staël: Lumières et Liberté* (Kincksiek, 1979), p. 88.

2. *De la Littérature considérée dans ses rapports avec les institutions sociales*, ed. Paul Van Tieghem (Geneva: Droz and Paris: Minard, 1959), II, 319.

3. *Dix années d'exil, Oeuvres Complètes* (Treuttel et Wirtz, 1820–1821), XV, 3.

4. *Préface, Delphine*, ed. Béatrice Didier (GF Flammarion, 2000), p. 58.

5. Paul Gautier, *Madame de Staël et Napoléon* (Plon, 1903), p. 95.

6. Balayé, *Lumières*, p. 118 note 209.

7. Letter to Claude Hochet, March 3, 1803, *Correspondance générale*, ed. Béatrice Jasinski (Pauvert, 1962), IV, part ii, p. 593.

8. Benjamin Constant, *Cécile, Oeuvres*, ed. Alfred Roulin (Gallimard, Bibliothèque de la Pléiade, 1957), pp. 183–184.

9. Jean-Denis Bredin, *Une Singulière famille: Jacques Necker, Suzanne Necker, et Germaine de Staël* (Fayard, 1999), p. 71.

10. Gouverneur Morris, *Diary and Letters*, ed. A. C. Morris (London: Kegan Paul, 1889), I, 278–279; G. E. Gwynne, *Madame de Staël et la Révolution française* (Nizet, 1969), p. 14.

11. Jean-Denis Bredin, *Sieyès* (Editions de Fallois, 1988), p. 216.

12. *Lettres sur les écrits et le caractère de Jean-Jacques Rousseau, Oeuvres complètes*, I, 71–72.

13. *Considérations sur la Révolution française*, ed. J. Godechot, p. 229.

14. *De l'Influence des passions sur le bonheur des individus et des nations, Oeuvres complètes*, III, 5-6.

15. Ibid., p. 173.

16. Ibid., p. 293.

17. *Réflexions sur la paix intérieure*, Ibid., II, 139–140.

18. *De l'Influence des passions*, Ibid., III, 34; Madame Necker de Saussure, *Notice sur le caractère et les écrits de Madame de Staël*, in Madame de Staël, *Oeuvres complètes*, I, ccxcix.

Notes

19. Benjamin Constant, *Journal*, January 26 and April 10, 1803, June 18, 1804, *Oeuvres* (Pléiade), pp. 233, 254, 321.

20. *Réflexions sur la paix adressées à M. Pitt et aux Français*, *Oeuvres complètes*, II, 52, 87.

21. *Réflexions sur la paix intérieure*, Ibid., II, 121.

22. *Des Circonstances actuelles qui peuvent terminer la Révolution et des principes qui doivent fonder la République en France*, ed. Lucia Omacini (Geneva: Droz, 1979), p. 210 note 14; *Préface*, 2nd ed., *De la Littérature*, ed. P. Van Tieghem, I, 14.

23. *Des Circonstances actuelles*, pp. 351–352 note.

24. Ghislain de Diesbach, *Madame de Staël* (Perrin, 1983), p. 198.

25. *Des Circonstances actuelles*, p. 122.

26. Ibid., pp. 26–27.

27. Prosper de Barante, quoted by Balayé, *Lumiéres*, pp. 66–67.

28. Jean Tulard, *Napoléon ou le Mythe du Sauveur* (Fayard, 1987), p. 159.

29. Madame Necker de Saussure, *Notice*, in Madame de Staël, *Oeuvres complètes*, I, clxxxi.

30. Ibid., p. cccvii.

31. Paul Gautier, *Staël et Napoléon*, p. 402.

32. *De l'Allemagne*, ed. S. Balayé (GF Flammarion, 1968), II, 188.

33. *Dix années d'exil*, ed. S. Balayé and M. V. Bonifacio (Fayard, 1996), p. 230.

34. *Corinne ou l'Italie*, ed. S. Balayé (Gallimard, Folio, 1985), p. 98.

35. Diesbach, *Staël*, pp. 399–400.

36. *De la Littérature*, ed. P. Van Tieghem, II, 280.

37. *Corinne ou l'Italie*, ed. S. Balayé, p. 53.

38. Gautier, *Staël et Napoléon*, p. 225.

39. *Dix années d'exil*, ed. S. Balayé and M. V. Bonifacio, p. 266.

40. Norman King, "Madame de Staël et la Chute de Napoléon," in *Mme de Staël et l'Europe, Colloque de Coppet*, July 1966 (Klincksiek, 1970), p. 72 note 54.

41. Balayé, *Lumières*, pp. 225–226.

42. Gautier, *Staël et Napoléon*, p. 369.

Chapter 6. George Sand: The Struggle with Class

1. Marie d'Agoult to George Sand, November 22, 1835, Marie d'Agoult, George Sand, *Correspondance*, ed. Charles F. Dupêchez (Bartillat, 2001), p. 24.

2. George Sand to Marie d'Agoult, end September, 1835, *Correspondance*, ed. Georges Lubin (Garnier, 1964–1991), III, 44 [henceforward known as C.]; Marie d'Agoult to George Sand, November 22, 1835, *Correspondance*, ed.

Notes

Dupêchez, p. 25; George Sand to Marie d'Agoult, beginning January, 1836, C. III, 223–224.

3. Juliette Adam, *Mes premières armes littéraires et politiques* (Lemerre, 1904), pp. 252–253.

4. *Horace* (1841) (Calmann-Lévy, 1880), pp. 123–124.

5. To Aurélien de Sèze, October 24, 1825, C. I, 214–215, 218, 221.

6. Aurélien de Sèze to Aurore Dudevant, end November 1825, C. I, 299–300.

7. To François Duris-Dufresne, July 19, 1830, C. I, 674–675.

8. Madame de Genlis, *Les Battuécas*, I, 38–39, 65.

9. *Histoire de ma vie, Oeuvres autobiographiques* (Pléiade), I, 629.

10. François Furet, *La Révolution française (1814–1880)* (Hachette, Collection Pluriel, 1997), II, 149.

11. To Charles Meure, August 15, 1830, C. I, 690–691.

12. To Charles Meure, September 17, 1830, C. I, 704–706.

13. To Madame Gondouin Saint-Agnan, October 12, 1830, C. I, 715; to Charles Meure, October 31, 1830, C. I, 724.

14. To Casimir Dudevant, February 20, 1831, C. I, 807.

15. To Charles Meure, February 25, 1831, C. I, 808–810; to Alexis Duteil, February 25, 1831, C. I, 811.

16. To Charles Meure, May 20, 1831, C. I, 874; to Jules Boucoiran, July 17, 1831, C. I, 917.

17. To Adolphe Guéroult, April c. 12, 1835, C. II, 854–855.

18. To same, end October 1835, C. III, 73.

19. *Mauprat*, ed. Claude Sicard (Garnier Flammarion, 1969), pp. 312–313.

20. To Louise Colet, February 28 [?], 1843, C. VI, 72; see also to same, C. V, pp. 506–507, and C. VI, 62ff; also to Luc Desages C. IV, 14–16.

21. To Adolphe Guéroult, end October 1835, C. III, 73–74; to same, November 9, 1835, C. III, 115.

22. To the Parisian Saint-Simonian Family, April 2, 1836, C. III, 326.

23. To Maurice Dudevant, November 6, 1835, C. III, 109; to François Buloz, July 3, 1836, C. III, 457, and July 11, 1836, C. III, 481–482.

24. To Giuseppe Mazzini, January 25, 1848, C. VIII, 258.

25. To Charles Poncy, November 25, 1845, C. VII, 194.

26. *Notice* (1851), *Le Compagnon du Tour de France* (1840) (Michel Lévy, 1869), I, 10.

27. To Charles Poncy, November 24, 1845, C. VII, 186.

28. *Le Compagnon du Tour de France* (Calmann-Lévy, 1885), II, 183.

29. To Charles Poncy, November 25, 1845, C. VII, 193.

30. To same, Ibid., p. 194.

31. To same, December 23, 1843, C. VI, 327–328.

Notes

32. To Alphonse Fleury, March 20, 1844, C. VI, 487; to Louis Blanc, end November 1844, C. VI, 719; to René Vallet de Villeneuve, November 18 or 19, 1845, C. VII, 175.

33. *Horace*, p. 204; see also François Buloz to George Sand, October 3, 1841, C. V, 457; to Buloz, September 15, 1841, C. V, 421.

34. To Apolline and René Vallet de Villeneuve, January 19, 1848, C. VIII, 251; *Aux Riches* (March 12, 1848) in *Questions politiques et sociales* (Calmann-Lévy, 1879), pp. 230, 253–254.

35. Karl Marx, Letter to Wedemeyer, March 5, 1852, quoted in George H. Sabine, *A History of Political Theory* (London: Harrap, 1941), p. 690.

36. D. O. Evans, *Le Roman Social sous la monarchie de juillet* (Presses Universitaires de France, 1930), p. 45.

37. David McLellan, *Marx Before Marxism* (London: Pelican, 1972), pp. 199–200, 237–238.

38. Note of Georges Lubin in C. VIII, 792.

39. To Karl Marx, July 20, 1848, C. VIII, 546–547.

40. To Maurice Dudevant, March 23, 1848, C. VIII, 359.

41. To René Vallet de Villeneuve, March 4, 1848, C. VIII, 317.

42. Alexis de Tocqueville, *Souvenirs* (Calmann-Lévy, 1893), p. 204.

43. To Frédéric Girerd, March 6, 1848, C. VIII, 324–325; to Maurice Dudevant, March 23, 1848, C. VIII, 361; to same, April 7, 1848, C. VIII, 389.

44. *16ᵉ Bulletin de la République*, C. VIII, 423 note 3.

45. Daniel Stern, *Histoire de la Révolution de 1848*, quoted in C. VIII, 419 note 1.

46. *Un mot à la classe moyenne*, March 3, 1848, in *Questions politiques et sociales*, p. 198; *Lettres au peuple*, March 7, 1848, Ibid., pp. 209–210.

47. To the Editor of *Le Constitutionnel*, beginning January 1848, C. VIII, 236.

48. To Charles Delavau, May 13 [?], 1848, C. VIII, 451.

49. To Ledru-Rollin, May 28, 1848, C. VIII, 476; to Edmond Plauchut, October 4, 1848, C. VIII, 655; to the editors of *La Réforme, La Démocratie Pacifique,* and *Le Peuple*, December 1, 1848, C. VIII, 718.

50. To J.-P. Gilland, July 22, 1848, C. VIII, 550; to Charles Duvernet, August 15, 1848, C. VIII, 602; to Jules Hetzel, December 1848, C. VIII, 757.

51. To Prince Louis Napoleon Bonaparte, January 20, 1852, C. X, 659–660; see also Renee Winegarten, "Two Women in Politics: Germaine de Staël and George Sand," in *George Sand Today*, ed. David A. Powell (Lanham, Md.: University Press of America, 1992), pp. 155–166.

52. *Lettres d'un voyageur, Oeuvres autobiographiques* (Pléiade), II, 752.

53. For Marc Dufraisse, see W. Karénine, *George Sand: sa vie et ses oeuvres* (Ollendorf, 1899–1926), IV, 226–228; for Louis Blanc, see C. X, 795 note 2; Jules Michelet, *Journal*, ed. Paul Viallaneix (Gallimard, 1959), II, 187.

54. To Mazzini, February 10, 1843, C. VI, 35.

55. W. Karénine, *Sand*, I, 123; see also Renee Winegarten, "'Brilliant Nebulae': "George Sand's Views of the 18th Century" (New York: *George Sand Studies*, 1999), pp. 87–93.

A Note on Sources

APART FROM WORKS quoted in the text and acknowledged in the Notes, I have consulted many authorities for the historical, political, social, literary, and cultural background, and for the movement of ideas and opinions. The following offers a selection of these books. Articles in journals have been omitted. The place of publication is Paris unless stated otherwise.

General

For the regency period, see Christine Pevitt, *The Man Who Would Be King: The Life of Philippe d'Orléans, Regent of France* (London: Weidenfeld and Nicolson, 1997). For the middle and later years of the eighteenth century, mention must be made of the splendid three-volume biography of *Jean-Jacques Rousseau* by Maurice Cranston (London: Allen Lane, 1991; Chicago: University of Chicago Press, 1996 and 1997); Jean Starobinski, *Jean-Jacques Rousseau: la transparence et l'obstacle* (Gallimard, 1971) and his *Montesquieu* (Seuil, 1953); P. N. Furbank, *Diderot* (London: Secker and Warburg, 1992); Élisabeth and Robert Badinter, *Condorcet: un intellectuel en politique* (Fayard, 1988); and Claude Arnaud, *Chamfort* (Laffont, 1988). To these should be added Daniel Roche, *La Fin des Lumières* (Fayard, 1993), and Robert Darnton, *Mesmerism and the End of the Enlightenment in France* (Cambridge, Mass.: Harvard University Press, 1968), along with François Bluche, *La noblesse française au XVIIIe siècle* (Hachette, 1973) and his *La vie quotidienne au temps de Louis XVI* (Hachette, 1989). Among nu-

A Note on Sources

merous works on the salons, particularly enlightening are Pierre de Ségur, *Le Royaume de la rue Saint-Honoré: Madame Geoffrin et sa fille* (Calmann-Lévy, 1897), and Benedetta Craveri's wide-ranging *Madame du Deffand et son monde* (Seuil, 1987).

For the Revolutionary era I have relied on historians too numerous to mention, from Louis Madelin to Simon Schama. Works on women in the Revolution range from Jules Michelet's pioneering account to Linda Kelly's *Women of the French Revolution* (London: Hamish Hamilton, 1987), Olivier Blanc's *Olympe de Gouges* (Skyros, 1981), and Elisabeth Roudinesco's important psychological study *Théroigne de Méricourt* (Seuil, 1989).

As regards the Napoleonic age, besides works by the noted authority Jean Tulard, I have profited from Dorothy Carrington's innovative *Napoleon and His Parents* (London: Viking, 1988), Peter de Polnay's *Napoleon's Police* (London: W. H. Allen, 1970), Pieter Geyl's essential *Napoleon: For and Against* (London: Jonathan Cape, 1949), and Alan Palmer's *An Encyclopedia of Napoleon's Europe* (New York: St. Martin's Press, 1984).

For the Restoration period, G. de Bertier de Sauvigny's *La Restauration* (Flammarion, 1955) remains invaluable. François Furet charts the intellectual currents of this era, as well as those of the years from the July Revolution of 1830 to the Revolution of 1848, in the second volume of his *La Révolution* (Hachette, 1988). See also, among many works on the ideas and upheavals of this era, Sébastien Charléty, *Histoire du Saint-Simonisme* (Hartmann, 1931), and D. O. Evans, *Social Romanticism in France, 1830–1848* (Oxford: Clarendon Press, 1951).

Two compilations, *French Women Writers*, ed. E. M. Sartori and D. W. Zimmerman (Westport, Conn: Greenwood Press, 1991), and *The Feminist Encyclopedia of French Literature*, ed. E. M. Sartori (Westport, Conn.: Greenwood Press, 1999), are helpful. Mona Ozouf's *Le Mots des femmes; essai sur la singularité française* (Fayard, 1995) offers useful insights. Ellen Moers, in her *Literary Women* (New York: Doubleday, 1976), was the first to provide a remarkable overview.

A Note on Sources

Prologue

Sources for the political and social attitudes and opinions of the French women writers under review, and their role in political life, are scattered and various. There are many gaps. In the decades before 1914 a number of ground-breaking French scholars devoted their researches and their editorial skills to some women writers of the past: their efforts are recognized in the Notes.

Chapter 1. Alexandrine de Tencin: Scandal, Intrigue, and Politics

The colorful life of Alexandrine de Tencin is so intriguing that her political and social views have not always been taken as seriously as they should be. Documentation concerning Madame de Tencin is scattered in French and European archives. Although her biographers treat of her political involvement and activities, these are not their primary concern. There is room for a more detailed inquiry into her political stance and her significance. Modern editions or reprints of her novels are to be found, for instance *Mémoires du comte de Comminge* (1969, 1996) and *Le Siège de Calais* (1983). A modern collected edition of her lively correspondence is eminently to be desired.

Chapter 2. Manon Roland: The Making of a Revolutionary

Manon's letters to the Cannet sisters, to her future husband, and to others are vital for an understanding of her prerevolutionary and revolutionary views. A modern collected edition of her correspondence would be helpful. There exist numerous biographies of Madame Roland in French and English, among them Guy Chaussinand-Nogaret, *Madame Roland* (Seuil, 1985). Gita May's important study *Madame Roland and the Age of Revolution* (New York: Columbia University Press, 1970) is essential. Édith Bernardin, *Jean-Marie Roland et le Ministère de l'Intérieur (1792-1793)* (Société des Études Robespierristes, 1964), makes very few allusions to Madame Roland's role in its 618 pages. Manon Roland, whose memoirs transformed her into a revolutionary icon, merits a full and detailed study of her political and social contribution in her own right.

Chapter 3. Claire de Duras: Dilemmas of a Liberal Royalist

There is no modern collected edition of Madame de Duras's letters, as there is for those of Chateaubriand and of Germaine de Staël. The correspondence between Claire de Duras and Rosalie de Constant has not been published separately in a modern edition, whereas the letters that passed between Mademoiselle de Constant and Benjamin Constant have been collected and edited (Gallimard, 1955). There are modern editions or reprints of Madame de Duras's novels but no new comprehensive study of the ideas, opinions, and political activities of this appealing and important woman writer. Her *bête noire* has merited a relatively recent biography: Françoise Wagener, *Madame Récamier* (Lattès, 1986).

Chapter 4. Félicité de Genlis: The Cover-up

Very few of the numerous works of Madame de Genlis have been republished, notable exceptions being historical novellas like *Mademoiselle de Clermont* (1802, 1977, 1996) and *La Duchesse de La Vallière* (1804, 1983). The rest are mostly to be found gathering dust in libraries. Her writings of the revolutionary period have not been republished either. Her memoirs, pillaged by social historians from the Goncourt brothers onward, have yet to appear in a modern critical edition. Only some of her letters, much praised by her contemporaries, have been collected and edited—see *Lettres à son fils adoptif Casimir Baeker 1802–1830*, ed. H. Lapauze (Plon, 1902); A. Castelot, *Dernières lettres d'amour: correspondance inédite avec le comte Anatole de Montesquiou* (Grasset, 1954). A modern collected edition of her letters might contribute to a fuller understanding of her social and political attitudes and involvement.

A Note on Sources

Chapter 5. Germaine de Staël: Against the Wind

The political importance of Madame de Staël is widely recognized today. André Jardin, distinguished authority on Tocqueville, devotes an extremely important chapter to her ideas and her place in his *Histoire du libéralisme politique* (Hachette, 1985). The condescension of some of his predecessors—for instance the snide tone and the animosity present in Henri Guillemin's *Madame de Staël, Benjamin Constant et Napoléon* (Plon, 1959), reedited as *Madame de Staël et Napoléon* (Bienne: Panorama, 1966, and Seuil, 1987)—is outmoded. Much has been learned from the researches of Simone Balayé and her diligent colleagues about Madame de Staël's developing ideas and political activities. Modern editions of Germaine de Staël's writings, including the invaluable *Carnets de voyage*, ed. S. Balayé (Geneva: Droz, 1971), have contributed to this reassessment. There is room for a work that attempts to disentangle the difficult and complex political relationship of Germaine de Staël and Benjamin Constant, as distinct from their fraught personal imbroglio, which appears to be well documented.

Chapter 6. George Sand: The Struggle with Class

Without Georges Lubin's masterly edition of George Sand's correspondence I should not have been able to write this chapter. Her letters provide an important counterbalance and corrective to her autobiography. They reveal her early interest in political and social matters and make it possible to trace the nature and extent of her personal involvement. Edouard Dolléans, *Féminisme et mouvement ouvrier: George Sand* (Editions Ouvrières, 1951), and J. P. Lacassagne, *Pierre Leroux et George Sand: histoire d'une amitié* (Klincksieck, 1973) remain helpful. Isabelle Hoog Naginski's *George Sand: Writing for Her Life* (New Brunswick and London: Rutgers University Press, 1991) is illuminating on the spiritual aspects of the writer's political and social views. A comprehensive study that would compare George Sand's socio-political outlook with that of writers like Marie d'Agoult, Hortense Allart, Louise Colet, and Flora Tristan, among others, would be challenging.

Epilogue

The words of the Catholic novelist François Mauriac are taken from his *Bloc-Notes*, ed. Jean Touzot (Seuil, 1993, II, 138), entry of September 27, 1958. Mauriac justified the political commitment shown by major writers of the past, like Chateaubriand and Constant, as well as by his own leading contemporaries. For a novelist to ignore the fate of the nation and the sufferings of the people, Mauriac observed, is to condemn himself to zero. Women writers (who shared that concern and compassion) did not form part of his purview. Mauriac's remarks connect with those of Rivarol quoted at the head of the Prologue and bear witness to the element of continuity. According to the noted historian Pierre Rosenvallon, author of *La Démocratie inachevée*, in his inaugural lecture at the Collège de France, the notion of political life is vital. In his view, the experiences of women as well as men in the past blend with those of the present day to form an ensemble of political life distinct from the themes of politics concerned with the modes and institutions of power.

Index

Index

Index

Index

Index

Index

A NOTE ON THE AUTHOR

Renee Winegarten was born in London and studied modern languages at Cambridge University. She has written for a great many literary and cultural magazines, including *French Studies*, the *Modern Language Review*, *Encounter*, *Commentary*, the *American Scholar*, and *The New Criterion*. She is the author of *Simone de Beauvoir: A Critical View*; *Madame de Staël*; *The Double Life of George Sand*; *Writers and Revolution*; and *French Lyric Poetry in the Age of Malherbe*. She lives in Edgware, Middlesex.